THE COMPLETE IDIOT'S GUIDE® TO

Natural Health for Dogs and Cats

WITHDRAWN

by Liz Palika

ALPHA

A member of Penguin Group (USA) Inc.

ALPHA BOOKS

Published by the Penguin Group

Penguin Group (USA) Inc., 375 Hudson Street, New York, New York 10014, USA

Penguin Group (Canada), 90 Eglinton Avenue East, Suite 700, Toronto, Ontario M4P 2Y3, Canada (a division of Pearson Penguin Canada Inc.)

Penguin Books Ltd., 80 Strand, London WC2R 0RL, England

Penguin Ireland, 25 St. Stephen's Green, Dublin 2, Ireland (a division of Penguin Books Ltd.)

Penguin Group (Australia), 250 Camberwell Road, Camberwell, Victoria 3124, Australia (a division of Pearson Australia Group Pty. Ltd.)

Penguin Books India Pvt. Ltd., 11 Community Centre, Panchsheel Park, New Delhi—110 017, India

Penguin Group (NZ), 67 Apollo Drive, Rosedale, North Shore, Auckland 1311, New Zealand (a division of Pearson New Zealand Ltd.)

Penguin Books (South Africa) (Pty.) Ltd., 24 Sturdee Avenue, Rosebank, Johannesburg 2196, South Africa

Penguin Books Ltd., Registered Offices: 80 Strand, London WC2R 0RL, England

Copyright © 2011 by Liz Palika

International Standard Book Number: 978-1-61564-120-8
Library of Congress Catalog Card Number: 2011908146

13   12   11   8   7   6   5   4   3   2   1

Interpretation of the printing code: The rightmost number of the first series of numbers is the year of the book's printing; the rightmost number of the second series of numbers is the number of the book's printing. For example, a printing code of 11-1 shows that the first printing occurred in 2011.

Printed in the United States of America

Note: This publication contains the opinions and ideas of its author. It is intended to provide helpful and informative material on the subject matter covered. It is sold with the understanding that the author and publisher are not engaged in rendering professional services in the book. If the reader requires personal assistance or advice, a competent professional should be consulted.

The author and publisher specifically disclaim any responsibility for any liability, loss, or risk, personal or otherwise, which is incurred as a consequence, directly or indirectly, of the use and application of any of the contents of this book.

Most Alpha books are available at special quantity discounts for bulk purchases for sales promotions, premiums, fund-raising, or educational use. Special books, or book excerpts, can also be created to fit specific needs.

For details, write: Special Markets, Alpha Books, 375 Hudson Street, New York, NY 10014.

Publisher: *Marie Butler-Knight*
Associate Publisher: *Mike Sanders*
Executive Managing Editor: *Billy Fields*
Executive Editors: *Randy Ladenheim-Gil, Lori Cates Hand*
Development Editor: *Lynn Northrup*
Senior Production Editor: *Kayla Dugger*

Copy Editor: *Christy Hackerd*
Cover Designer: *Kurt Owens*
Book Designers: *William Thomas, Rebecca Batchelor*
Indexer: *Johnna VanHoose Dinse*
Layout: *Brian Massey*
Proofreader: *John Etchison*

This book is dedicated to two men who have been very important in my life:

My dad, Wray Allen Stout (October 13, 1929–December 8, 2008), taught me there was no such phrase as "I can't." I have never forgotten that. My dad was always my biggest fan, and at book signings he wore a sweatshirt he had made that said on the front, "I'm the Father of the Author."

My husband, Paul Allen Palika (June 30, 1950–March 21, 2011), passed away during the writing of this book. He supported my writing efforts, was proud of my successes, and commiserated during my failures. I love you, Paul, and miss you.

Contents

Appendixes

Introduction

I was first introduced to natural remedies, especially herbal remedies, by my grandmother. Several herbs were staples in her kitchen: peppermint, chamomile, willow bark, ginger, milk thistle, slippery elm, and red clover. I helped her garden, too, and as we planted, weeded, and harvested her flowers and herbs, she taught me about those plants—what they needed to grow, how they should be dried, and what uses they provided. I loved going down into her basement to see all the herbs drying in bunches. I loved the smell of all those herbs.

What I didn't know at the time was that Grandma was whetting my appetite for more knowledge. I began doing more research into the value of herbs first, then nutrition, followed by other natural health techniques. All of this research paid off when one of my dogs was diagnosed with a serious illness for which there was no cure. I used my powers of research to find some nutritional and herbal remedies that could support my dog and hopefully keep her healthier, even if she couldn't be cured. After consulting with my veterinarian, I implemented those techniques and my dog lived to the age of 13—when she died of old age, not the disease.

I have implemented several natural health techniques into the lifestyle I share with my dogs and cats. I also incorporate those techniques with conventional veterinary medicine. I have found a balance between the two that is comfortable for both me and my veterinarian. What I do may not work for you; you're going to have to find the balance that you will be happy with. However, I am more than happy to lead you along on this journey of discovery. I find natural health techniques to be fascinating. I hope you do, too.

How to Use This Book

Part 1, An Overview of Natural Health, talks about what natural health care is—and what it isn't. In addition, I introduce you to a wide variety of natural health techniques from around the world.

Part 2, Start with the Basics, details the foundation of pet health care, including vaccinations, grooming and body care, and the importance of play and exercise.

Part 3, Good Food for Better Natural Health, examines the subject of nutrition. Because the adage "you are what you eat" is as true for our pets as it is for us, I discuss the various options available for feeding your pet, from commercial pet food to cooking for your pet. I also include several recipes, and I talk about supplementing your pet's diet.

Part 4, Your Pet's Health from A to Z, discusses a wide range of health issues faced by dogs and cats as well as natural remedies that can be used. In addition, I offer suggestions as to when to call your veterinarian for additional help.

You'll also find three helpful appendixes: a glossary of terms that I use throughout the book, a list of additional resources, and several recipes you can make to treat your dog or cat.

Extras

Throughout this book, you'll find a variety of sidebars that provide extra information:

DOG TALK

These sidebars offer information of particular interest to dog owners.

CAT CHAT

Check out these sidebars for information that applies exclusively to cats.

GO NATURAL

These sidebars provide tips for how to use natural techniques when caring for your pet, as well as other related information.

PET ALERT

These sidebars alert you to cautions and misconceptions about natural pet health.

DEFINITION

In these sidebars, you'll find words and terms related to natural pet health that may be unfamiliar to you.

Thanks to the Veterinarians

Four veterinarians assisted me with this book. They shared their knowledge, provided valuable information, and sometimes disagreed with me. Even the disagreements were good—after all, many natural health techniques aren't proven by scientific studies. I've shared that information with you, too.

Robin Downing, DVM, is a graduate of the College of Veterinary Medicine at the University of Illinois. She's the director of The Downing Center for Animal Pain Management, the first comprehensive pain prevention and management practice for pets in Northern Colorado. She's a certified veterinary acupuncturist, a certified canine rehabilitation practitioner, and a certified Tui-na practitioner. She's also certified in canine medical massage and animal chiropractic.

Greg Martinez, DVM, is a graduate of the University of California at Davis. He has been a practicing veterinarian for 30 years, and practices today in Gilroy, California, at the Gilroy Veterinary Hospital. His particular interest is the effect diet and nutrition has on pet health, and for the last decade he has been emphasizing this with his clients. His book *Dr. Greg's Dog Dish Diet: Sensible Nutrition for Your Dog's Health* (Riparian Press, 2009) has been warmly received by pet owners and veterinarians alike.

Shawn Messonnier, DVM, is a graduate of Texas A&M University, and holds a doctorate of veterinary medicine. His Acupuncture and Holistic Animal Health Care Center is the only pet hospital in the area to offer both conventional and complementary therapies for dogs and cats. He has written extensively about complementary and alternative remedies and treatments. His book *Natural Health Bible for Dogs & Cats* (Prima Pets, 2001) is still the reference of choice for many pet owners.

Narda Robinson, DO, DVM, MS, DABMA, FAAMA, is a medical acupuncturist, osteopathic physician, and veterinarian. She has taught at Colorado State University's College of Veterinary Medicine and Biomedical Sciences since 1997 and is an assistant professor in the Department of Clinical Sciences. She directs the CSU Center for Comparative and Integrative Pain Medicine. She teaches acupuncture to veterinarians from around the globe.

Any mistakes or problems in this book are to be considered my mistakes and should not be blamed on these helpful, wonderful veterinarians.

Trademarks

All terms mentioned in this book that are known to be or are suspected of being trademarks or service marks have been appropriately capitalized. Alpha Books and Penguin Group (USA) Inc. cannot attest to the accuracy of this information. Use of a term in this book should not be regarded as affecting the validity of any trademark or service mark.

An Overview of Natural Health

Natural health for dogs and cats encompasses a wide variety of health-care techniques, from acupuncture to Reiki healing. However, before you go exploring, we need to first define natural health care. We see words like "natural," "holistic," and "organic" in pet food advertisements all the time. But what do those words really mean? I help you sort it out in the first chapter.

I then guide your explorations through the variety of natural health techniques for dogs and cats. These widely different health-care systems come from all over the world: acupuncture and traditional Chinese veterinary medicine from China, Ayurveda from India, Reiki from Japan, Native American techniques from North America, homeopathy from Europe, and herbal remedies from around the world.

What Does "Natural" Mean?

In This Chapter

- What does natural health mean?
- A look at alternative health techniques
- The integrative care approach
- Ask questions and do your research
- Exploring a natural approach with your vet
- Small changes that make a big environmental impact

About 10 years ago, our then 6-year-old Australian Shepherd, Dax, was diagnosed with a congenital and potentially lethal liver disease. Our vet advised us to reduce Dax's exposure to as many chemicals and toxins as possible. Because one of the liver's functions is filtering toxins from the system, doing so would ease the burden on her liver. "Provide a natural lifestyle for her as much as possible," we were told by her veterinarian.

We were willing to try to do that, but we first had to define *natural*, which has many meanings, especially in relation to care and health. We had to find a means of providing care for Dax, as well as our other dogs and our cat, that was as natural as possible yet that would also fit our lifestyle and maintain the quality of life we wanted them to have.

The Many Definitions of Natural Health

For thousands of years, our ancestors used plants and other things found in nature to treat illnesses and injuries. Willow bark, for example, is a pain reliever, and evidence shows it has been used in that manner in every region where willow trees grow.

Eventually, ancient people began combining ingredients and forming supplements or pills. Archaeologists excavating an ancient shipwreck found a medicine chest that contained a sealed tin of medicinal tablets. Those pills, more than 2,000 years old, were comprised of carrots, parsley, celery, cabbage, alfalfa, and wild onion. Perhaps ancient sailors used these pills to prevent scurvy? We don't know their exact purpose, but these pills confirm that people have been using natural remedies for a long time.

In the last 200 years, natural remedies were often referred to as *home remedies*. Techniques for preparing these remedies were often passed down from mother to daughter, generation after generation. A hot Epsom salt bath, for example, eased sore muscles, and a paste made of oatmeal relieved itching. Although modern medicine has made many of these unpopular, natural remedies kept people and their pets comfortable for many generations.

DEFINITION

Home remedies are natural health techniques passed down from generation to generation. They often include plants, spices, or other items found in the home.

My grandmother, who was of Native American ancestry, learned many lessons from her grandmother, a member of the Lakota tribe, and she passed those lessons to me. She used willow bark, peppermint, wild turnips, and a variety of other plants native to where her people lived.

Natural Today

Most of us probably have a definition in mind when we think of natural. A friend of mine defines *natural* as, "How Mother Nature created it." A bright, shiny apple, fresh from the tree, is certainly natural, right? But what if farmers sprayed insecticides onto that apple while it was growing? Is it still natural? What if the ground under the apple tree was treated with herbicides?

The first thing to understand is that natural doesn't mean organic. *Natural* has no legal definition, whereas *organic* does. That bright and shiny apple might be considered organic if it was produced with no pesticides or herbicides, and all the other requirements were met.

DEFINITION

Organic means the food or product is grown or produced using environmentally sound techniques, with no synthetic pesticides, chemicals, or fertilizers. Organically processed foods don't contain genetically modified organisms, nor do they contain chemical food additives.

Businesses have known for a long time that *natural* is a word consumers like to see, so it's plastered on the sides of buses and featured in magazine advertising, in yellow page ads, and on television. *Natural* is used everywhere to promote a huge variety of products and businesses.

Food is often labeled "natural," as are ingredients used in foods. Cleaning supplies, pest repellents, clothing fibers, and even landscaping techniques have been called natural.

The lack of a legal definition for what constitutes a natural product makes it difficult to understand what products really are and aren't as nature made them. The Natural Products Association (www.npainfo. org), however, is trying to clear up the confusion. They have created standards and certification processes for a variety of products, including household cleaning supplies. As of this writing, the organization hasn't created standards for pet products, but perhaps they will do so in the future.

Setting aside the fact there's no legal definition for *natural*, the consensus among various sources seems to be that something marketed as natural shouldn't be artificial or include artificial ingredients. There should be little or no processing, and no chemical additives.

Of course, the lack of guidelines means buyer beware. Read labels and use common sense. Keep in mind, advertising firms and product manufacturers know people are paying attention to this word.

Veterinarians Define Natural Health

If we define *natural* as "not artificial," then what does natural health mean in regard to our dogs and cats? Again, the concept that our pets' care shouldn't be artificial is one definition, but what does that really mean?

Narda Robinson, DO, DVM, MS, of Colorado State College of Veterinary, and founder and director of the Medical Acupuncture for Veterinarians Program, says "Natural health care, in my opinion, would be avoiding the use of drugs and surgery. Instead, it would involve utilizing the patient's own innate healing capacity. It would also involve encouraging that with bodywork, diet, exercise, and so on. It might also involve using herbs."

Robin Downing, DVM, of The Downing Center for Animal Pain Management in Windsor, Colorado, says, "When I talk to clients about natural health care, I explain that I'm speaking of pet ecosystem management. This is a geeky phrase, but one that implies all the details involved. We are then talking about taking care of the whole animal in its environment and within the family dynamic and relationships. It means paying attention to all the nuances that influence not just the health of the pet, but that foster healthy relationships between the human and animal members of the family."

Dr. Downing provides some examples of natural health:

- Making educated choices regarding vaccinations and a vaccination schedule
- Making nutritional choices based on facts—not marketing

- Maintaining a healthy body weight using nutrition and exercise

- Providing joint protection with nutrition and supplements, based on scientific evidence

- Using physical medicine modalities to enhance wellness and to treat specific conditions, including acupuncture, medical massage, physiotherapy, chiropractic, and strength building

Greg Martinez, DVM, author of *Dr. Greg's Dog Dish Diet* (see Appendix B) and a practicing veterinarian in Gilroy, California, says, "I believe the average pet owner and veterinarian thinks that natural health refers to acupuncture and herbal treatment for medical conditions. Even though much more widely accepted, especially in California, it is still not widely practiced."

Natural health practices can certainly be effective in preventing or treating some of our pet's illnesses. Obesity, for example, is preventable by feeding a good-quality diet, limiting treats, and making sure the dog or cat gets sufficient exercise. Many digestive upsets and even gastrointestinal diseases can be prevented, cured, or controlled through diet.

A natural health technique that is not widely understood yet is vital to your pet's good health is that of simply paying attention to your pet. If you watch your pet on a daily basis and pay attention to how he walks, runs, breathes, eats, and relaxes, you'll notice when there's a problem. You can then evaluate the problem and take action. That might be giving your pet a massage or an herbal remedy, or contacting your veterinarian.

Essentially, natural health includes many aspects of the animal's life, and requires making decisions as to whether or not to use medications, vaccinations, surgery, and other aspects of conventional veterinary care. It also encompasses diet and nutrition, grooming and body care, play and exercise, and pet and human relationships. Alternative remedies, which I discuss a little later in this chapter, might be a part of this equation.

Pet Owners Define Natural Health

Veterinarians define natural health for dogs and cats from their professional points of view, of course, although most are also pet owners themselves. Pet owners who aren't veterinarians may look at natural health from a different perspective.

Food is important to most pet owners who wish to use more natural methods of caring for their pets. Heather Houlahan, a Search and Rescue Dog handler and trainer, says, "I raise all my animals as naturally as I can. I use nutritional supplements and feed raw and homemade foods. In addition, I believe that in many cases, the most natural choice is no product at all. I don't spend top dollar for a bag of food with the picture of a carrot on it; I just feed the dog a carrot."

Houlahan also says she approaches training in a *holistic* manner. A pet owner or trainer using a whole animal approach takes into consideration the individual dog and his or her health, genetics, environment, past experiences, and reactions to training. This holistic approach is therefore different for every dog trainer as well as every dog.

DEFINITION

The **holistic** approach to pet care subscribes to the idea that the whole pet—that is, all aspects of the pet's life—must be considered.

Tammy McKinnon, a pet-owning graphic designer, says, "I'm of the opinion that a really good diet can mitigate a lot of potential problems so our holistic approach largely goes for diet. We feed a primarily raw diet." McKinnon notes that, when dealing with health issues, "I do a lot of personal research and I don't blindly follow what the veterinarian says." She adds she and her husband even switched veterinarians because a previous vet wasn't listening to what was important to them.

"I do for my dogs as I would do for myself," says Renea Dahms, a Canine Behavior Consultant who uses a primarily natural approach to raising her dogs. She feeds her dogs, sheep, horse, ducks, and chickens natural diets; in the case of her dogs, she provides them with raw foods. She uses homeopathic and herbal remedies and Reiki healing to care for her animals as well.

Many pet owners, pet professionals or not, seem to agree on several points, beginning with the idea that natural health encompasses many different things. It does seem, for most people, though, to begin with diet and nutrition.

Alternative Health Techniques

An interest in natural health techniques for pets seemingly grew out of natural health interests for people. Many pet owners feel as Renea Dahms does, endeavoring to treat pets as they do themselves. Pet owners often use *alternative medicine* or alternative techniques as a part of natural health for dogs and cats.

DEFINITION

The generally accepted definition for **alternative medicine** is anything used for health care or prevention that falls outside the scope of conventional medicine.

Techniques generally considered alternative medicine include the following:

- **Acupuncture:** A practitioner placing fine needles in specific areas of the pet's body to alleviate symptoms and ailments. This is discussed in more detail in Chapter 2.

- **Aromatherapy:** Using scented oils for a healing purpose. You learn more about this in Chapter 4.

- **Ayurveda:** Complementing conventional medicine (rather than replacing it) with the traditional medicine of India. You learn more about Ayurveda in Chapter 5.

- **Chiropractic:** A practitioner treating and preventing musculoskeletal system disorders. This technique is discussed in more detail in Chapter 2.

- **Flower essences:** Using diluted formulas of plant parts— including flowers, leaves, stems, and roots—to prevent or treat mental or emotional stresses. This homeopathic technique is covered in Chapter 4.

> **PET ALERT**
>
> Compared to dogs, cats are more sensitive to certain substances. Only use herbs and flower essences when that substance is well known to be safe for cats. Never use oils because most are toxic for cats.

- **Herbal remedies:** Using plants and plant parts—flowers, leaves, roots, and stems—to prevent or treat health issues. The use of herbal remedies is one of the most commonly known and used alternative techniques. See Chapter 3 for more information.

- **Homeopathy:** Using highly diluted preparations in a medicinal fashion to prevent or treat health disorders. This controversial alternative remedy is discussed in Chapter 3.

- **Nutrition:** Defining and feeding the right food to your dog or cat. I discuss nutrition in Part 3.

- **Nutritional supplements:** Adding whole foods and supplements for specific purposes to your pets' diets. Chapter 13 talks about supplements of various kinds.

- **Reiki:** Often called "the laying on of hands," Reiki is a Japanese technique of using the warmth and placement of the hands to assist in healing. Reiki is explained in Chapter 5.

- **Traditional Chinese medicine:** Using Chinese herbal medicine, massage, acupuncture, and nutritional therapies. This is discussed in Chapter 5.

Some pet owners choose one alternative technique, such as herbal remedies or homeopathic remedies. Others prefer to combine techniques, using what they feel is needed at the time or for a particular situation.

Renea Dahms uses a variety of alternative techniques with her pets and farm animals, but if her animals need veterinary care, she makes sure they get that as needed. Dahms says, "My overall theory is 'The lesser of two evils.' I look at my options, weigh the effects on my dog, and opt to use what is going to ensure their ultimate health."

The National Center for Complementary and Alternative Medicine (www.nccam.nih.gov) defines complementary and alternative medical (which includes veterinary) techniques as, "A group of diverse medical and health-care systems, practices, and products, that are not currently part of conventional medicine." That statement is wide open to interpretation.

Using Integrative Care

Some proponents of natural health techniques or alternative medicine feel these must be used apart from conventional medicine. Dr. Downing believes natural health and conventional veterinary medicine don't have to be an either/or relationship. She says, "Pitting natural against conventional seems to imply that conventional medicine is somehow unnatural. I would suggest that a more accurate description might be *integrated care*."

DEFINITION

Integrated care encompasses many aspects of animal health, including the relationship with the owner, the environment, natural remedies, as well as conventional veterinary medicine.

The decision to use one or more natural health techniques for your pet doesn't mean that conventional veterinary medicine cannot be used. Many injuries, especially traumatic ones, are best dealt with using conventional veterinary medicine, at least initially. This is especially important should surgery be warranted.

Although some illnesses can be treated quite effectively with natural products, sometimes conventional veterinary care is also needed. Sudden-onset illness and life-threatening illness are times when you may need veterinary intervention. Veterinary medications, especially antibiotics and cortisones, have saved many lives. Pain relievers and anti-inflammatories can make life much more comfortable while an animal is healing. Although there are natural remedies that can approximate these medications, none are quite as effective, or as fast-acting, as conventional veterinary medicines.

But again, this doesn't have to be an either/or situation. Talk to your veterinarian about what you can do during and after the health crisis to support his efforts. That's what integrative care is all about. Shawn Messonnier, DVM, says combining conventional veterinary care with complementary or alternative treatments is often the best medicine. For example, he says milk thistle is a wonderful herb that can help heal the liver, and there's no conventional medication that can do the same thing.

Do Your Research

Many aspects of natural health for our pets are rooted in sound evidence. No one can deny that good nutrition, exercise, grooming, and body care are important for good health. Nor can anyone debate the importance of a sound relationship between pets and their people. Not all aspects of natural health are scientifically proven, which can be an issue when a pet is ill or injured. Dr. Downing says, "Anecdotes are fascinating but they do not form the foundation for making reasonable medical decisions." Bypassing veterinary care and relying on an unproven and possibly ineffective natural technique may be harmful to your pet.

Of course, just because a natural health technique isn't scientifically proven doesn't necessarily mean it isn't effective. It could also mean that it hasn't been tested scientifically yet.

GO NATURAL

Research and studies are often funded by corporations who wish to prove a point about a product or a line of products. Therefore, when the media reports on a study, it's important for consumers to know who funded the study and any potential bias influencing the result or interpretation of the data.

It doesn't hurt to be a skeptic. It's important to ask questions and research potential products and remedies to ensure what you choose to use is safe for your pet and has minimal side effects. For example, although most herbal remedies are safe, some are toxic. Cats in particular can be sensitive to many different things.

There can also be problems with some natural remedies. For example, in May 2010, the Government Accountability Office (GAO) released a report to Congress concerning diet supplements and herbal remedies. In brief, the report noted widespread deceptive marketing practices, such as manufacturers making untested and unproven claims regarding their products' health benefits. In addition, the GAO tested 40 supplements for heavy metal and pesticide contamination, and found contaminants in 37 of the 40 products.

Commercial Products

The Food and Drug Administration (FDA) doesn't test or govern alternative remedies such as herbs and supplements, which means just about anything can be labeled, produced, and sold as a natural remedy or supplement. In addition, the amount of the herb or supplement contained in a tablet, capsule, or tea may vary from product to product.

When choosing a commercially produced natural product, choose wisely:

- Choose only products from well-known, recognized companies.

- Do some research to find out whether a particular product, supplement, or herb has been the subject of any tests regarding its use and efficiency.

- Research each product's potential side effects. What are they?

- Talk to your veterinarian. What does he or she think about a product and the company that produces it? Could this product be beneficial or detrimental to your pet's health?

Chapter 13 discusses supplements in detail.

Other Natural Health Techniques

Apply skepticism to all natural techniques. If something sounds too good to be true, it probably is. There isn't anything magical about natural health techniques; they're simply something else you can use to provide a better life for your dog or cat.

So ask questions, do research, and choose wisely. Natural health techniques can be good for your pet, but at the same time, you want to make sure these techniques don't cause harm.

Working with Your Vet

When done wisely, a natural, holistic approach to natural pet health can be beneficial to your cat or dog. That means looking at your pet's overall life, including your pet's relationship with you and the home environment, body care and grooming, and exercise. A more natural diet, taking into account your pet's nutritional needs, is the usual first step toward natural health care.

It's vital to find a veterinarian who's willing to work with you as you explore natural health techniques and care. Dr. Downing says, "Allopathic veterinary medicine can and should blend seamlessly with the detailed day-to-day hands-on relationship of the pet owner and the pet; weaving into the picture the medicine we know can help make pets healthier."

When our dog, Dax, was diagnosed with liver disease, my husband Paul and I were willing to use modern medicine to help her, but there weren't beneficial treatments available in conventional medicine. Thankfully, our veterinarian worked with us when we turned to natural remedies to treat Dax. Not all veterinarians are open to natural health care for pets.

Have a frank talk with your veterinarian. Ask whether he or she is willing to work with you as you try new things. Ask what background or knowledge your vet has in natural health techniques. If you aren't comfortable with your vet's answers, ask more questions—after all, many natural health techniques are scientifically unproven. Let your vet explain his or her concerns. Then, find a balance that will satisfy both of you.

If your veterinarian doesn't use or believe in the use of natural health techniques, it's perfectly acceptable to get a second opinion. To find a veterinarian in your area who practices natural health techniques, go to the website of the American Holistic Veterinary Medical Association (www.holisticvetlist.com).

Helping the Planet

Many pet owners begin using natural techniques for themselves, their family, and their pets out of concern for the world around them. Making even small changes can make a difference. We've all read articles or seen on the news that plastic grocery store bags are a blight in landfills. In response to this, many people now bring reusable tote bags with them to the grocery store. This small change will make a big difference, especially as more people make the change.

Pet owners can make a difference, too, as so many have discovered:

- When you feed your pet a better diet, your pet produces less waste.

- If you feed a homemade diet, choose to buy meat from animals raised locally and naturally, rather than from factory farm animals.

- Pick up after your dog using biodegradable bags.

- Use a more natural litter—such as one made from wheat—for your cat.

- Buy toys and other products made from naturally sustainable sources or recycled materials.

- Choose pet shampoos, conditioners, and other products made from natural ingredients rather than from chemicals.

CAT CHAT

If you decide to change cat litters, do so gradually. Every few days, add a small scoop of the new litter to the old kind so your cat can get used to it gradually. Abrupt changes can cause even a fully housetrained cat to avoid the litter box.

Many businesses are becoming aware that pet owners are concerned about the environment and their pet's carbon footprint. Planet Dog has been producing dog toys from recycled materials for a long time. The company even has a program in which consumers can send old toys back to the company to be recycled. The giant pet supply corporation Petco has a new line of green products that includes leashes and collars made from recycled materials, toys made from environmentally friendly materials, shampoo free of artificial dyes, and even kitty litter made from recycled paper.

The easiest way to provide for a pet and protect the environment is to be a wise consumer. Read labels and understand what's on them. Then, make small changes. Even small changes can add up to something big!

The Least You Need to Know

- Natural health for your dog or cat can encompass many things, including good nutrition, exercise, quality time with you, acupuncture, and herbal remedies.
- Integrative care, or combining natural health techniques with conventional veterinary care, is a good practice for many pet owners.
- Many aspects of natural health care are not scientifically proven, and although that doesn't mean they don't work, being a little bit of a skeptic is not a bad idea.
- It benefits your pet and helps the planet when you use natural health-care techniques, use fewer chemicals, read labels, and choose products made from sustainable practices.

Natural Healing Therapies

In This Chapter

- Discovering acupuncture
- Understanding acupressure's relationship to acupuncture
- Taking a look at chiropractic therapy
- How effective are these treatments?

In recent years, acupuncture, acupressure, and chiropractic therapies have become increasingly popular in pet care. Acupuncture is especially well accepted as a therapy that can work alongside conventional veterinary medicine. Acupressure is relatively new to pet care, but many pet owners appreciate that it's something they can do at home to help their pets. Most veterinarians don't yet accept chiropractic therapy as a viable care option, but it's gaining more acceptance among pet owners.

All three therapies have multiple applications for pets. They're often used to alleviate discomfort from joint pain, such as pain associated with hip or elbow dysplasia, and other musculoskeletal disorders. These therapies can help treat a number of different diseases, and experts continue to explore other applications for future use. As with most natural techniques, however, there are skeptics.

The Ancient Therapy of Acupuncture

Acupuncture is an ancient healing art with roots in China that go back thousands of years. Archeologists have found acupuncture needles in China that date back at least 7,000 years. Many experts believe practitioners in India were also instrumental in the development of acupuncture.

According to Chinese philosophy, acupuncture corrects energy imbalances in the body. This energy is called the *Qi*. An imbalance in one's Qi can lead to injuries, disease, or an inability to heal.

> **DEFINITION**
>
> A living body's **Qi** (pronounced *chee*) is its vital energy or life force. There are two sides to this energy, a negative and a positive. For a body to remain healthy, both sides to the body's Qi must be in balance.

According to many documented histories of acupuncture (and they all vary to a certain extent), it was first practiced on livestock, then on humans, and then on pets. Horses, in particular, respond well to this therapy. Because horses have been so essential to human survival throughout history, it's easy to understand why caretakers used acupuncture to treat them.

There has been a lot of research done for both people and animals regarding the effectiveness of acupuncture. It has been found to be effective in a wide range of situations. Acupuncture can be used to treat a variety of problems for dogs and cats, including the following:

- Musculoskeletal problems, including the pain and inflammation from hip and elbow dysplasia

- Pain and inflammation from performance sports injuries or those incurred when a working dog is hurt

- Neurological disorders of various kinds, including problems with the spinal cord

- Digestive disorders, including spasms of the intestinal tract

Luanne Burton of Dana Point, California, offers a personal account of the effectiveness of acupuncture: "My Australian Shepherd, Jake, had been a very active dog throughout his life, playing catch, jumping, leaping, participating in agility and flyball. But all of his activities began to catch up with him as he grew older." Jake developed arthritis and back problems. Burton says, "I had heard about acupuncture as an alternative to pain medications and decided to give it a try. Jake went once a week for a month for treatment. He was incredibly relaxed for the treatments, much to my surprise. After each treatment he would trot out the door, apparently in no pain."

Combining the Physical and Spiritual

A practitioner performs acupuncture by applying very fine needles to specific spots on the patient's body. These spots, called *acupuncture points*, are located along energy lines known as *meridians*.

Physically, acupuncture works because these meridians contain connective tissue, small blood vessels, and nerve endings. When the practitioner inserts the needles, they cause the body to release endorphins, hormones, and other healing and pain-relieving mechanisms that also trigger the body's healing processes.

Spiritually, acupuncture's proponents believe the practice strives to balance the body's opposing forces—the yin and the yang. The body's yin and yang can be considered the opposing forces for just about anything: balanced and unbalanced, happy and sad, and so forth. If you think about acupuncture as restoring the proper balance, that is reasonable.

Meridians and Points

In traditional Chinese medicine (TCM; see Chapter 5), these meridians are channels along which the body's Qi, or life force, travels. Each side of the body has meridians that run parallel down the body, and each meridian is associated with a particular organ.

The two most important meridians are the Governor and the Conception. The Governor, or Governor Vessel (GV), runs along the center of the back and up to the head. The Conception, or

Conception Vessel (CV), begins at the head and runs down the center of the body in the front. The other meridians are named according to the organs they affect, and include the following: Heart (HT), Pericardium (PC), Lung (LU), Small Intestine (SI), Large Intestine (LI), Kidney (KI), Stomach (ST), Liver (LR), Spleen (SP), Gallbladder (GB), and Bladder (BL).

In addition, each therapeutic point along the meridians is numbered for easy identification. For example, the fourth point along the meridian for the heart is labeled HT4. Veterinarians who practice acupuncture have charts listing all of the meridians and their dozens of therapeutic points.

DOG TALK

Most veterinary acupuncturists agree that dogs have 73 therapeutic points. There is often debate among experts about this number, however, because some believe there are more therapeutic points.

It may seem the locations of the meridians and points and the organs they affect don't make any logical sense.

For example:

- Point KI3 is the third point along the meridian that affects the kidneys. This point is inside the hock of a rear leg and is nowhere near a kidney.

- BL60 is the sixtieth point along the meridian that affects the bladder. It's located on the outside of a rear leg, above the hock.

- PC6 is the sixth point along the meridian that affects the pericardium. It's located inside a front leg, just above the wrist.

However, just because the meridians and therapeutic points don't follow any obvious rhyme or reason doesn't mean they don't work. Numerous studies and trials have shown that acupuncture does work.

CAT CHAT

Generally, there are 44 therapeutic acupuncture points on cats. Some practitioners use additional therapeutic points on cats, just as many use additional points on dogs.

Alone and Together

Acupuncture has been a standalone medical and veterinary technique for thousands of years. In many parts of the world, it still is. Today, however, veterinarians more often use it in conjunction with conventional veterinary medicine. Depending on your pet's health issues, acupuncture can be a part of your pet's treatment or physical therapy. Your vet may offer it before or after surgery, or with medications.

Acupuncture has many applications and uses. If your veterinarian hasn't recommended acupuncture for your pet, ask whether he or she believes it may be beneficial.

A Variety of Techniques

The original acupuncture technique, practiced for thousands of years, involved practitioners placing many tiny needles along the body's meridians at specific acupuncture points. Traditionalists still believe this is the true method of practicing acupuncture. However, a variety of techniques are now available, including the following:

- *Aquapuncture* involves injecting tiny amounts of vitamins, sterile water, antibiotics, or other therapeutic fluids at the acupuncture sites.

- *Electro-acupuncture* is the technique of using small amounts of harmless electricity to stimulate the acupuncture points.

- *Implantation* is the technique of implanting small metal beads, usually gold, at acupuncture points.

- *Laser acupuncture* involves using a cold or low-power laser to stimulate acupuncture points.

Your veterinarian can recommend the acupuncture technique best suited to your dog or cat, depending on the health problem. If you contact a veterinary acupuncturist who isn't your pet's regular veterinarian, ask the two professionals to discuss your pet's health needs so they can work together and stay fully informed.

> **PET ALERT**
>
> Acupuncture is a beneficial, safe health-care technique, but never attempt to perform it on your pet in the home. Because it involves inserting needles into your pet's body, it can cause infection or even more serious issues if done incorrectly or under unsanitary conditions. Only allow a veterinarian trained and licensed in acupuncture or a professional acupuncturist to perform acupuncture on your pet. For more information, see the website of the American Academy of Veterinary Acupuncture (www.aava.org).

Acceptance by Pets

Although the idea of someone inserting fine needles into the skin may bother many people, most dogs and cats accept acupuncture treatments very well. Some twinge as the needles are inserted, but they usually remain quiet and still for the 20- to 30-minute procedure.

Connie Kelly, a dog trainer from Carlsbad, California, says of her Australian Shepherd, Taco, "Taco has elbow dysplasia and has had surgery, various treatments, and medications. He's still often uncomfortable, so I decided to try acupuncture. Thankfully he accepts it well." Although acupuncture treatments can't cure Taco's elbow dysplasia, each treatment keeps him relatively comfortable for two to three weeks, depending on his activity level during that time.

Jennifer Acquire of Denver, Colorado, notes her long-haired tabby cat, Sassy, injured her back jumping from a high bookshelf when she was younger. Now, at 14 years old, Sassy is arthritic and stiff. Acquire says, "Sassy was having trouble with pain medications—too many side effects—so I had our veterinarian begin acupuncture treatments and they work wonderfully for Sassy. She had weekly treatments for a month and now just one a month." Acquire says Sassy relaxes during the treatments and purrs the entire time.

Acupressure

Acupressure grew out of the science of acupuncture. The difference is that with acupressure, as the name suggests, practitioners use pressure on the acupuncture points instead of needles. Because there is no penetration of the pet's skin, this is something that many pet owners learn to perform on their pets at home and feel comfortable doing.

Acupressure is related to massage, which can also be therapeutic for your pet. Most pets learn to enjoy a massage very quickly, and therefore learn to accept acupressure as well. Acupressure can be used by itself to benefit your pet, or it can be used as a treatment at home, by the owner, in between acupuncture treatments. The range of injuries and illnesses that can be treated by this technique are the same as for acupuncture.

CAT CHAT

Introduce cats to massage and acupressure slowly. Begin by stroking the cat, and then over several weeks, gradually increase the pressure of the petting. If you apply the massage or acupressure too firmly, the cat may panic.

Physical and Spiritual

Just as with acupuncture, acupressure has two aspects: the physical and the spiritual. In fact, the only real difference between the two therapies is one is performed with needles and the other without.

Acupuncture purists don't believe acupressure is a legitimate therapy, believing it's a copycat or less effective technique, but that belief isn't universal. Shawn Messonnier, DVM, of the Acupuncture and Holistic Animal Health Care Center in Plano, Texas, says, "Owners can be taught to apply acupressure on pets at home using the acupuncture points that have been used during veterinary treatments. This can give the pet further relief from pain and inflammation."

Acupressure Basics

Veterinary acupuncturists have thoroughly detailed charts that display the many acupuncture meridians and points for dogs and cats (as well as humans and horses). Generally, though, not all of these are used for acupressure.

You can feel most acupressure points as small indentations, depressions, or dimples on the dog's or cat's body. By using these specific points rather than the wide range of acupuncture points, it's much easier for a pet owner to find them. Use only enough pressure during the massage to maintain contact with the dimple. Larger dogs may require slightly more pressure, while cats and small dogs may require less.

Most veterinary acupuncturists who recommend acupressure treatments suggest daily treatments. Each session should be for no longer than 5 to 10 minutes, and shorter if the animal is anxious and trying to squirm away. Some pets may be uncomfortable with the pressure point massage initially, but they get used to it. However, if your pet whines, growls, or otherwise shows discomfort with this technique, stop.

Acupressure may be helpful in treating the following conditions:

- **Allergies:** Raise one of your pet's front paws and bend the elbow. Feel for the crease on the outside of the elbow. At the end of the crease, feel for an indentation. Massage or put pressure at the indentation.

- **Allergies—dermatitis:** On the inside of the rear legs, at the thigh, find the indentation in the large muscle just in front of the femur. Massage or put pressure at the indentation.

- **Diarrhea:** On the rear legs, apply pressure or massage the indentation just below the ankle, on the inside of the leg.

- **Digestion:** There's an indentation in the middle of the muscle of each rear leg, just below the knee, toward the front of the leg. Massage or put pressure at the indentation.

- **Digestion—vomiting:** On the back of each front leg, behind the wrist, there's an indentation between the two tendons. Massage or put pressure at the indentation.

- **Ears—pain or infection:** There's an indentation on the head, in front of the ear. (Note: its location can vary depending upon the breed and the breed's ear set.) Massage or put pressure at the indentation.

- **Eyes—conjunctivitis:** There's an indentation in the skull directly under the center of the eye. Very gently massage or put pressure at the indentation.

- **Eyes—tearing:** At eyebrow level, there's a slight indentation above the inner corner of the eye. Very gently massage or put pressure at the indentation.

- **Heart—calming:** Count the ribs from the last one, moving up toward the head, until you reach the fifth rib. Massage or put pressure at the small indentations on either side of the spine, where the fifth rib meets the spine.

- **Lungs—bronchitis and coughing:** There's an indentation in the muscle below the shoulder joint, at the front of the chest. Massage or put pressure at the indentation.

- **Lungs—respiratory problems:** On the front legs, at the wrist, feel for an indentation on the inside of the wrist. Massage or put pressure at the indentation.

As you massage a specific point, you may sense some heaviness at that spot. The energy may be stopped or clogged, or the blood flow may be impeded by a tight muscle, a pooling of blood, or another blockage. This usually signifies you've found the right point for your pet's health problem. You may find your dog or cat winces when you massage that spot. Just be gentle!

A few seconds of gentle massage usually releases that heaviness. You may need to come back to that spot a couple times per day, or once a day for several days, to fully release it.

Although there aren't as many acupressure points as there are acupuncture points, these are just a sample of the full list of points. If you would like to try acupressure, either in conjunction with acupuncture or with another therapy, talk to your veterinarian. If he or she is educated in acupressure, your vet can show you the appropriate acupressure points and coach you in this therapy's use. If your veterinarian is not knowledgeable on this subject, contact a veterinary acupuncturist.

> **DOG TALK**
>
> Most dogs relax during acupressure, but some dogs are ticklish (especially on their paws) and may pull the paw away. If your pet resists the acupressure, ask your vet if there's an alternative pressure point you can use.

Using Acupressure

You can perform acupressure on your pet on a daily basis, or depending on your pet's health problem, you can even apply it a couple of times each day. A daily massage isn't going to cause any harm, and could potentially do a lot of good. However, if your pet pulls away from your hands, winces, or shows signs of soreness, there may be a problem:

- Your pet may be reacting to the original ailment and is wincing at the massage of that particular meridian point.

- You may be using too much pressure on the meridian point.

- You may be massaging too deep, on a bone, or in a muscle.

- Your pet may have unrelated soreness where you are massaging.

If the soreness continues, talk to your veterinarian about it. Be prepared to explain and demonstrate what causes your pet to wince.

Chiropractic Therapy

Chiropractic therapy is a more recent addition to the medical and veterinary community than is acupuncture. It was founded in 1895 by Daniel David Palmer, who theorized that manipulation of the spine may cure disease. His son, B. J. Palmer, continued his father's profession by taking over and promoting the Palmer School of Chiropractic, the first school to teach the discipline.

Chiropractic medicine involves understanding the body's skeletal anatomy, as well as the nerves and spine. Many chiropractors use a variety of tools to diagnose problems, including x-rays or other imaging, hands-on assessments, and neurological evaluations. The animal's stance, gait, ability or inability to move normally, and pain or soreness are evaluated.

Standalone and Mixed Together

There are two fields of chiropractic therapy: *straight chiropractics* and *mixed chiropractics*. Unfortunately, these two fields don't always get along. The two groups' disagreements can make it difficult for medical practitioners outside the chiropractic profession to accept chiropractic therapies as legitimate medical techniques.

> **DEFINITION**
>
> **Straight chiropractors** adhere to the Palmers' principles. They believe, among other things, that problems with the spine are a leading cause of all disease. **Mixed chiropractors** believe using chiropractic techniques alongside other therapies is beneficial.

Straight chiropractors don't use their techniques in conjunction with other medical therapies. These practitioners hold strong metaphysical beliefs concerning the body, its vitality, and innate intelligence. Mixed chiropractors believe problems of the spine may be just one cause of disease; that is, they believe not all diseases originate in the spine. Mixed chiropractors also believe in using chiropractic therapies in conjunction with other therapies, including conventional medicine, nutritional supplements, herbal remedies, and more.

Chiropractic Theory

Chiropractic therapy works with the relationship between the spine, the spinal column, and the nervous system. The spine is comprised of vertebrae, which are separated by intervertebral discs. The discs provide a cushion between the vertebrae. The vertebrae protect the spinal cord, which passes through the center of the vertebrae.

Chiropractors believe illness can result when something is wrong in this system, such as a problem with a vertebra, a disc, the spine's range of motion, or the nerve impulses from the brain to the spinal cord to the body. Experts often recommend chiropractic therapy for pets with arthritis, elbow or hip dysplasia, back injuries, athletic injuries, and even weaknesses associated with old age.

Veterinary Chiropractic Therapy

Chiropractic therapies have been used for horses since the early 1900s, but vets only recently began using it for dogs and cats. In fact, the American Veterinary Medical Association (AVMA) didn't delineate policies detailing animal chiropractic care until 1994. The AVMA recommends a veterinarian first examine the dog or cat and decide upon a course of treatment, which may include chiropractic therapy.

Veterinarians have used chiropractic therapy extensively for race horses, working horses, racing greyhounds, working dogs, as well as other pets. Studies have found that chiropractic manipulation raises pain thresholds and enables animals to move more freely after treatments. Few studies have been performed regarding efficacy in dogs and cats, and the few that do exist don't provide definitive proof of its value for these animals. Dr. Narda Robinson says, "There is no research on veterinary patients stating whether or how chiropractic works on animals. While anecdotal reports say that it helps some pain or spinal issues, we can't say much about the risk-benefit ratio without research."

Not for Home Use

Pet owners must never try to practice chiropractic therapy on their pets at home. This therapy requires a complete and thorough knowledge of the dog's or cat's anatomy, and someone without adequate knowledge may do more harm than good. Manipulating the spine incorrectly may cause serious damage to the spine or spinal cord. Even trying to adjust a leg, shoulder, hip, or other extremity can potentially cause your pet great harm.

> **PET ALERT**
>
> Only a veterinarian who has studied chiropractic veterinary therapy should perform chiropractic adjustments on your pet. Ideally, the veterinarian should be a member of the American Veterinary Chiropractic Association (www.animalchiropratic.org).

Are These Treatments Effective for Pets?

Acupuncture, acupressure, and chiropractic therapies are certainly becoming more popular for pets. Growing enrollment in professional organizations for acupuncture and chiropractic therapies is indicative of increasing interest. The American Veterinary Chiropractic Association has members in the United States, Canada, Europe, and Australia. Contact the American Veterinary Chiropractic Association (www.animalchiropratic.org) for a referral in your area.

However, popularity isn't necessarily proof positive that a technique works. Many pets whose owners take them to acupuncturists or chiropractors are on other therapies as well, including medications, herbal remedies, and physical therapy. Although acupuncture or chiropractic therapy may have helped the pets, there's no way to determine exactly which—if not all—of those therapies was the most effective.

There Are Skeptics

Many alternative and natural health techniques, including chiropractic therapy, are said to be alternative therapies because they are not proven through rigorous studies to be effective.

Acupuncture also comes under fire from critics. Some say that just because a therapy has existed for thousands of years doesn't mean it's effective. Perhaps it's been in existence this long because there weren't alternatives for so many years.

Although these skeptics certainly have a point, there are skeptics for all treatments, including conventional human and veterinary medicine and other alternative therapies. Disagreements regarding efficacy are why so many people get second and even third opinions prior to accepting medical advice.

Alternative Therapies Are Just That ... Alternatives

Shawn Messonnier, DVM, says, "Skeptical veterinarians do not approve of using natural therapies that they consider to be unproven. According to the skeptics, unless the therapy has been proven to work through numerous rigidly controlled scientific studies, that therapy would be considered to be an alternative and unproven therapy. That therapy should not be used in the practice of medicine." However, many times pet owners turn to alternative therapies when conventional ones haven't been effective or have caused side effects that were too numerous or too harmful for their pet.

The Least You Need to Know

- Acupuncture is an ancient medical art that combines physical and metaphysical applications.
- Acupressure is an offshoot of acupuncture that pet owners can use on their pets at home.
- Chiropractic therapy involves manipulation of the spine for disease prevention and healing.
- As with all alternative and conventional therapies, there are skeptics who feel pet owners should avoid unproven therapies.

Homeopathy and Herbal Remedies

In This Chapter

- Defining homeopathy
- Turning plants into natural remedies
- Are these remedies effective?
- Using homeopathic remedies safely

Homeopathy is a controversial alternative health technique that uses minute amounts of substances to affect a change in the body. Skeptics question the minute, often immeasurable amounts of medicinal substances in the remedies and doubt their effectiveness. Still, homeopathy—for people and for pets—has a very dedicated and growing following.

A great number of people use herbal remedies; many often don't even know they're using one. For example, do you drink chamomile tea to calm down before going to bed? Do you like to take some peppermint when your stomach is upset? These are herbal remedies. Increasingly in recent years, pet owners have been using herbal remedies for their dogs and cats.

Discovering Homeopathy

Dr. Samuel Hahnemann (1755–1843) is considered the inventor and father of *homeopathy*. He practiced the traditional medicine of his era, but he became dissatisfied with the results—after all, medicine in the

1700s was primitive. Although many of the herbal remedies we know today were in use at that time, there were no antibiotics, and no sterilization of the hands or even the instruments was used.

DEFINITION

Homeopathy is an alternative medicine that uses highly diluted remedies to cure diseases.

The causes of disease were unknown, too. The night air, for example, was often the cause of disease, according to doctors of that era. It wasn't unusual for patients to get worse or even die under a doctor's treatment. It's easy to see why a doctor who cared about his patients could become so frustrated.

Dr. Hahnemann began experimenting while trying to find ways to help his patients. He understood that itching, for example, was not the actual disease, but instead a symptom of something else that was causing the itching. Dr. Hahnemann believed in the law of similars (discussed in detail in the upcoming section). If he could find a substance that could also cause itching, he could use that as a remedy for the disease that was causing itching in the patient. He began formulating remedies made from things in nature: animal organs, including those of reptiles; oyster shells; fish; minerals such as sulfur; volcanic ash; insects, including the venom from bees; and the roots, leaves, bark, and flowers of many plants. Very small amounts of these substances were added to water or alcohol, shaken vigorously, and then diluted again.

Although some folks disagree about how to classify homeopathy (some call it the most basic of natural health remedies because natural substances are the primary ingredients in the remedies; others call it alternative medicine because the substances are considered medicines), homeopathy today has not changed much at all. In fact, many of Dr. Hahnemann's remedies are still in use, made with his original recipes. More recipes have been added, but they are still made according to his original directions.

The Vital Life Force

Dr. Hahnemann believed everything in the world contained a *vital life force*. Today, homeopathic practitioners still believe birds, reptiles, mammals, plants, rocks, and everything else on the planet contains this vital life force. When they make remedies using these animals, plants, or other substances, that substance's life force is transferred to the remedy. When a patient uses the remedy, the patient benefits from the substance's life force, which can then help the patient heal.

Dr. Hahnemann diluted his remedies over and over, making them more and more dilute, because he believed the more diluted the remedy, the more life force the remedy contained. For example, consider crushed peppermint leaves soaked in alcohol. After soaking up the life force from the leaves and some of the sap, it's now in the alcohol. Add 1 drop of that mixture to 9 drops of clean distilled water. That formula—1 to 9—is a 1x potency remedy.

If you add 1 drop of the original single drop of alcohol and peppermint to 99 drops of water, you've created a 1c potency remedy. Even though the second formula is considerably more diluted than the first, homeopathic practitioners believe it contains more vital life force and is therefore the stronger formula of the two. This way of thinking is counterintuitive to most people—anything severely diluted should be weaker than the original, right? If I take 1 drop of pancake syrup and add it to 9 drops of water, that mixture is sweeter than 1 drop of syrup added to 99 drops of water. Still, proponents say homeopathic remedies work.

The Law of Similars

Dr. Hahnemann documented the primary principle of homeopathy, the *law of similars*. Basically, he said that like cures like. For example, consider a health problem that causes a specific symptom, such as itching. According to the law of similars, this health problem can be treated by a remedy that, in its original form, also causes itching. The severely diluted remedy no longer causes itching, but because of its dilution, it now contains a life force so strong it promotes the healing of the person's health problem.

Dr. Shawn Messonnier gives an example: "One homeopathic remedy that may be used to control itching is Rhus tox, which is made from poison ivy. In full concentration, poison ivy causes sores and itching. Yet the homeopathic preparation of Rhus tox is often used in the treatment of poison ivy and other itching disorders. Therefore, we see that a substance which causes itching in an undiluted, pure, concentrated form can also be used to treat itching when in the diluted form."

The Most Common Homeopathic Remedies

The following are a number of common homeopathic remedies. Many treat a variety of disorders because the original form of the remedy may normally cause a variety of symptoms. Due to the law of similars, some remedies may be effective for a variety of health problems. Unless otherwise directed by a homeopathic veterinarian, these are given via drops in the mouth.

- **Aconitum napellus:** This comes from the root, stem, leaves, and flowers of an herb in the family Ranunculaceae. For dogs, use it for respiratory disease and fevers. For cats, use it for muscle and joint pain and arthritis.

- **Apis mellifica:** This remedy contains honey bees, including the poison sac. Use this on dogs and cats who have fluid in the lungs or swelling in musculoskeletal joints.

- **Arnica montana:** This comes from plants in the family Compositae. The entire plant is used in the remedy, including the roots. Both dogs and cats can take this remedy to reduce shock, help heal bruises and wounds, and help control bleeding. It also assists with an easy labor and delivery.

- **Arsenicum album:** This remedy is derived from the potent poison arsenic. Both dogs and cats can take it to treat skin conditions, including dry, itchy, and scaly skin, and to help with pneumonia.

- **Belladonna:** Belladonna is an herb in the family Solanaceae, and can help calm a dog's or cat's racing heart.

- **Bryonia alba:** Bryonia is a perennial vine. This remedy is made from the roots of the plant. Use it on dogs and cats suffering from respiratory illnesses.

- **Calcarea carbonica:** This remedy originates from crushed and powdered oyster shells; the active ingredient is calcium carbonate. Puppies with pica (that is, they eat strange objects) benefit from this remedy. It's also beneficial to dogs and cats with bone and joint problems.

- **Calendula officinalis:** Calendula is a flowering plant in the marigold family. Its leaves and flowers make up a remedy that helps heal open wounds in dogs and cats.

CAT CHAT

Wounds from mice and rat bites often become infected and are slow to heal. Calendula officinalis is often effective at helping these wounds to heal more quickly.

- **Carbo vegetabilis:** This remedy comes from charcoal and is safe to use with cats and dogs. Use for animals with flatulence and exhausted animals (such as dogs participating in sports).

- **Cortisone:** This extremely diluted form of the drug cortisone is effective in treating inflammation, allergies, and arthritis.

- **Hecla lava:** This remedy comes from lava ash or ground lava stone. You can use it for a dog or cat with dental problems or problems with the bones of the jaw or face.

- **Hepar sulphuris calcareum:** This is a combination of powdered sulfur and finely ground oyster shell. Use this for a dog or cat with a pus-producing infection.

- **Hypericum perforatum:** This is made up of the flowers, leaves, stems, and roots of St. John's wort. Use it for both dogs and cats for cuts, especially when there's a damaged nerve. It's also used for spinal cord injuries and dogs with allergies.

- **Lycopodium clavatum:** This remedy contains the spores on the flowers of the lycopodium evergreen plant, and can help dogs and cats suffering from a variety of digestive, urinary, and respiratory illnesses.

- **Nux vomica:** This remedy comes from the seeds of the berry of the nux vomica evergreen tree. Frequently, pet owners use this for dogs and cats with digestive issues, including flatulence and diarrhea.

- **Rhus toxicodendron:** This remedy is derived from the leaves of the poison ivy plant. It can help dogs and cats with skin problems (including itching) and with muscle and joint pain.

- **Ruta graveolens:** This is a plant, and the entire plant is included in the remedy. In dogs and cats, this remedy can help the bones and cartilage, as well as eye disorders.

- **Spongia tosta:** This remedy comes from toasted ocean sponges. It helps both cats and dogs with respiratory problems or swollen lymph glands.

- **Sulphur:** This is derived from the mineral sulfur, and is used for both cats and dogs. It has a variety of uses, including skin problems such as dermatitis, flea allergies, and mange.

- **Thuja occidentalis:** This remedy comes from an evergreen coniferous tree. The remedy is good for skin warts, tags, and other small growths, as well as for vaccine reactions.

These are some of the most common remedies, but there are many others. If you have questions about these or other remedies that may help your pet, talk to your veterinarian or a homeopathic practitioner.

Alone or Together?

Expert opinions differ on whether pet owners should give their pets individual homeopathic remedies or in combination with other remedies or therapies. Those who believe strongly in the original homeopathic guidelines feel a pet should only take one homeopathic remedy at a time, and the pet shouldn't take it with other homeopathic or alternative remedies—especially not with conventional medicines.

Today, however, most people feel those guidelines are blurry. Many pet owners combine homeopathic remedies with other alternative therapies, including herbal remedies, acupuncture, and nutritional supplements.

Many veterinarians who incorporate alternative therapies into their treatment options recommend homeopathic remedies in conjunction with other treatments, including conventional medications and alternative therapies. If you aren't sure how to proceed with homeopathy, talk to your veterinarian. Share your concerns for your pet, and with your vet's help, you can decide which options are best for your pet.

Finding Homeopathic Remedies

Homeopathic remedies are available from a variety of sources, including health food stores, pharmacies, and even pet supply stores. You can even buy them online (see Appendix B). However, because these remedies are not regulated in any fashion, buy only from reputable companies. If you have doubts about any particular company, ask your veterinarian for recommendations.

Homeopathic Safety

Homeopathic remedies are quite safe for dogs and cats, but as with anything, nothing is 100 percent safe. To prevent problems, keep these suggestions in mind:

* Before giving your pet a remedy, talk to a homeopathic practitioner. If this isn't your veterinarian, ask the practitioner to talk to your veterinarian so the practitioner can become familiar with your pet's health history.

* Buy only well-known, name-brand homeopathic remedies or those the practitioner made specifically for your pet. A remedy with an unknown brand or sold at a street fair booth may be fine—then again, maybe not.

* Don't use any homeopathic remedy as a substitute for medical care. If your pet has a serious illness or injury, take your pet to the veterinarian's office right away. Once there, ask about using homeopathic remedies in conjunction with the veterinary care your pet needs.

> **PET ALERT**
>
> Although a severely diluted homeopathic remedy might seem quite safe—and many are—it's still important to follow the directions for its use.

If a homeopathic remedy isn't working, talk to the homeopathic veterinarian or practitioner who recommended it. As with conventional medicine, it sometimes takes more than one try to find exactly what works for your pet.

Homeopathy Effectiveness Questioned

Many people question a remedy's effectiveness if it's so diluted the original substance can't even be detected through chemical analysis. After all, it doesn't make sense that something in such infinitesimal amounts can cure disease.

The placebo effect is often mentioned in debates about homeopathy's legitimacy. For people, this effect is a very real phenomenon. If a person takes a remedy and believes it will work, it may do just that— or he or she may imagine it is working. The placebo effect doesn't have the same outcome on dogs and cats, however, because our pets have no idea we've given them a remedy.

Sometimes an ill person or pet will get better, no matter what the remedy. Perhaps the medicine or homeopathic remedy helped, or perhaps the body simply healed using its own devices.

There are few studies to prove the effectiveness of the numerous homeopathic remedies. Most supporting evidence comes from homeopathic practitioners and pet owners, and such evidence is considered anecdotal in the scientific community. Dr. Messonnier says, "While we should encourage further studies in the area of veterinary homeopathy, the lack of studies shouldn't discourage pet owners from trying homeopathic remedies prescribed by their veterinarians. While not effective in every case (just as conventional medicines are not effective in every case), they do have their place in the treatment of a variety of medical disorders in dogs and cats."

Herbal Remedies

Using herbs and plants for healing is one of the oldest known forms of medicine. Early mankind used plants as food and as medicine from as far back as archeologists have been able to track human activities. A man who perished more than 5,300 years ago and whose body was found frozen in the Alps by two German hikers had medicinal herbs in his pack. Hippocrates, widely considered the father of modern medicine, described how to make a pain reliever from the bark and leaves of the white willow tree. His formula was a precursor to aspirin.

In every part of the world, people developed uses for the plants native to their region. They used the grasses, grass seeds, leaves and stems of plants, roots, and flowers, depending on the individual plant. My grandmother, a Lakota Indian, was taught the healing arts of her people by her mother. Although the Lakota Indians believed in a spiritual world that worked alongside the physical world, plants were valued for their healing abilities as well as their nutritional value.

These remedies were used for people, but also for their domesticated animals. Because horses in particular were integral to human survival in many cultures, they were often the recipient of herbal and plant therapies.

The Most Common Herbal Remedies

You can give your pet herbal remedies as the fresh plant or as parts of a newly picked plant. Depending upon the type of plant and remedy, you can also use them dried or put them in teas, juices, or *tinctures*. Commercial formulations may be in tablet form or capsules.

DEFINITION

A **tincture** is a liquid solution of an herb mixed with alcohol. The herb and alcohol are mixed and allowed to steep for a period of time, and then the solid matter is strained off.

Many plants have different chemical compositions in various parts of the plant. Therefore, some remedies may contain the plant roots while others may have just the flowers.

There are hundreds of plants with medicinal properties, most of which are safe for dogs and cats. Some of the most commonly used herbal remedies include the following:

- **Alfalfa:** This nutritious plant is high in plant proteins, vitamins, and minerals. The leaves and flowers reduce inflammation. Alfalfa also has anticancer properties. The high vitamin K content makes it effective for animals with bleeding disorders. It aids the bladder and digestion, and helps promote normal growth.

- **Aloe vera:** This succulent is used primarily to heal wounds. Apply the sap, mixed with a salve or ointment, directly to a cut or scrape. In dogs and cats, it reduces inflammation and speeds healing.

- **Arnica:** This is a flowering plant with bright yellow daisylike flowers. The entire plant helps with healing, especially open wounds, sprains, bruises, and broken bones. Arnica also aids the circulatory system.

PET ALERT

If you use arnica on an open wound, don't let your dog or cat lick it off. Many pets will have an upset stomach if they consume it, so keep the wound bandaged.

- **Burdock:** This herb has lavender to purple blossoms and grows along ditches and the edges of plowed fields. The root of the plant is medicinal, and is effective fresh, dried, or as a tincture. This herb is good nutrition, but it also aids liver function by helping to remove toxins from the system, and reduces inflammation.

- **Calendula:** This is a flowering plant in the marigold family. The flowers are useful in tinctures, poultices, salves, and ointments. When you mix a tincture with petroleum jelly or another salve, it's an excellent first aid ointment. It aids healing, prevents infection, relieves pain, and reduces swelling. A tincture of calendula aids digestion and relieves colitis.

- **Cayenne:** This pepper helps dilate blood vessels, which in turn aids circulation. Externally, it has anti-inflammatory and analgesic properties. Use dried peppers soaked in oils (such as olive oil) medicinally in food or mixed in a salve for external use. Caution should be taken when using or ingesting cayenne, as it can burn.

- **Chamomile:** This is one of the most common herbal remedies ever, second only to willow bark. Chamomile is a daisylike plant with lovely flowers. The flowers are used medicinally in tinctures, dried, and as teas. It's wonderful for the digestive system, where it calms everything down and relieves flatulence. It also expels worms. It calms the nervous pet and aids in sleep. To help teething puppies, rub chamomile extract on the gums directly where the new teeth are coming in.

- **Clover (red):** This invasive plant grows wild, but you can also grow it as a cultivated plant. It has red flowers you can use fresh (in the pet's food), dried, or as a tea. This is a useful herb that aids the liver's function, helps cleanse the body of toxins, and aids in fertility in female animals. It's also good nutrition.

- **Comfrey:** This common garden herb has pink, purple, or yellow flowers. You can use the stems, leaves, and flowers medicinally. Mash fresh or dried herbs with water to make a paste you can place over a wound. It aids healing and has anti-inflammatory qualities, and treats flea bites, cuts, scratches, bites, and stings.

> **PET ALERT**
>
> Don't let your pet lick or eat the comfrey paste. Always cover comfrey paste with a bandage because ingesting comfrey may be toxic to your pet.

- **Dandelion:** This weed is every gardener's nightmare, but it's every herbalist's dream. All parts of the plant are useful medicinally. It stimulates digestion and is a good anti-inflammatory. The plant is good nutrition; it's high in vitamins and minerals. Mix some chopped leaves and flowers into your pet's food.

- **Dill:** This herb is best known for curing pickles, but its leaves, flowers, and seeds actually have useful medicinal properties. Dill is soothing to the intestinal tract, easing nausea and expelling gas. According to some herbalists, it may have anticancer properties.

- **Echinacea:** This flowering plant's claim to fame is its ability to stimulate the immune system. (My grandmother always urged my mother to put us kids on Echinacea just before school began each year so we wouldn't catch all the colds that went around at the start of school. It seems to me we were pretty healthy.) Puppies can take Echinacea before beginning puppy class. Dogs and cats can start it before a dog or cat show. Use it dried or in a tea.

- **Feverfew:** This plant has tiny white flowers and serrated leaves. It is a strong anti-inflammatory herb that can ease arthritis pain. It dilates blood vessels; by doing so, it helps flush toxins from the system. It also has insecticidal properties. Use it dried or in a tea.

- **Flaxseed:** This native American plant with tiny leaves and purple flowers grows throughout the prairies and meadows of mid-America. Its seeds have medicinal properties. Flaxseed helps the digestion of fat-soluble vitamins and nervous system function. Consumed whole, the seeds will either pass through your pet undigested or cause gastrointestinal distress. Bake and then crush raw flaxseed, and then mix it into your pet's food. Or steep the seeds in olive oil, strain the seeds, and add the oil to your pet's food.

- **Ginkgo:** For thousands of years, the nuts of the ginkgo tree have been used in China as both food and medicine. Ginkgo dilates blood vessels, increasing circulation. It also helps to prevent blood clots. Use it dried or in a tea.

- **Goldenseal:** Native Americans have used this herb as a natural remedy for respiratory and digestive problems for hundreds of years. It also helps expel parasites from the intestinal tract. Use the dried, ground roots in a tincture or in a tea.

- **Hawthorne:** Use the small purple berries of the hawthorne tree in tinctures, in teas, or dried. They're particularly effective in increasing blood flow, especially to the heart, and dilating blood vessels. They are particularly effective in older animals with heart disease.

PET ALERT

If you have a dog or cat with heart disease, talk to your veterinarian before giving your pet hawthorne. Make sure it won't interfere with any medications your vet has prescribed for your pet.

- **Licorice:** This North American plant is an anti-inflammatory and an expectorant. It also soothes and protects mucus membranes. It has antiviral properties and stimulates the immune system. Use it dried or in a tea.

- **Marshmallow:** This plant has 2-inch pink flowers that grow on spires. Marshmallow's roots make a soothing wash for irritated skin, including flea bites, abscesses, and wounds. Marshmallow tea is soothing to an upset stomach. It's also good for the urinary tract and boosts the immune system.

- **Nettle:** Use the dried leaves to make a tea that's good for the immune system; it's particularly helpful during allergy season. It's a natural antihistamine.

- **Oats:** Oats are a familiar food, but they also have medicinal properties. The green seeds—picked before they're ripe—are useful fresh or dried, crushed, and made into a tincture. Oats have anti-inflammatory properties and can soothe depression.

- **Peppermint:** Peppermint is very soothing to the intestinal tract. It can stop nausea and vomiting, calm an irritated bowel, and help a pet expel gas. It's also wonderful for motion sickness. Use it dried, in a tincture, or in a tea.

- **Raspberry:** Dry raspberry leaves and use them in tinctures to soothe the intestinal tract and help calm an irritated bowel. It's also calming for nervous animals, especially newly adopted ones. Female dogs and cats in season, being bred, or having cramps can benefit from some raspberry tea.

- **Sage:** Dried sage leaves make an effective astringent and antiseptic wash for skin irritations and wounds. It also fights fungal infections. A sage tea makes a good mouth rinse for dogs and cats with gum infections, mouth ulcers, or wounds. Don't worry if your pet swallows some of the tea; sage is soothing to the intestinal tract and may kill harmful bacteria, such as E. coli.

- **Sarsaparilla:** This herb's tiny white flowers can stimulate natural hormone production. As such, pet owners often give it to their pets to treat reproductive disorders. It's also effective for skin disorders and allergies. Use it dried and in tinctures or teas.

- **Slippery elm:** The inner bark of this large tree is useful in tinctures and teas. It's soothing to the intestinal tract, and it's good for colitis, diarrhea, and stomach irritations. It can ease constipation without causing colon spasms.

- **St. John's wort:** This herb has lovely yellow flowers. The top third of the plant, including new leaves and the flowers, has medicinal uses when dried and included in tinctures and teas. Often called the "herbal Prozac," this herb can ease depression and calm a nervous animal. It also stimulates the immune system.

- **Valerian:** Dry the roots of this plant and use it in tinctures or teas. It calms nerves, relaxes the body, and allows even the most nervous dog or cat to fall asleep. It may prevent seizures, too.

- **Yarrow:** A member of the sunflower family, you can use this herb dried in tinctures and teas or in poultices. In a poultice, yarrow stops bleeding and works as a pain reliever. Yarrow is quite strong, so use it with caution. Although most pets can use it with no trouble, if your dog or cat begins panting, has swelling, or vomits or has diarrhea, stop using it immediately and call your veterinarian.

PET ALERT

There are many plants that should not be used medicinally, as they can be toxic to your dog or cat. The American Society for the Prevention of Cruelty to Animals (ASPCA) has a website that maintains a list of toxic plants. Go to www.aspca.org/pet-care/poison-control/plants/ if you have any doubts about using a specific plant.

Alone or Together?

Most herbal remedy enthusiasts look upon herbal remedies as one tool in their toolbox to provide good natural care for their pet. Most don't believe that herbal remedies must be used alone. In fact, you can use many herbal ingredients together—such as chamomile and peppermint in the same tea—or use multiple remedies at the same time.

Often, pet owners use herbal remedies in conjunction with conventional medicine, homeopathic remedies, acupuncture, chiropractic, and a wide variety of other health-care techniques. Rather than standing alone, herbal remedies are team players. Remember that herbal remedies, like homeopathy and other natural health techniques, are not a substitute for veterinary care. If your pet has a sudden illness or injury, or is not getting better after a couple days' use of herbal remedies, call your veterinarian.

Finding Herbal Therapies

Herbs used for cooking and food preparation are usually limited to specific common plants, such as ginger, pepper, and sage. The term *herb*, however, includes just about any plant with medicinal properties when one uses it in conjunction with remedies. This may include thousands of plants with a variety of uses.

You can grow your own herbs; many do quite well in backyard gardens, in outdoor pots, or under indoor grow lights. You can use some herbs, such as peppermint, fresh off the plant. Just drop a clean leaf in hot water, and let it steep. Voilà! Peppermint tea. For other herbs, you must dry them before use. Tie picked stems together, with the leaves and flowers still on the stems. Then hang the plants with cut stems hung highest in a cool, dry place.

Sometimes natural food stores and farmers' markets sell dried herbs. Usually they sell them at very reasonable prices, especially if they're grown locally. Most people use commercial herbal remedies, however, usually in tablet or capsule form. You can find these remedies with single herb ingredients or with several grouped together. What you choose should depend on what you're looking for and what your pet needs. For more information, see Appendix B.

Look at Both Sides

There is no one form of healing that everyone is going to support. Even conventional veterinary medicine can be controversial. The same applies to alternative medicine and therapies.

Usually, being a little skeptical is a good thing. Look at natural health, healing, and alternative therapies from both sides. What are the claims concerning these therapies? After all, if something sounds too good to be true, it probably is. Can the remedy be harmful to your pet? How effective is it? Can you use it in conjunction with other therapies? After you've obtained answers to all your questions and consulted your vet, you can make a decision regarding whether to use a remedy or not.

Confusion About Herbs

There are many completed studies concerning the effectiveness of herbs for homeopathic remedies. St. John's wort and Echinacea have both been well studied in the United States and in Europe. However, not all herbs have been studied as well, and the effectiveness of many available herbs has yet to be proven. When the varied forms of the herbs—tinctures, teas, tablets, capsules, poultices, and more—are taken into account when considering a study, proving their effectiveness may be virtually impossible.

Commercial herbal supplement companies produce products with varying recipes. Some may contain exactly what the label states, with unadulterated, good-quality herbs. Other products may not be as good. This variance makes choosing herbs difficult and giving them to your pet less safe.

Identifying herbs can be difficult. The plants my grandmother identified by their Native American names are not identified the same way by someone who uses the Latin scientific nomenclature. This difference can create confusion and possibly misidentification.

 CAT CHAT

Cats are sensitive to some herbs, so never give your cat an herbal remedy without checking to make sure it's safe for cats. Cats may require less per pound of body weight than dogs take, so check the dosage carefully.

Keep Safety in Mind

Herbs are effective because they have an identifiable effect in the body. Because of this, they may also have a detrimental effect. To keep your pet safe, keep a few things in mind:

- Herbs are not innocuous foods; consider them medicines and give them to your pet only when he or she needs it.

- Talk to your veterinarian or a veterinary herbalist prior to giving your pet an herbal remedy. Make sure you understand how, when, and how much to give your pet.

- Buy only recognized name-brand herbs, or grow your own.

- Some herbs interact with conventional medications, so always tell your veterinarian what herbs you're considering giving your pet.

As with homeopathic remedies and conventional medicines, you may need to try more than one remedy to find the best treatment for your pet.

The Least You Need to Know

- Homeopathic practitioners follow the law of similars: a substance that causes a specific symptom at full strength is a remedy for that symptom when in a highly diluted form.

- Homeopathic remedies come from sources that originate in the earth and include animals, plants, stones, minerals, and other natural substances.

- Herbal remedies include more than kitchen herbs; they can come from a wide variety of plants and may include roots, stems, leaves, flowers, seeds, or even the entire plant.

- Skeptics question the use and effectiveness of homeopathic and herbal remedies. Consider natural health, healing, and alternative therapies from both sides and remain objective when evaluating claims concerning these therapies.

Flowers, Oils, and Pheromones

In This Chapter

- Flower remedies for many situations
- Healing essential oils
- How pheromones affect behaviors
- Some commonly used remedies

Although most people think of natural health therapies as organic foods or herbal remedies, or perhaps a lack of conventional medicine, that's not the complete picture. Natural remedies can be found in a variety of forms.

Flower remedies aren't new; just as herbal remedies have been available for thousands of years, so have flower remedies. Although not as well known as many other natural therapies, more people have been learning to use essential oils. The use of pheromones to change unwanted behaviors is a relatively new technology; although not completely natural, it's based on the science of natural behavior.

Flowers as Natural Remedies

Flower essences are homeopathic remedies made from flowers and parts of flowering plants. While Dr. Hahnemann's homeopathic remedies (discussed in Chapter 3) were made using a wide range of ingredients—from volcanic ash to animal organs—flower essences use only flowering plants. They were originally made by floating flowers or flower petals in water. After an established period of time for that specific remedy, the water would then be used as the original substance, and drops of this water were used to create more diluted remedies—just as other homeopathic remedies are made.

DEFINITION

Flower essences are homeopathic remedies created from flowers and the parts of flowering plants. The base of the remedy can be water or alcohol, often brandy.

Today, flower remedies are made using either water or alcohol, depending on the flower essence used and the recipe. Brandy is often used when an essence is created ahead of time and needs to be preserved.

Most homeopathic remedies are used with one ingredient diluted in water or alcohol. Although many flower essences are created this way, it's also not at all unusual for a remedy to contain several flowers. Custom combinations are often created by holistic veterinarians or flower essence practitioners depending on the individual pet's need.

Many experts suggest flower essence remedies made from flowers grown in the user's local area are more effective than flowers grown elsewhere. They say locally grown flowers are better suited to those living in the same region, breathing the same air, and so on. Not everyone agrees with this, however, and many commercial flower essence companies ship their products all over the world.

Flower essences are often used for the following:

- **Behavior problems:** The cat who claws the furniture, the dog who barks too much, jealousy, or aggression.

- **Emotional issues:** Fear after surgery; panic after an accident; or grief when a pet loses an owner, another pet, or its home.

- **Health issues:** Allergies, infections, illnesses, and injuries.

- **Other natural remedies:** In conjunction with and assisting herbal remedies, nutritional supplements, or acupuncture.

Flower essences are usually dropped in the mouth, as are other homeopathic remedies. However, a flower essence practitioner or your veterinarian may recommend that the remedy be mixed in the pet's water so that the pet receives some each time he or she drinks.

As with most natural health remedies, researchers continue to find additional uses all the time. As people and pets change, and the world around us changes, so do the remedies and their uses.

Bach Flower Remedies

Dr. Edward Bach (1886–1936), an English physician, homeopath, and spiritual writer, developed what are now called Bach Flower Remedies. Whereas most homeopathic remedies use a variety of ingredients— including animals, birds, reptiles, and insects—Dr. Bach wanted to find simpler ingredients for his remedies that didn't require creatures to die to create them.

As with many homeopathic practitioners, Dr. Bach believed that diseases of the body were caused by imbalances in the body and the spirit. He wanted his remedies to help on both levels. He created 38 remedies, which at that time he felt would correct all the possible imbalances in people.

Bach Flower Remedies are probably the best-known natural remedies of any kind. They're sold in health food stores worldwide, as well as in many other stores. Today, there are formulas for people as well as pets, and the yellow Bach Flower label is instantly recognizable.

Even More Sources

Although Dr. Bach's remedies are the best known, there are several other companies and organizations producing reputable flower essences:

- **Australia Bush Essences** (www.ausflowers.com.au/) is an Australia-based company that produces flower essences from Australia's native plants. They have 50 well-researched essences created by Ian White, a naturopath.

- **BlackWing Farms** (www.blackwingfarms.com) created their flower essences to assist with problem behaviors and emotional distress. Their combination formulas include several flowers in one remedy. They recommend their formulas for a variety of problems, including fears, bullying, changes, and more.

- **California Essences** (website not available) is a nonprofit organization founded by Patricia Kaminski, a counselor who has studied flowering plants and flower remedies extensively, and Richard Katz, a scientist, psychologist, and expert on flowering plants and their uses in remedies. The extensively researched program has three goals: to research the therapeutic uses of flower essences, to train and certify practitioners, and to create referrals between consumers and practitioners.

- **Green Hope Farm Flower Essences** (www. greenhopeessences.com) include the flowers of fruit trees, shrubs, annual flowers, perennials, herbs, and vegetables. The creators' philosophy behind the flower essences is that the spiritual and physical worlds should work together.

Many other flower essences are available from a variety of sources. To find those produced locally, talk to a holistic veterinarian. You can also search online for local sources.

Specific Flower Essences

You can use flower essences individually or in combination with others. Although experts most often recommend flower essences for emotional issues, some also treat physical ones. What you use for your pet is up to you and the issues you're trying to treat. Here are some common flower essences and their uses:

- **Aspen:** Helps ease fear and anxiety.

- **Beech:** For pets who don't care for other animals.

- **Bleeding heart:** Helps ease grief.

- **Centaury:** For overly submissive pets and those with submissive urination problems.

- **Chamomile:** Calming, particularly for emotional issues as well as for physical issues.

- **Cherry plum:** For aggression issues, biting, and a loss of self-control.

- **Chestnut bud:** For pets who tend to repeat behavior patterns and don't learn from past mistakes.

- **Chicory:** For pets who demand too much attention and those who suffer from jealousy.

- **Clematis:** For pets who have trouble concentrating, especially dogs in training, cats who need to learn housetraining skills, and those who appear disconnected from the world around them.

- **Crab apple:** Used in conjunction with medication when the pet needs help cleansing toxins from his system.

- **Gentian:** Helps build confidence and increase mental strength.

- **Heather:** For separation anxiety.

- **Holly:** Eases jealousy.

- **Honeysuckle:** Combats homesickness.

- **Impatiens:** Helps calm the hyperactive pet and decrease hyperactivity.

- **Larch:** Eases the anxiety of the shy or fearful pet and builds confidence.

- **Lavender (for dogs only):** Calms, relaxes, and soothes an anxious dog.

- **Mimulus:** Helps overcome fear.

- **Olive:** Helps exhausted pets and helps pets heal from a chronic illness.

- **Pink yarrow:** Helps pets cope with negative emotions, such as grief when a loved one has passed away.

- **Rock rose:** Excellent for panic attacks.

- **Star of Bethlehem:** Helps pets recover from physical or emotional trauma.

- **Tiger lily:** Good for aggressive pets who tend to bite or snap, or who show hostility toward those around them.

- **Vervain:** Good for the overly enthusiastic or overbearing pet, or to help ball-crazy dogs relax.

- **Vine:** Helps with a bullying pet.

- **Walnut:** Helps pets cope with transitions: moving, a new home, or a new stage of life.

- **Water violet:** Helps the introverted pet relax.

- **Wild oat:** Helps the scatter-brained pet focus.

- **Willow:** Helps the resentful pet accept changes.

Although these tend to be the most common flower essence therapies, there are many others. For example, Australian Bush Essences uses plants native to Australia, including a wide variety of plants that don't normally grow anywhere else. A few of these include:

- **Banksia robur:** For frustration and renewing enthusiasm for life.

- **Bauhinia:** For pets who are reluctant to change.

- **Bluebell:** For pets who are greedy and overly possessive.

If you don't see what your pet needs in these lists of common essences, take a look at other suppliers. A wide variety of flower essences are available.

Flower Essence Combinations

Just as some herbal remedies work well together—like peppermint and chamomile to calm an upset stomach—several combinations of flower essences have become standards for certain situations. Although you can use each essence individually, sometimes the combinations are more effective:

- Bach Flowers' best-known Rescue Remedy combines star of Bethlehem, clematis, rock rose, impatiens, and cherry plum and treats shock, trauma, fear, and panic. It can be used to help a newly adopted pet get over the initial fear of being in a new place, or for when a pet hurts himself and is afraid. Rescue Remedy can be found at grocery stores in the pharmacy section and at pharmacies, pet stores, and health food stores.

- Australian Bush Essences also has a remedy for emergency situations. It contains angelsword, crowea, dog rose, fringed violet, grey spider flower, sundew, and waratah. As with Rescue Remedy, this can be used when a pet might be afraid—after an accident or injury, after a sudden change in location, or after a change in owners.

- Holly and hickory make a good combination to treat jealous pets.

- A combination of cerato and chestnut bud is effective in helping young dogs with their training.

- Shy cats come out of their shell with a combination of mimulus, aspen, and larch.

- For the overly possessive pet, try a mixture of chicory and heather.

These ingredients can generally be mixed in equal amounts. However, your veterinarian or practitioner may recommend different proportions depending on your pet's needs.

> **CAT CHAT**
>
> Newly adopted cats may be anxious and afraid. A good combination for these cats is aspen, impatiens, red chestnut, and mimulus.

Flower Essence Safety

Flower remedies are generally quite safe, and enthusiasts truly believe these remedies are effective. They are homeopathic remedies, however, and although greatly diluted, they aren't inert. Therefore, give as recommended and never overdose your pet.

If your pet is taking any medications, talk to your veterinarian prior to giving any flower essences. Rescue Remedy is commonly given in conjunction with medication; however, talking to your vet about it is always a good idea.

> **CAT CHAT**
>
> Cats are particularly sensitive to many substances that dogs do not react to at all. However, flower essences are often recommended for cats, and they rarely suffer adverse reactions.

Using Essential Oils

Essential oils come from plants. They can be from roots, stems, leaves, flowers, and seeds, depending upon the plant. Whereas your pet may take herbal remedies, homeopathic remedies, and flower essences internally (except for poultices for wounds), essential oils aren't consumed. Essential oils repel insects, help heal wounds and skin problems, and provide aromatherapy. They may also relieve pain, ease stress, and invigorate the entire body.

Researchers believe aromatherapy was established in ancient Egypt, where they used oils for massage, bathing, and medicine. They even embalmed the dead in cedar oil. The Europeans used essential oils, too, and during the Black Plague, oils were used to ward off disease as well as to mask the smell of decomposing bodies. These were found to be ineffective, however, and were often used as a scam.

GO NATURAL

Essential oils aren't the same as oils used as food supplements. Food supplement oils—such as fish oil, salmon oil, and flaxseed oil—are for ingestion. Essential oils are for external use only.

Essential Oils Can Heal

Rene-Maurice Gattefosse (1881–1950) was a French chemist who discovered that oils can be healing. Amazingly, an accident in his laboratory led Gattefosse to become a proponent of healing with essential oils. During an explosion in his lab, he burned his arm and so he plunged it into the nearest container of water. It turned out there was lavender oil in the water. Not only did the lavender oil help suppress the pain of his burn, but over the next few days he also realized his arm was healing very quickly and with little scarring.

Depending on the individual plant, essential oils can have antibacterial, antiviral, antifungal, or anti-inflammatory properties, or they can clear the body of toxins. From an emotional standpoint, essential oils can be relaxing or stimulating.

One of the most popular essential oils is tea tree oil. Dr. Shawn Messonnier says, "There is little question that tea tree oil is an effective antiseptic, active against many bacteria and fungi. It also has penetrating qualities that may make it particularly effective for infected wounds." The best tea tree oils are from the melaleuca tree in Australia.

Tri-Animals (www.tri-animals.com) is a combination of essential oils in an apple cider vinegar base. It contains catnip, cedar, citronella, eucalyptus, lavender, marigold, myrrh, tea tree, coconut, and valerian tea. The maker says that, when sprayed on dogs and horses, it will repel ticks, fleas, and mosquitoes; help skin irritations heal; and reduce scarring. Because it contains lavender, which is toxic to cats, this should not be used on cats or on cat's furniture or bedding.

Aromatherapy

Aromatherapy is the technique of using essential oils for their fragrances. Many people don't even think about the importance of smells, but scents definitely can set a mood, bring back memories, or help one heal.

Today, corporations know scents are important. Many manufacturers of cleaners, air fresheners, and even cosmetics use carefully selected fragrances in their products. Think about it: why do so many cleaners contain a lemon or orange scent? Citrus scents are uplifting and create a positive mood. So after you clean with a citrus-scented cleaner, not only is your house clean, but you feel good about it.

Scents can also be healing. If you've had a hard day at work and come home with a headache, grab the lavender and head for the bathtub. Take a hot bath with lavender oils, and your stress and headache will disappear. Not only that, but you'll also be relaxed enough to sleep. The hot bath is certainly a part of your relaxation, but the lavender helps, too.

Does aromatherapy work as well on our pets as it does for us? No one really knows. Anecdotal evidence seems to show it does, but there haven't been studies to document aromatherapy's effectiveness in pets.

> **PET ALERT**
>
> Essential oils are metabolized in the cat's liver. Because cats lack the enzyme glucuronyl tranferase, they can't rid the liver of toxins as quickly as some other animals. The toxins can build up over time, causing a toxic situation. Use them with caution around cats; never use essential oils directly on cats. If you would like to use a specific essential oil around your cat, talk to your veterinarian first.

Some Popular Essential Oils

Even though pet owners should use essential oils with caution, especially for cats, they continue to grow in popularity. Some of the most common essential oils include the following:

- **Calendula:** This oil, just like in herbal form, is wonderful for healing wounds.

- **Catnip:** This is an excellent pest repellant. Plus, most cats love it!

- **Chamomile:** Just as with the herb, you can use this to help calm the mind and the body.

- **Citronella:** This is an excellent pest repellent.

- **Eucalyptus:** This oil is antibacterial and antifungal, and it helps skin irritations heal quickly.

- **Lavender:** Lavender is calming, although not as much as chamomile. Lavender is also healing for skin irritations and wounds.

PET ALERT

Although lavender is a common scent for cosmetics, colognes, household cleaners, room fresheners, and more, it can be toxic to cats. Never use it on a cat's bedding or on the cat.

- **Myrrh:** This oil has anti-inflammatory properties and decreases scar tissue as the skin heals.

- **Tea tree oil (melaleuca):** Tea tree oil is excellent for skin irritations and wounds. Use a commercial product, or dilute the essential oil with witch hazel or water.

A variety of other essential oils are available commercially. Don't use them on your pet, however, until you know for sure they're safe. Many oils people can use aren't safe for dogs, and few should be used around cats.

Essential oils are concentrated and can be potent. Talk to your veterinarian before using these oils.

Essential Oil Safety

Essential oils are very strong substances. For safety, always be sure to dilute them before use. A few drops of an oil mixed with a quarter cup of olive oil or sweet almond oil can ensure the essential oil isn't too strong.

Even diluted, some oils are potentially dangerous for use on cats and dogs, particularly because our pets lick themselves. Oils that might be safe on our skin can be a serious problem for our pets if they ingest the oil as they groom themselves.

> **PET ALERT**
>
> A few plants that are safe and medicinal as dried herbs or flower essences are toxic in oil form because the oil is so concentrated. Potentially toxic essential oils include yarrow, anise, birch, camphor, hissop, juniper, white thyme, and wintergreen. Pet owners often use pennyroyal as a flea repellent, and it works well that way, but it's much too strong and very dangerous in oil form. It's toxic to the kidneys and can damage the nervous system. Cats are more sensitive to oils than dogs. In addition to the ones listed previously, don't use these oils on cats: cinnamon bark, citrus, melaleuca, tea tree, lavender, and peppermint.

Pheromones

Pheromones are naturally produced chemicals that tend to cause a reaction from other members of the same species. Some pheromones trigger a reaction when danger is present, while others are sexual in nature. It's widely thought bees use a pheromone to let other members of the hive know where they've located food.

Here are some other uses for pheromones:

- **Aggregation:** This pheromone supplies a call to gather and may be what causes ladybugs, butterflies, and other insects to gather in large groups. It may also be a precursor to reproduction.

- **Aggression:** This pheromone can trigger an attack by ants or a dangerous swarm of bees.

- **Information:** Used along with territory markers, this phero-mone identifies an individual.

- **Maternal:** This pheromone makes the babies feel loved, wanted, and welcome.

- **Territorial:** This pheromone claims territory, especially when present in urine.

Pheromones also tell other members of the same species when females are ready to breed and where they are. Males also produce pheromones to let the females know they're ready, willing, and able.

Mammals detect pheromones through their sense of smell. When dogs and cats process pheromones, they may lift their top lip and draw air in through the mouth. They may drool a little or move their lips on the side of the muzzle. They may repeatedly return to the spot where the pheromones are present.

Dog Appeasing Pheromone

Like most mammals, nursing mother dogs produce an "appeasing" pheromone to help calm their newborn puppies. These are secreted by the sebaceous glands of the abdominal skin so the puppies are in contact with it as they nurse.

Researchers have synthesized this in both a collar and a household mister so pet owners can use it for dogs who are no longer nursing. This pheromone, called the Dog Appeasing Pheromone (DAP), can help a newly adopted dog adapt to a new home by making the dog feel welcome and wanted. It can aid puppies as they go through the socialization period, helping them cope with new sights, sounds, and experiences. It's also useful for dogs who tend to be fearful in new situations.

 DOG TALK

Many dog trainers and dog behaviorists recommend the DAP collars or misters for fearful dogs, newly adopted dogs, and dogs with adjustment issues. Use DAP in conjunction with behavior modification and training to help your dog.

The DAP collars and misters aren't magic wands; by themselves, they don't cure behavior problems, nor do they turn fearful dogs into bold ones. Still, they're useful tools for dog owners and trainers. Several companies market these collars and misters. They can be found in most pet supply stores or at online pet supply stores.

Calming Pheromones for Cats

A product similar to DAP is available for cats. As with the products for dogs, it mimics the pheromones secreted by nursing mother cats and creates a sense of calm acceptance. It is also useful for newly adopted cats and fearful cats. The synthetic feline pheromone is available in a mister or diffuser. You can use it by itself or in combination with the herbs valerian root and St. John's wort. As with the products for dogs, several companies make these products. They can be found at most pet supply stores and online pet supply stores.

Pheromone Safety

These synthetic pheromones have been well tested and are considered safe. The dog pheromone is available in collar form. If the dog chews on and eats the collar, that can be an issue. The concern is not related to the dog ingesting the pheromone, though; instead, the issue is with the animal ingesting the collar itself.

Most pet owners see a positive change in their pet when they use synthetic pheromones. As with any product, however, it doesn't have the same affect on all pets. Few owners have said they see no change at all.

The Least You Need to Know

- Flower essences are made from the flowers of plants and include herbs, shrubs, trees, and even some weeds.
- Flower essences are safe for most pets and are useful for a variety of purposes.

- Essential oils are concentrated, very strong plant oils that you must use with extreme caution. Avoid using essential oils on or around cats, as they are toxic to cats.

- Synthetic pheromones aid in implementing changes in a pet's behavior, especially in changing a pet's response to fear.

Natural Healing Around the World

In This Chapter

- The ancient art of Ayurveda
- The healing techniques of TCVM
- Reiki: channeling energy through the hands
- A variety of Native American healing methods

Every culture has its own healing techniques that its people have used for generations. Conventional modern veterinary medicine is a fairly recent innovation, so it's easy to understand that people needed ways to keep their animals healthy prior to its introduction. Even today, many cultures tend to distrust modern technology, and their people are far more comfortable with the ancient ways.

It's very interesting to see the similarities between the many ancient healing arts. Herbal remedies are quite common, for example, and many share a belief in the spiritual world and call on it for healing.

Ayurveda: India's Native Medicine

Ayurveda originated in India thousands of years ago. This holistic system of medicine emphasizes preventing as well as curing disease. It also focuses on living in balance with nature. As with many other natural healing techniques, one of Ayurveda's goals is to balance the body, mind, and spirit. Its philosophy is that all things in the universe—living and nonliving—are joined together.

One of the world's oldest medical techniques, Ayurveda was used for people exclusively for most of its history. However, Dr. Tejinder Sodhi of the Animal Wellness and Rehabilitation Center in Bellevue, Washington, says, "Ayurveda's focus on living in harmony with nature can be applied to every living creature, including pets."

Ayurveda's Life Forces

Ayurveda, like homeopathy and flower essences (discussed in Chapters 3 and 4, respectively), says that all living things have life forces that are vital to good health. Each life form (human, animal, or other) has a constitution, which is a unique combination of physical and psychological characteristics that affect how that life is lived. The constitution is made up of elements called *doshas*. Each dosha consists of two of the five basic elements, which include fire, water, earth, air, and ether (space).

GO NATURAL

The National Center for Complementary and Alternative Medicine (NCCAM) says Ayurveda is a Complementary and Alternative Medicine (CAM). The NCCAM considers it a whole medical system—or an all-encompassing one—because it's focused on health and illness and ways to prevent, manage, and treat health problems.

Here are the most common doshas:

- **Kapha: water and earth.** This dosha maintains the immune system and helps keep the body strong. A bad diet, too much sugar or salt consumption, and sleeping too much can aggravate it. Pets with this dosha are prone to diabetes, cancer, obesity, and asthma.

- **Pitta: fire and water.** This dosha controls the digestive system and hormones. Too much time in the sun and a poor diet can aggravate it. Pets with this dosha are prone to digestive problems and infectious diseases.

- **Vata: air and ether.** This powerful dosha controls the heart, breathing, and the mind. Fear or grief can aggravate it. Pets whose main dosha is vata are more susceptible to heart disease, skin conditions, arthritis, and anxiety.

Most living things are a combination of all three doshas, in some manner, but there is usually a dominant dosha. Each dosha has certain dietary or lifestyle needs, and maintaining good health means working to achieve balance with each dosha. How a dosha and elements are balanced or changed in each life form is a well-studied and complete science within Ayurveda, which has the single goal of creating (or re-creating) balance and harmony with nature.

Ayurveda Veterinary Medicine

A veterinary practitioner of Ayurveda first determines the pet's doshas and dosha balance. To determine this, the practitioner will ask you as the pet's owner about the pet's health, diet (including treats), exercise, sleeping habits, strength, and other lifestyle and health questions. The practitioner will examine the pet, looking at the overall appearance and any problems. He or she will also evaluate the animal's urine and stool.

Treatment depends on a pet's health, illnesses, and/or injuries, as well as the pet's dosha(s). Treatments can include the following:

- **Diet:** A healthy and appropriate diet is important to this medical technique. The diet must be clean, comprised of good foods, and appropriate to the pet. Depending on the pet's condition and his or her doshas, certain foods may be recommended or eliminated from the diet.

- **Increase harmony:** The pet owner must create harmony in the pet's home to bond strongly with the pet and alleviate stress.

- **Other remedies:** Ayurveda practitioners often recommend a variety of herbal remedies and nutritional supplements, both as medicine and to increase the value of the diet. More than 600 herbal remedies are included in the list of Ayurveda treatments.

- **Strength:** Physical exercises, stretching, breathing exercises, and massage help the pet's body grow stronger.

- **Strengthen resistance to disease:** Herbs or nutritional supplements boost the immune system.

- **The sun:** The pet must lie in the sun, a vital energy source, to absorb its warmth and strength.

CAT CHAT

Cats have long known the healing properties of the sun. After all, they are the ultimate sun worshippers.

The Ayurveda practitioner may make a number of other recommendations, including eliminating many chemicals from the pet's home such as air fresheners, perfumes, and cleaners. You can use green, or natural, products instead. The practitioner may also recommend stopping pest control treatments, including those for heartworm, fleas, and ticks. Obviously, make these changes wisely, with research and after speaking with your veterinarian, and with thought on your part as to the potential consequences.

Ayurveda Safety

As with most alternative medical techniques, there are some safety concerns. Independent testing has revealed that some over-the-counter, prepackaged Ayurveda herbal remedies contain metals, including lead and mercury, and others contain arsenic. Obviously, these are poisonous to people and pets.

Although people have been practicing Ayurveda medicine for thousands of years, there are few studies available regarding its effectiveness. The existing studies are small and weren't conducted according to Western medicine's research standards.

If you're interested in Ayurveda techniques for your pet, talk to your veterinarian or an Ayurveda veterinary practitioner. Make sure the practitioner also talks to your veterinarian so he or she has a good understanding of your pet's health and history.

In addition, keep these cautions in mind:

- Make sure the practitioner knows what medications your pet is presently taking.

- Don't stop any medications without first consulting the prescribing veterinarian.

- If the Ayurveda practitioner recommends changing your pet's diet, change it gradually to prevent digestive upset.

- Buy herbal remedies from a known source, or buy those sold by a known manufacturer. It is difficult to ensure the quality of unknown or off-label herbs, and they may be contaminated with other materials.

Ayurveda is a well-known, ancient form of medicine and may be the right choice for your pet. It's a complicated form of medicine, however, so only approach this with the help of an Ayurveda practitioner who's willing to consult with your pet's veterinarian.

Traditional Chinese Medicine

Traditional Chinese medicine (TCM) is an ancient healing art that originated in geographical regions that are now part of China. TCM's basic philosophy is that every aspect of a life must be a part of the healing process, and that includes body, mind, spirit, and emotions.

Traditional Chinese veterinary medicine (TCVM) is an offshoot of TCM, but it's not new; it originated more than 3,500 years ago. It adheres to the same principles as TCM. The basis of TCVM is that you must treat and change the root cause of illness, not its symptoms. TCVM encompasses several different types of treatments, including food, herbal remedies, massage, acupuncture, and acupressure, which I'll discuss in the next several sections.

The Five-Element Theory

The five-element theory states that a human or animal body is a microcosm of the universe, and that what happens in the body happens in the universe and vice versa. This theory is the foundation of TCM and TCVM. The development of this theory helped explain things in the universe that otherwise couldn't be explained, from the character of people and animals to changes in the weather.

The five elements are wood, fire, earth, metal, and water. The division of five continues throughout TCVM. There are also five major organ groups in human and animal bodies: liver and gallbladder, heart and small intestine, spleen and stomach, lung and large intestine, and kidneys and urinary system (including the bladder). Tastes for food are also broken down into five groups: sour, bitter, sweet, pungent, and salty.

All of these divisions of five can be related to a variety of things by TCVM practitioners, including the season of the year, the time of day, colors, and foods. This is an incredibly complicated health-care method, but it gives the practitioner a means of choosing particular treatments for his patients.

Food

TCVM practitioners believe food does more than simply nourish the body. Because foods contain vital energy, they are also medicinal. If your pet eats bad foods—either the wrong kind or contaminated foods—then it will upset the energy balances in the body, leading to illnesses. Eating the right foods can prevent or help heal illnesses. According to TCVM, a balanced diet includes a variety of foods offered based on the pet's individual needs.

In TCVM *food therapy*, foods are associated with the five universal elements: wood, fire, earth, metal, and water. In addition, they are divided by the five basic tastes: sour, bitter, sweet, pungent, and salty. Here's how it breaks down:

- *Foods associated with wood* include chicken and wheat. Their flavor is *sour*. A diet in excess of these foods may result in muscle injuries, a weakening of the spleen, and the liver overproducing saliva. Balance these foods with pungent foods from the metal element.

- *Foods associated with fire* include lamb and corn. Their flavor is *bitter*. Too much of these foods may cause problems with the spleen and stomach, dry skin, and coughing. Counteract these by adding salty foods from the water element.

- *Foods associated with earth* include beef and grains. Their flavor is *sweet*. These foods are harmonizing, but an excess can cause kidney disease. Achy bones and joints and hair loss may also result from too many earth foods. Balance these with sour foods from the wood element.

- *Foods associated with metal* include horse meat and rice. Their flavor is *pungent*. Too many of these foods may cause muscle cramping, unhealthy toenails, and an irregular pulse. Counteract these by adding bitter foods from the fire element.

- *Foods associated with water* include pork and beans. Their flavor is *salty*. An excess of these foods may cause a lack of muscle tone, a lack of bone strength, and mental depression. Balance these with sweet foods from the earth element.

Determining what foods your pet needs according to TCVM can be quite complicated, but a consultation with a TCVM practitioner can help. To find one in your area, go to the website for Alternative Pet Health (www.alternativepethealth.com) or traditional Chinese veterinary medicine (www.tcvm.com).

DEFINITION

In TCVM, **food therapy** consists of combining foods based on the energy they contain. That doesn't mean caloric energy, but rather the energetic effect the food has on the body after your pet has eaten.

Herbal Therapy

TCVM uses many different herbs and herbal combinations for healing. Many of the herbs are familiar to people around the world, such as ginkgo biloba. There are more than 500 herbs and herbal therapies in TCVM, and practitioners may use them when they are fresh, dried, or in capsules, tablets, teas, tinctures, poultices, and creams. Most TCVM herbal therapies use herbs in combination with several others. Several herbs may be used as one medicinal compound.

Herbs, like foods in TCVM, are classified according to their usage. The same five flavor classifications are used for herbs as for foods: sour, bitter, sweet, pungent, and salty. In addition to that, they're classified according to the five temperatures: hot, warm, neutral, cool, and cold. You can choose the herbs or herbal combinations according to the patient's needs.

> **PET ALERT**
>
> In most parts of the world, herbal remedies are made only from plants or parts of plants. In TCM and TCVM, however, herbal remedies may contain a variety of substances, which may include animal parts and metals. Before giving any remedy to your pet, read the label, understand all the ingredients, and check with your veterinarian.

Tui-Na

Tui-na is a combination of acupressure and massage, with some chiropractic techniques thrown in the mix. The goal is to enhance the flow of Qi (vital energy or life force) throughout the body through hand motions, massage, and manipulation of the body.

The history of Tui-na is interesting. Originally, martial arts instructors taught it to their students. Students injured during training used Tui-na to heal.

Tui-na for pets tends to include more massage and acupressure because dogs and cats tend to be more accepting of these techniques. Chiropractic manipulation isn't widely applied to pets because they're generally less tolerant of this.

CAT CHAT

Cats don't seem to appreciate chiropractic (or similar) therapies. Most cats, when manipulated in this way, react by leaving, biting, or scratching. Never force a cat to accept this therapy because it may be uncomfortable or frightening to the animal.

Acupuncture and Acupressure

Acupuncture originated in China, so it's no surprise that it's an integral part of TCM and TCVM. In TCVM, acupuncture is usually paired with other therapies, including herbal remedies and Tui-na.

Acupressure has its roots in acupuncture, but whereas acupuncture must be performed by a practitioner, pet owners can learn to do acupressure at home. It can be a beneficial therapy between acupuncture treatments. See Chapter 2 for more about providing acupuncture, acupressure, and other chiropractic therapies for pets.

The Downside to TCM and TCVM

TCM and TCVM have a side that offends many people, especially Westerners. Some remedies recommended by TCM and TCVM practitioners are made from animal parts—which in and of itself isn't unusual in many parts of the world—but many are made from endangered animals. For example, the penis of a tiger, a severely endangered species, is a remedy for impotence in men and male animals.

Other animals are killed by hunters for just one part of their body, and the rest of the carcass goes to waste. Many times, poachers kill the animal illegally. Rhinoceros horn is made of keratin—the same thing hair and fingernails are made of—and is supposed to be good for fevers. Unfortunately, black market demand for rhinoceros keratin has decimated the world's population of these animals by more than 90 percent in the last 40 years.

Other animals are cruelly farmed for their parts. Farmers keep bears in very small cages with barely enough room to turn around, and they insert drains into each bear's gallbladder to harvest the bile for medicinal uses.

Most people understand that cultures vary in their treatment of animals. Should you wish to follow TCVM, be aware these practices do occur and be knowledgeable about what may be in some TCVM products.

Reiki Healing

Reiki is not an ancient healing technique; in fact, it was founded by Mikao Usui in the early 1920s in Japan. Usui was going through a Buddhist training course when, through meditation, fasting, chanting, and prayer, he gained knowledge of a healing technique he called Reiki.

According to Reiki practitioners, like several other healing arts, all living things contain a life force. This life force isn't simply the energy of the physical life; it also includes the spiritual life. A practitioner can channel this life force from himself or herself into the patient by the positioning of his or her hands. Reiki's followers believe doing so activates the patient's own natural healing abilities.

GO NATURAL

Reiki followers believe Reiki is the most natural form of healing because practitioners use only their hands and energy to heal.

Usui created the Five Reiki Precepts, which were summarized and condensed from the works of Japan's Emperor Meiji. They are as follows:

- Reiki is the secret art of inviting happiness.
- Reiki is the miraculous medicine for all diseases.
- At least for today, do not be angry. Do not worry. Be grateful. Work with diligence. And be kind to people.
- Every morning, join your hands in meditation and pray with your heart.
- Make statements in your mind and chant with your mouth.

As these show, traditional Japanese Reiki is concerned with more than simply healing the body. The mind, the emotions, and even social order are all involved in the process.

American Reiki

Japanese Reiki students learn they will know where to place their hands on their patients—that the knowledge will come to them when the patient needs it. In American Reiki, often called Western Reiki, the acupuncture meridians are the guidelines for placing the hands (see Chapter 2). There are seven standard positions: the top of the head, the forehead, the neck, the heart, the solar plexus, the groin, and the base of the spine. Many American practitioners also use multiple acupressure points along the meridians.

The practitioner's hands may touch the patient, or he or she may hold them slightly above the skin. The practitioner generally holds the hands in one position for a few moments, and then moves to the next position. Patients often report feeling heat or a tingling feeling in the area being treated by the practitioner.

Reiki for Pets

Practitioners provide Reiki for dogs and cats with a variety of health issues, ranging from ear infections to arthritis, often in conjunction with other alternative and conventional health-care techniques. Practitioners say Reiki healing can help pets heal after surgery or an injury, and it can stimulate the immune system. It's also relaxing to your pet and can help you bond with your pet.

To find a Reiki practitioner in your area, or classes so you can learn to do it yourself, go to the International Association of Reiki Professionals website (www.iarp.org).

 DOG TALK

Reiki practitioners often recommend this form of healing to help solve behavior problems, saying it calms the dog and helps the animal focus.

Many Are Skeptical

Many stories exist about people who could heal just by touching others with their hands. When similar stories exist in a variety of cultures and geographical locations, one may surmise there's some basis in fact for them. Still, Reiki healers face many skeptics. After all, as one skeptic says, "Healing through the laying on of hands seems pretty far-fetched."

Unfortunately, studies and clinical trials haven't proven the validity of Reiki healing techniques. A 2009 review in *The Journal of Alternative and Complementary Medicine* couldn't state that Reiki healing was effective.

Native American Healing

There are hundreds of Native American tribes in North America. Each individual tribe has its own history, culture, and traditions that include healing techniques. Although some tribes that lived near each other, or have intermingled through the years, may share healing techniques, there are still unique traits to each tribe's techniques.

There are also many common characteristics. All tribes believed everyone and everything on Earth is interconnected and all lives are interwoven. Every living thing and everything on Earth—including the earth itself and the air above it—has a spirit or essence.

In Native American beliefs, illnesses occur when a life is out of balance. There may be spiritual problems, an unhealthy lifestyle, a poor diet, mental issues, or other problems that have caused or allowed a disease to invade the body. Healers looked for a way to re-create balance so the body can be healthy again. To re-create balance, practitioners used a number of different healing techniques that varied according to the tribe. A shaman, a medicine man or woman, or a spiritual leader may have performed the healing.

Purification

Purification and cleansing the body is a healing technique that was used by many Native Americans. Sweat lodges, which are very hot and cause the person within to sweat out impurities and toxins, are still used by some today. They're intended for people only, but there are other techniques available to animals.

Although they didn't use sweat lodges for animals, if the tribe's healer determined a valuable animal—a horse or a dog—was ill and needed purification, he or she provided other treatments. The healer may have exposed the animal to smoke from special substances believed to cleanse the body and spirit, or he or she may have offered the animal special teas to cleanse the body from the inside out.

DOG TALK

In most Native American communities, dogs hunted, warned of trespassers, and acted as beasts of burden. They kept children company, warmed feet on cold nights, and kept predators away from valuable horses.

Healing Rituals

Most Native American people believed in the spirit world. Rituals that appeased the spirits or asked for help from the spirits were very much a part of life and still are in some tribes. Although these rituals were intended primarily for people rather than animals, a fast, brave war horse or a courageous, talented hunting dog was—and is—worthy of help.

The rituals may have been private, with just the healer, the owner of the animal, and the animal present. Sometimes these occasions included the entire community. After all, if the spirits are going to be called for assistance, it might be a good idea to put on a show. With everyone participating, the spirits couldn't help but realize how seriously the community looked upon the request.

Herbal Remedies

Plants were a source of food, food supplements, and medicine to Native American people. They ate grains, fruits, and seeds, or they fermented them to make alcoholic drinks for ceremonies and rituals. Sometimes the healer, not the patient, drank the fermented drink.

Fresh or dried plants also provided herbal remedies in the form of teas, tinctures, and salves. Native Americans used these remedies for people, dogs, and often horses. Some remedies include the following:

- **Creeks:** They use boneset, steeped in a tea, to ease aches and pains.

- **Iroquois:** They use boneset tea to treat fevers.

- **Lakota:** They create a combination remedy that includes boswellia, willow bark, sarsaparilla, and feverfew leaves in a poultice that eases sore muscles and joints.

- **Menominees:** They boil witch hazel leaves and rub the resulting liquid on sore muscles.

- **Mohegans:** They allow ripe wild cherries to ferment and then use the juice throughout the year to combat diarrhea. They also use a tea made of dandelion roots to treat digestive upsets.

- **Navajo:** They use osha, also called bear root, as a tea or tincture for respiratory problems. Also, they boil the Fendler's bladderpod in a tea they use to treat spider bites.

- **Plains Indians:** They mash purple coneflower blossoms, mix them with water, and apply the poultice to treat insect bites and stings.

The plants and herbs the Native Americans used depended upon the plants available in the tribe's geographical region. Native Americans in the Southwest, for example, used aloe vera extensively as a healing plant for people and animals. This wasn't available or known as a healing plant to Native Americans in other geographical locations.

The Healer Has the Last Word

In most Native American cultures, the healer—a medicine woman, a medicine man, a shaman, or another type of healer—has the last word on how to treat an ill person or animal. The healer has the knowledge of both the physical and the spiritual world, and the tribe's members aren't allowed to question the healer.

Often, Native American healing techniques were, and still are, passed down from generation to generation, from grandmother to mother to granddaughter. My grandmother, a medicine woman, was taught by her mother, and my grandmother in turn taught me; she skipped my mother's generation. The healers use these techniques equally with tribal members and their animals, pets, and livestock. My grandmother kept goats and chickens, and I remember as a young child watching her treat a milk goat who had lost her milk.

Most Native American healers restrict their healing practices to those who belong to their individual tribes. However, a great deal of information is available about their healing techniques. You can begin your exploration at the Native American Healing Arts website (www.healing-arts.org/nativelinks.htm).

The Least You Need to Know

- Ayurveda medical techniques originated in India, and focus on disease prevention and healing illnesses.
- Traditional Chinese veterinary medicine (TCVM) is more than 3,500 years old and encompasses food, herbal remedies, massage, acupuncture, and acupressure.
- Reiki healing began in Japan. Practitioners use their hands to channel healing energy to the patient.
- Native American healers concentrated on both the physical and the spirit world to heal the sick.

Start with the Basics

Everything has to start at the beginning, and when it comes to natural health for pets, often one of the first topics to come up is vaccinations. Since their introduction into the veterinary world, vaccinations have saved thousands—if not millions—of dogs' and cats' lives, but that doesn't mean vaccinations are without risk. In this part, you learn about both sides of this argument.

The basics also include natural body care: brushing the coat, cleaning ears, and clipping toenails. In these chapters, you also learn more about the importance of exercise, play, and quality time shared between you and your pet.

In This Chapter

- How vaccinations protect your pet
- Core and noncore canine vaccines
- Core and noncore feline vaccines
- Why more is not always better
- Vaccinosis and other health risks
- A homeopathic alternative

Vaccinations were developed to save lives, and they do. Before vaccinations, dogs and cats died by the thousands from diseases we see rarely today. Years ago, distemper wiped out entire kennels of show, working, and hunting dogs. Cats also died from a variety of diseases that we now can prevent with vaccinations.

Vaccinations aren't innocuous, however, and they can cause some problems. Reactions are uncommon, but unfortunately, they do happen. Some concerned owners and professionals believe vaccinations may be responsible for some serious health problems.

How Vaccinations Work

When an animal gets sick because of an infectious disease, his or her immune system creates *antibodies* against that disease. The process of creating these antibodies is called an *active immunity*, and they prevent the animal from getting sick from this particular disease in the future.

DEFINITION

An **antibody** is a substance made out of protein and produced by the immune system. It protects against disease.

The animal's immune system continues to make antibodies against a disease long after the original infection is gone. If the animal is exposed to the same disease again, the body will produce even more antibodies. Generally, this protection lasts the animal's lifetime.

Vaccinations provide a controlled exposure to an infectious disease to allow the animal's body to produce antibodies to fight that disease. Modified live virus vaccines contain the living virus, but the virus has been modified so the animal won't get sick when it receives the vaccine. The immune system tends to react quickly to these vaccines and begin producing antibodies right away.

Killed virus vaccinations contain a sample of the dead virus. Killing the virus before administering the vaccination ensures the dog or cat won't get sick. The body will make antibodies in response to killed virus vaccines, but it'll do so at a slower rate.

The primary difference between natural exposure and exposure via a vaccine is that a vaccination may not produce lifetime immunity to the disease. Whether it does or doesn't depends on the vaccine, the animal's immune system response, and the number of exposures the animal has had to the disease or to vaccinations.

GO NATURAL

Some natural health advocates believe natural exposure is the best way for a pet to develop immunities to diseases. Although certainly a natural approach, it leaves the pet vulnerable to illness.

Canine Vaccines

A variety of vaccinations are given to puppies and adult dogs on a regular basis. Veterinary professionals consider some vaccinations essential—these are called *core vaccines*. Others are needed by some dogs depending on the dog's geographical location, whether the dog travels or not, and other aspects of the individual situation. These are called *noncore vaccines*. There's a third category of vaccines available under specific circumstances (I'll cover these later in the chapter).

Core Canine Vaccines

For the following diseases, dogs must receive core vaccinations:

- **Distemper vaccine:** Canine distemper is a virus similar to the human measles virus, and it is a potentially fatal disease. It can affect many of the dog's organs, including the skin, eyes, and intestinal and respiratory tracts. The virus is transmitted through urine, feces, and saliva. The first symptoms are usually nasal and eye discharge.

- **Hepatitis vaccine:** Canine hepatitis is a virus that exists worldwide. It's spread through nasal discharge and urine, usually through direct contact to the infected substance. The first symptom of the virus is a sore throat; the dog may avoid swallowing, drinking, and eating. It spreads rapidly to other organs and develops quickly; dogs can die within hours of exhibiting the first symptoms.

- **Parvovirus:** This deadly virus, often referred to simply as *parvo*, has killed thousands of dogs, usually puppies. Because the virus continues to mutate and change, it's still a deadly threat. Symptoms include diarrhea, vomiting, and severe dehydration. This virus is widely considered the most dangerous and fatal disease known to dogs.

- **Rabies:** This virus is almost always fatal once the animal has contracted the disease. Usually, it's transmitted through contact with an infected animal, such as a bat, skunk, squirrel, or raccoon. The first symptom is usually drooling because the animal has difficulty swallowing. This symptom is followed quickly by staggering, seizures, and behavioral changes. Many states and regional governments require rabies vaccinations.

Most veterinarians recommend all puppies and dogs be vaccinated with these vaccines because these diseases are serious, difficult to treat, and often fatal.

> **PET ALERT**
>
> Wait in your veterinarian's office for half an hour after your pet receives a vaccination. If your dog or cat is going to have a reaction to the vaccine, it usually begins within that time period.

Noncore Canine Vaccines

The diseases and vaccines that are considered noncore—or not essential—include:

- **Bordetella bronchiseptica:** Bordetella are bacteria that cause coughing and other respiratory problems. This disease is often attributed to canine or kennel cough, too. It's very contagious and spreads easily from one dog to another through coughing. It's rarely dangerous to healthy dogs, but puppies can get quite sick.

- **Leptospirosis:** These potentially fatal bacteria affect the kidneys. It's passed from the kidneys to the urine, and it's transmitted to other dogs when they sniff contaminated urine. Lepto, as it's often called, can spread to other species and even people. Symptoms include fever, nausea, and severe dehydration. It's not uncommon for dogs to have adverse reactions to the leptospirosis vaccine. These can be as minor as redness, itching, and swelling at the injection site, or as serious as anaphylactic shock and death.

- **Lyme disease:** This bacterial disease is spread by infected ticks, flies, and fleas, although ticks are the primary host. Originally limited to the state of Connecticut, it now exists in all 48 contiguous states. A fever is the first symptom, followed by muscle soreness, weakness, and joint pain. Severe, permanent joint damage is possible, as is neurological damage.

- **Parainfluenza:** This virus is one of several viruses attributed to canine or kennel cough. It is easily spread when a dog coughs, and coughing happens to be one of the first and primary symptoms. Parainfluenza can lead to pneumonia, but it's generally just a cough that goes away in a week or two.

Discuss these noncore vaccinations with your veterinarian. He or she may recommend one or more of them, depending on your dog's location and activities.

Specific Circumstances

Scientists continue to develop new vaccines, and most have some specific applications. These include the following:

- **Coronavirus:** The first symptom of this virus is diarrhea, which can range from mild to severe, and the animal may have blood in the feces. Although puppies may be at risk for dehydration, the disease is usually quite mild.

- **Giardia:** A giardia vaccine is available for pets, and vets often recommend giving it to dogs who live near wildlife areas. Giardia is a protozoa that's transmitted when the dog ingests the organism, usually while in a wildlife environment. The primary symptom of giardia is diarrhea.

- **Porphyromonas:** These bacteria cause periodontitis. There is vaccine available, and vets often recommend administering it to dogs with periodontitis when routine cleaning techniques are not working.

- **Rattlesnake venom:** If you live in an area where rattlesnakes are common and your dog likes to chase reptiles, this vaccine may gain your dog some time to find emergency veterinary help after a snake bite. However, the vaccination will not protect your dog from all reactions from a rattlesnake bite.

Usually, veterinarians only recommend these vaccines in specific situations. Talk to your veterinarian about them.

Feline Vaccines

Cats are amazing animals, with strong and agile bodies, but they're just as susceptible to diseases as dogs and people. As with other animals, vaccinations can help prevent diseases in cats. There is a variety of vaccines available for cats; some are considered essential, and others not.

Core Feline Vaccines

The following are all potentially serious diseases that can be fatal to cats, even with treatment. Most veterinarians recommend all cats should be vaccinated against the following diseases:

- **Feline calicivirus (FCV):** This highly contagious disease affects the respiratory tract. Once a cat has the disease, he or she never totally gets rid of it, and the cat can continue to infect other cats.

- **Feline panleukopenia (FPV):** Also called feline distemper, this is a very contagious and potentially deadly viral disease. FPV causes listlessness, diarrhea, vomiting, dehydration, and fever, and treatment is very difficult. The virus is very strong and can live outside the cat's body for a long time—up to a year!

- **Feline viral rhinotracheitis:** This highly contagious virus causes an upper respiratory tract infection. It causes sneezing, eye discharge, and loss of appetite, and it becomes an increasingly serious illness. Even if a cat recovers from the symptoms of the infection, the cat may continue to shed the virus and infect other cats throughout his or her life span.

- **Rabies:** In many localities, the law requires that pet owners get all cats vaccinated for rabies. Cats who go outside and especially those who hunt should definitely receive the vaccination.

Noncore Feline Vaccines

Several noncore feline vaccinations are for extremely contagious and potentially serious diseases. If your cat stays inside and has no contact with stray or unvaccinated cats, these may not be an issue. If your cat goes outside, attends cat shows, does cat therapy work with other animals at a nursing home, or in other ways comes in contact with other cats, ask your veterinarian if he or she recommends giving your cat these (or some of these) vaccines:

- **Feline chlamydophlia:** This is a bacterial respiratory disease. It's extremely contagious and cats can pass it to people through direct contact.

- **Feline immunodeficiency virus (FIV):** This virus is passed from one cat to another through bites during cat fights, and it can hibernate in the bitten cat's system for years. It can cause a number of chronic health issues, including diarrhea, skin infections, dental disease, and seizures.

- **Feline infectious peritonitis (FIP):** This is a dangerous disease that causes the formation of abscesses throughout the cat's body. Fluids can leak from blood vessels, causing fluid to gather in the chest and threaten breathing.

- **Feline leukemia (FeLV):** This disease can hibernate in the cat's system for months or even years after exposure, and the cat can infect others while the disease lies dormant. As the cat's immune system is slowly destroyed by FeLV, the cat may begin to suffer from secondary infections or even develop cancer.

A couple other vaccines are available for cats that are much like those for dogs, and include bordetella and giardiasis. Talk to your veterinarian to determine whether your cat needs any of these vaccines.

The Pros and Cons of Vaccinations

Vaccinations are important for both dogs and cats—they save lives. In fact, many of the diseases that killed thousands of pets—such as canine distemper—are extremely uncommon now because of vaccinations. Vaccines aren't innocuous, though, and they can cause problems. Therefore, they should be given wisely and with caution. More is not always better.

Dr. Marty Becker, a veterinarian, author, and speaker, says to make vaccinations safer for your pet, "Avoid giving multiple doses of vaccine at the same appointment as this has been shown to be associated with increased risk of an acute vaccine adverse reaction." By administering vaccinations in intervals of several weeks, the animal's immune system can heal in between shots. Most veterinarians recommend giving the core vaccines first and then giving any needed noncore vaccines when those are completed.

Testing Titers

Now that most pet owners and veterinarians are questioning the wisdom of giving booster vaccines every year, people have been asking how long vaccination protection lasts. Unfortunately, that's hard to say because every dog's and cat's immune system is different. There's a fairly easy way to tell if an animal is still immune: your vet may check the animal's antibodies for a particular disease. This is called testing the *titers*.

DEFINITION

A **titer** describes the concentration of a measured substance in the blood serum.

Although this test is a wonderful alternative to vaccinating a dog or cat every year—especially when it's not needed—as with everything else, this system isn't perfect. Antibody tests aren't available for all dog and cat diseases. Plus, standardized levels of antibodies have yet to be established. More research on antibody levels is needed to determine when a pet can be considered safe.

Considering the antibody levels is just one part of the equation; the pet's lifestyle is important, too. Dogs who compete in dog shows and performance sports events are more likely to be exposed to contagious diseases, as are cats who go to cat shows. Dogs and cats in boarding kennels, humane societies, and shelters are also more apt to pick up diseases. These animals may need higher titer levels to be safe.

Vaccine Reactions

Most vaccinations have a low risk of side effects, especially for dogs. Distemper, parvovirus, hepatitis, parainfluenza, bordetella, and coronavirus for dogs all have a low risk of adverse side effects. The rabies vaccine carries with it a moderate risk of side effects, as does the Lyme disease vaccine.

The leptospirosis vaccine has a high risk of side effects, with more than 30 percent of vaccinated dogs having some kind of side effect. Side effects range from seizures to not developing adequate immunity.

Cats are very sensitive to many medications, including vaccinations. Panleukemia, rhinotracheitis, calciviris, and rabies vaccines all have a low to moderate risk for side effects. The chlamydophlia vaccine has a high risk of adverse side effects, so vets don't recommend it for cats unless they are at risk for catching this disease.

Reactions to the chlamydophlia vaccine can be as mild as trembling after the shot, a fever later in the day, soreness at the injection site, or a mild case of the illness. Serious side effects include seizures, anaphylactic shock, and death.

Vaccination Schedules

Puppies and kittens receive immunities from their mothers through the colostrum (the first milk) that the babies ingest shortly after birth. This *passive immunity* helps keep the babies healthy for their first few weeks of life.

> **DEFINITION**
>
> **Passive immunity** is a type of immunity gained by the transfer of anti-bodies from one individual to another, such as from mother to offspring through the mother's milk.

Most veterinarians recommend puppies and kittens get their first vaccinations between 6 and 8 weeks of age. If the mother's antibodies are still effective in the puppy's or kitten's body, the first set of vaccinations may not be entirely effective. That's why most puppies and kittens get a series of vaccines early in life. The animals usually receive each stage of the vaccine series about three to four weeks apart.

Following the puppy or kitten shots, vets used to recommend that dogs and cats receive an annual booster for all of the vaccinations, except rabies. (Following a booster at 1 year of age, rabies is usually on a three-year schedule.) These recommendations have changed in recent years.

The American Veterinary Medical Association (AVMA) now says, "Dogs and cats at a low risk of disease exposure may not need to be boostered yearly for most diseases. Consult with your veterinarian to determine the appropriate vaccination schedule for your dog or cat." You need to consider many factors when determining what vaccines your pet should receive, including your pet's age, breed or mixture of breeds, and vaccination history. The health of your pet is also impor-tant. Is he suffering from any diseases? The risks your pet faces are important, too. Does your pet go to dog or cat shows? And last but not least, where you live must be taken into consideration. Are there any diseases prevalent in your area that your pet should be vaccinated against?

In the past, when vaccinations saved thousands of pets' lives annually, questioning whether a pet should receive any particular vaccination was not an issue. Dr. Marty Becker says, "I remember when I first started practicing as a veterinarian we robotically gave every pet who came in for annual shots exactly the same thing. No more. Now we carefully evaluate each patient and look at breed or mix, life stage, lifestyle, and emerging risks to determine exactly what vaccines and other preventive health-care measures are recommended."

When Making a Decision

Talk to your veterinarian about vaccines, keeping an open—not confrontational—dialogue. Your veterinarian is, of course, concerned with preventing disease. You may be concerned with the dangers of overvaccinating your pet. Meet in the middle and talk about it.

Some discussion points might include the following:

- What is your pet's risk of exposure? Does your dog go to dog parks, dog shows, training classes, or other places where he or she meets a variety of other dogs? Does your cat go outside on a regular basis or go to cat shows? Obviously, pets that spend time in these environments have a higher risk of being exposed to disease.

- Which vaccines are you concerned about? What are the risks to your pet should he or she get sick? Is the disease treatable with a high probability of success?

- What is the risk to people should the pet get sick?

- What is the risk to other pets in the home should the pet get sick?

- How old is your pet? What is his or her state of health? Would a vaccination do more harm than good?

- What is the potential for an adverse reaction from a specific vaccine? Has your pet had adverse reactions to vaccines in the past?

Once you and your veterinarian have discussed these issues, you can make a decision based on what's best for your pet.

Understanding Vaccinosis and Other Risks

No discussion of vaccinations is complete without the elephant in the living room—*vaccinosis*. Many pet owners and veterinarians are growing increasingly concerned about the number of animals—dogs, cats, horses, and other animals—with serious long-term health problems that appear to be related to vaccinations. Vaccinations have been implicated in certain health problems for several reasons. Vaccinations affect the animal's immune system—that's how they work. Many of the diseases causing concern are autoimmune diseases, including lupus, immune system suppression, and bone marrow suppression. Cats are susceptible to injection site sarcomas, an aggressive cancer that occurs at the site where they have received vaccinations.

DEFINITION

Vaccinosis is an illness or reaction that occurs as a result of being given a vaccination.

In addition, many pets who develop vaccinosis later in life suffered adverse reactions after getting vaccinations. The reactions may appear immediately after a vaccination has been given—within 30 minutes—or the reaction may appear after an animal has received multiple vaccinations over several years. The reactions may be mild—perhaps just lethargy and a lack of appetite for a day or two—but note even mild reactions and report them to the veterinarian.

It is vitally important that only healthy animals receive vaccinations. If the animal is sick or has a compromised immune system, don't get the animal vaccinated, at least not at that time. Although the animal may not get sick from the vaccine itself, the immune system could go wild in response and cause a number of autoimmune diseases, including arthritis, colitis, pancreatitis, cancer, and leukemia.

Modified live virus vaccines are implicated the most in these incidences. Combination vaccines—those containing the antigens of numerous diseases—are also a possible factor. Many veterinarians now recommend avoiding combination vaccines that contain more than three antigens. Some vaccines are available that may contain as many as seven antigens. If all seven diseases are a potential threat, then the dog or cat would be better served by having those vaccinations be given in smaller combinations.

Although some holistic veterinarians today seem to feel that vaccinations do our pets a great deal of harm, most veterinarians aren't
ready to give up on them. Dr. Marty Becker says, "Fewer, less
frequent, more targeted vaccines yes, but no vaccines at all? As a
veterinarian, I shudder at the suffering that could mean. And I'm
guessing almost all of my colleagues would, too."

Nosode Alternatives

Dr. Samuel Hahnemann, the father of homeopathy (see Chapter 3),
discovered that after people and animals received vaccinations, they
often became ill. He noted that some people and animals seemed
to have a sensitivity toward certain substances (minute amounts of
diseases given as vaccinations or homeopathic treatments for disease)
injected into the body—that what one person or animal could handle
with no reaction might cause a serious problem in another.

Many homeopathic veterinarians are now offering *nosodes* to replace
vaccinations. A homeopathic remedy comes from an infected animal,
and your pet receives the remedy in place of the vaccination.

DEFINITION

A **nosode** is a homeopathic remedy made from a product of disease,
such as a bit of infected tissue.

Homeopathic practitioners say that because the animal takes the
nosode orally, there's no pain or shock, and no inflammation afterward. Nosodes are less expensive than vaccinations, and they don't
cause a sick reaction. Unfortunately, controlled studies haven't shown
nosodes to be effective. Hopefully, future studies will have different
results.

The Least You Need to Know

- Vaccinations have saved many pets' lives, but never consider them innocuous; they do carry some risk.

- Core vaccines are considered essential; noncore vaccines are for specific situations.

- Decide what vaccinations your pet should receive after discussing your pet's age, health status, potential to be exposed to disease, and other risk factors with your veterinarian.

- Vaccines can adversely affect your pet's health, from mild reactions that occur immediately following the vaccination to more serious problems that could occur later in life after multiple vaccinations.

- Nosodes are homeopathic treatments that are used to replace vaccinations. They are controversial and have not yet been proven to be effective.

Natural Body Care from Head to Tail

In This Chapter

- Brushing your pet's coat
- Caring for ears, teeth, toenails, and claws
- Bathing your pet
- Grooming the anxious pet

Your dog or cat needs your help to keep himself clean, neat, and healthy. Although cats—and many dogs—are good about keeping themselves well groomed, that's not enough; only you can brush your pet's coat, remove grass seeds and burrs, and untangle matted fur. Caring for your pet doesn't have to be difficult. A regular grooming routine that includes massage, body care, and paying attention to details is all it takes.

A consistent grooming routine allows you to find potential health problems early. If you find a lump, bump, cut, or scratch earlier thanks to regular grooming, you ensure the opportunity to get the problem checked out and treated before it's able to become a bigger health risk. You can note and address dirty ears, a broken tooth, or a broken toenail before the issue develops into a bigger problem.

Choosing natural products to help you care for your pet can be a little more challenging than simply buying any product that looks attractive on the pet store shelf. Read the labels on all pet products to choose more natural products, and use homemade products or remedies when available.

Grooming Begins with Brushing

Most dog and cat owners know they need to brush their pets' coats on a regular basis. Brushing the coat helps keep it clean by pulling the dirt out. The brush also pulls out the dead undercoat, and you can find and untangle matted areas. Brushing stimulates the skin, which helps keep it healthy. Brushing your pet is just the beginning, though; there's more to caring for your pet than that.

Brushing your pet every day also helps build a good relationship with your dog or cat. Your gentle handling and kind brushing—stopping to comb out tangles, for example, rather than just continuing to pull on those tangles—teaches your pet to trust you. As you brush, you can also touch your pet all over. This will help you care for him or her and find any potential health problems. But this, too, helps build trust. By doing this on a daily basis, it also helps your pet become more comfortable with this personal care.

Ideally, begin this care as soon as your pet joins your family. If your pet is a puppy or kitten, keep these grooming sessions short, as these babies have very short attention spans. However, don't let your puppy or kitten dash away as soon as you bring out the grooming tools. Instead, pet your puppy or kitten first to help relax him. Then do some gentle brushing to get him or her used to it.

Introducing Brushing

If you have a puppy or kitten or a newly adopted pet, or you haven't been grooming your pet regularly, introduce brushing slowly. Because you're going to be grooming your pet on a regular basis, it'll be much easier if your pet enjoys it. Let's face it, if your dog or cat fights you, you'll both hate it. Then, because brushing is an awful experience for you and your pet, you won't do it as often as your pet needs it. So take it slow so your cat or dog can learn to love it.

CAT CHAT

If you have an adult cat who you've never brushed before, make sure groom activities are linked to good treats in the cat's mind. Show the cat the brush or comb and give him or her a treat; do this for a couple of days. Next, progress to touching him or her with the brush or comb and follow that up with a treat. Do this for several days, until your cat accepts the tool and you can begin a daily brushing routine without treats.

Start with Some Stroking

You can make brushing easier and less stressful for you and your pet if you introduce it with a little massage—not a deep tissue massage, but a slow, gentle, calming one. Doing so will teach your pet to accept handling. This is particularly important if your dog doesn't like you to handle his or her paws or your cat would rather have you stay away from the belly.

To begin, choose a place where you and your pet can be comfortable. You can hold a small dog, puppy, kitten, or cat on your lap or he or she can sit next to you on the sofa. If you have a large dog, try sitting on the floor where he or she can approach you.

Invite your pet to join you. Without forcing your pet into a specific position, begin stroking him or her gently with long, slow strokes. Be calm and move your hand slowly; fast petting will wake up your cat or dog and get him or her excited. You may need to calm and relax your pet first. As he or she calms down, your cat may stretch— that's fine; just keep stroking. If your dog rolls over and bares his or her belly, that's fine, too.

As you feel your pet relax under your hands, stroke all over the body—front and back, and left side and right side. Stroke his or her head, down each leg, and down the tail. At this point, maintain contact in a stroking motion only. Do this daily for a week. Then, introduce massage. You can do this by starting out with stroking your pet as you've been doing. When your pet is relaxed, begin rubbing his or her body with gentle finger pressure. Rub your pet's ears at the base, making small circles, and gradually progress to the cheeks, under the chin, and down the neck. Eventually, massage his or her entire body.

> **PET ALERT**
>
> If your pet begins flinching, making noise, or pulling away, your massage is too firm. Use your pet's reactions as a gauge to indicate how you're doing. Cats, small dogs, and thin dogs need more gentle handling than do larger dogs who have more muscle mass.

Fingertip Health Check

As you're stroking and massaging your pet, your fingers will learn what your pet feels like. Pay attention to his or her shoulder and hip muscles, the bone structure, and the texture of the skin. As you continue the stroking and massage process over time, you will instantly recognize a change.

A good example is my now 12-year-old dog, Riker. Like so many old dogs, he's changing. His muscles aren't as strong and prominent as they once were, and he has some lumps and bumps. As I massage him, I can tell when something has changed and can monitor it over time or call the veterinarian. For example, Riker has many lipomas (fatty benign growths) that his veterinarian has seen over time and assured me are not a problem. I can then watch them for changes. However, if you find something new, such as a new lump or bump or a change of any kind in your pet's body, call your veterinarian.

The fingertip health check also allows you to check for ticks, cuts and scratches, and hair tangles. Also, as you massage, your pet will let you know if something is sore.

> **DOG TALK**
>
> Some dogs are as reactive as cats and will let you know immediately if something is too rough or if something hurts. Others are stoic; if your pet is like this, watch for a lip twitch, a blink, a flinch of the skin, or a small whine.

Introduce the Brush and Comb

After a couple weeks of stroking and massaging your pet, begin introducing the brush and comb into the routine. First, use the same relaxation technique as you did previously, but have the brush or comb nearby. When your pet is relaxed, pick up the tool and begin brushing or combing slowly and easily. Don't use it roughly. If your pet reacts, stroke his or her coat again and talk in a soft voice. Then begin brushing again.

As your pet relaxes, brush or comb your pet from head to tail and all the parts in between. Take your time, and concentrate on keeping your pet relaxed.

Begin Gentle Brushing

When your dog or cat is relaxing under your hands during the stroking and massage process, and when your pet's comfortable with the grooming tools, you can begin grooming. Don't forget to precede grooming with a massage to feel for any new problems and to relax him or her.

Use the tools appropriate for your pet's breed (see the next section). Brush or comb in the direction the hair grows. I like to start at the head and work toward the tail. Don't forget potential problem areas: behind the ears, the back of the legs, and under the tail. If you find hair tangles, use your fingers or a comb to untangle the hair gently. Sometimes, applying a small amount of hair conditioner is effective in untangling matted hair.

PET ALERT

Never use scissors to cut out a tangle; it's too easy to cut the skin under the tangle.

If at any time during the brushing your pet gets worried, stop and give a little massage. When your pet is relaxed, begin again.

Grooming Tools

A large variety of grooming tools is available, but I prefer to keep things simple. For my dogs, I have a good brush that can get through the coat to the undercoat, a comb for tangles, a rake for matted areas, and a nail trimmer. For my cat, I have a soft-bristle brush and a comb. What you need depends on the breed of dog or cat you have and what your pet is able to tolerate.

You can brush a short-haired dog's coat easily with a soft-bristle brush. A pin brush—the kind with beads at the end of each pin—is effective with short haired cats. Medium and long-haired dogs require a metal comb or rake capable of going through thick coats. You can keep a long-haired cat gorgeous using a metal comb.

If you have questions about grooming tools for your breed (or mixture of breeds), talk to a professional groomer. He or she can identify the tools best suited for your dog or cat.

GO NATURAL

The key to keeping your pet looking awesome isn't so much what tools you use, but that you comb or brush your pet daily.

Other Parts Need Care, Too

Your pet's skin and coat are important, and the fingertip health check can potentially catch many health problems early. Other parts of your dog's or cat's body need regular care, too.

Dogs have a gland on either side of the anus called an anal gland. This gland contains a musky oil. A small amount is secreted as the dog passes feces. Sometimes these glands can become full and inflamed. If your dog is dragging his butt on the ground or trying to lick these glands, take him to the veterinarian. Don't try to express these yourself without veterinary instruction, as the full glands can rupture.

Cleaning the Ears

To clean your pet's ears, you need a cleaning solution and a few cotton balls. I use either witch hazel or tea tree oil to clean their ears, but ask your veterinarian for a recommendation.

Dampen the cotton ball in the cleaning liquid and squeeze out the excess. Make sure the cotton ball is damp but not wet.

Hold the ear flap in one hand and lift it so the inside of the ear is exposed. Gently clean the ear. Make sure you clean all the folds and crevasses in the ear. If the ear is really dirty, you may need a couple of cotton balls. Throw that cotton ball away and use a clean one for the other ear. Don't use a cotton swab in your pet's ear canal. Although the ear canal has a bend in it that makes it difficult to puncture the ear drum, you can still harm your pet.

If your pet's ear appears very dirty (with a brown, waxy buildup) or if it smells bad, clean the ear thoroughly and check it often. Your pet may be developing a problem. If the ear is dirty, red, and inflamed, call your veterinarian because your pet likely has an ear infection (see Chapter 15).

Ear mites can be another problem in both dogs and cats. As with an ear infection, the ear will be red and inflamed and look dirty. However, with mites the ear will also be itchy, and your dog or cat may paw and scratch at the ear or shake their head. This, too, needs immediate veterinary care.

Cleaning Those Pearly Whites

One grooming chore that far too many people ignore is cleaning their pet's teeth. Unfortunately, *periodontal disease* is one of the most common health problems veterinarians see. This is particularly sad because pet owners can usually prevent it.

DEFINITION

Periodontal disease is the inflammation of the gums and the deeper structures supporting the teeth.

When dogs and cats eat, food particles stick to the teeth. Pets who eat dry kibble often have food particles lodged in next to the gums at the base of the teeth. Bacteria coat these food particles, along with calcium salts and other organic materials, and then plaque forms. Over time, plaque hardens and becomes calculus. Calculus is hard, can form all over the surface of teeth, and leads to gum inflammation.

When the material is still in the plaque stage, you can remove it by providing brushing and tooth care. When calculus forms, though, the veterinarian will need to do a thorough tooth cleaning. Most veterinarians recommend cleaning your pet's teeth at least three times a week. If your pet already has dental problems, it's best to clean the teeth daily.

> **PET ALERT**
>
> If your pet has a broken or cracked tooth, or has swollen and red gums, call your veterinarian. Don't try to take care of these dental problems at home.

To clean your pet's teeth, you need baking soda and some gauze pads and a toothbrush made for pets (available at a pet supply store) or a small child's toothbrush. Mix the baking soda with just enough water to make a paste. Wrap the gauze around your index finger and dab it in the paste, or moisten the toothbrush and dab the bristles in the paste.

Begin rubbing the paste gently over your pet's teeth, both on the outside and inside. In the beginning, brush a few teeth at a time and then take a break. Give your pet a drink of fresh water in between brushing. If you do a few teeth each day for a few weeks, you can gradually get your pet used to this new grooming regime without stressing him or her out too much.

> **CAT CHAT**
>
> Cats don't often take kindly to teeth cleaning. The best way to approach this is to wrap your cat firmly in a towel to protect you from bites and scratches. Then gently clean the teeth using a small child's toothbrush or pet toothbrush.

Although cats don't chew enough to help keep their teeth clean, some dogs do. However, only some specific types of things will help.

Dry kibble dog food doesn't, nor do hard treats made from cereal grains. Crumbs from these treats tend to lodge between teeth or in the gum line and make dental problems worse. Hard treats made from rawhide, dried animal parts (like beef ears and meat), and raw bones can scrape the teeth as the dog is chewing. However, these types of treats do carry with them some risk. Here are some tips:

- Bones should always be raw; cooked bones are brittle and can splinter.

- If your dog breaks off bone shards, take the bone (and shards) away and don't give your dog bones in the future.

- Only give your dog bones that are too large for him to swallow. Beef, bison, venison, and elk are better than bones from smaller animals.

- Never give your dog poultry bones.

- Some dogs will chew off big chunks of rawhide, try to swallow it whole, and choke. If your dog does this, don't give him rawhide again.

- Always supervise your dog closely when giving him treats such as these.

Trimming Canine Toenails

As with other grooming chores, toenail trimming doesn't have to be an ordeal if you got your pet used to the procedure at an early age. When you massage your pet, make sure you touch the toenails, too. Touch each nail on each paw so your dog gets used to it.

You can trim dog toenails with nail clippers or you can shorten them with nail grinders. I prefer grinders because they make the job easier, and there's less chance of cutting the nails too short and making them bleed. However, if you're used to trimming the nails, that's fine; the scissors-type nail clippers are easiest to use.

When trimming nails, have some styptic powder on hand. This is made of alum that not only stops bleeding, but also prevents bacteria from moving into the bloodstream. Commonly used by veterinarians and groomers, styptic powder can be found anywhere dog and cat grooming supplies are sold.

Follow these steps:

1. Massage one paw and then grasp one toe gently but firmly.

2. Pull the hair back from the nail so it won't get pulled by the clippers.

3. Examine the nail. Note the wide base and the narrow tip. Cut off only the narrow tip.

4. If you cut into the quick and the nail bleeds, stop the bleeding with some styptic powder or scrape the nail along a bar of soap. Soap stops the bleeding until a clot forms.

> **DOG TALK**
>
> If your dog has white nails, you can see the pink of the quick. Cut only the white portion of the nail; don't cut the pink. If your dog has black nails, trim the nails multiple times, taking just a tiny bit off with each trim. Eventually you will see the center meaty part of the nail begin to appear. Stop trimming at that point.

To use a nail grinder, be sure to get your dog used to it first. Let your dog see and smell the grinder, and give him or her a treat. Repeat this several times.

Turn the grinder on and give your dog a treat. Praise him or her when he or she investigates the grinder. Then, touch the vibrating grinder handle to your dog's side, tell him how silly that grinder is (in a happy voice), and give him a treat. When your dog thinks that the vibrating grinder is the silliest thing in the world, you're ready to continue.

Each grinder has directions for use; follow those directions. If your dog begins to panic, stop, repeat the introduction steps, and try again.

Trimming Feline Claws

Make sure your cat is used to you touching his or her paws before you attempt to trim the claws. Gently press on the top and bottom of one toe so the claw extends. Release it and praise your cat. If your cat likes a special treat, offer it as you praise him or her. Repeat the process for each nail.

Don't use a grinder on your cat's nail. Use a small-sized, scissorlike nail trimmer because they're easiest to use on cats and because you can cut the nail quickly.

As with dogs' nails, take only the tip off each claw. With the cat on your lap, extend the claw with one hand and trim with the other. Don't be slow or your cat will get impatient. You will be able to see the quick, and it's important not to trim into the quick. That's painful and will cause your cat's nail to bleed.

When Your Cat Claws Everything

Many cat owners know this sound: *r-i-i-p-p-p*. Your cat is clawing the furniture again. Contrary to what you might think, cats don't claw up the carpet, furniture, or drapes just for fun, nor do they do it to get a reaction out of you. Cats claw for a couple reasons: First, when the cat reaches above to furniture or ahead to the carpet, he or she grabs with the claws and then stretches. This moves the body, limbers up the muscles, and keeps him or her strong and agile. Second, cats claw to remove a transparent sheath on the nail that has become worn and dull. When that's pulled off, a bright, shiny, sharp nail is underneath. Cat owners often find this shed nail on the floor or imbedded in the furniture.

To prevent damage to your furnishings but still allow your cat to stretch and scratch, you should provide him or her with a cat tree or scratching post. Cat trees are generally wooden or hard cardboard poles with resting places for the cat. They are generally covered in carpet, but some may also have sisal rope wrapped around sections. Scratching posts are usually smaller than cat trees. Some scratching posts will have cardboard sections that cats will also like clawing.

To encourage a cat to use a cat tree or scratching post, add some catnip. Spray liquid catnip or sprinkle dried catnip on several areas of the tree or post. Refresh the catnip often. You can also place an attractive cat toy in a spot where the cat will need to climb on the tree or stretch to reach it.

Giving Your Pet a Bath

You need to know how to give your pet a bath should he or she need it, but bathing your pet doesn't need to be a part of the regular grooming schedule. A healthy dog or cat smells clean and healthy. Many cats can go their entire lives without a bath. This doesn't mean the cat owner is negligent; rather, it means the cat is healthy and cleans himself or herself. A bad odor may be a sign that something isn't right, either in the animal's health or with the diet.

Some dogs get wet and dirty, or may work hard; in these cases, the dogs may need bathed. Therapy dogs must be clean prior to visiting clients. Some breeds have oilier skin than others, requiring regular baths. Bath schedules are an individual thing. Remember, however, that you can bathe a dog or cat too often, drying out the skin and coat.

Finding natural shampoos is easier than it used to be because more people are expressing concern about the products available for their pets. Only Natural Pet (see Appendix B) offers a shampoo and a conditioner that are 70 percent organic, and both are *paraben* and *sodium laurel sulfate* free.

DEFINITION

Paraben is a preservative in many cosmetics and shampoos. However, it has been linked to the development of cancer. **Sodium laurel sulfate** is a strong cleaning agent that creates suds; it is found in many cosmetics and shampoos, and it's been linked to several nasty side effects, including skin irritations and ulcers.

Other makers also produce shampoos that contain safe ingredients. Avoid shampoos that contain insecticides or medications, especially if your pet doesn't need them. Get in the habit of reading the labels and doing an Internet search for any ingredients you don't recognize.

You can bathe small dogs and cats in a large sink, but large dogs are easier to bathe in the bathtub. A friend of mine bathed her large Mastiff in the walk-in shower. During the summer you may be able to bathe your dog outside using the garden hose. Just choose a practical spot to do it, and get your pet used to the cooler water from the hose before the bath. And remember, if it's too cold for you, it's too cold for your pet.

Be calm, gentle, and patient when getting ready to bathe your pet. If you're impatient, in a hurry to get it over with, or anticipating trouble, your pet is going to know this. Instead, be calm, be ready to get wet, and laugh. It will go easier for you and your pet.

Follow these steps for stress-free bathing:

1. Always brush your pet thoroughly before bathing.

2. Hold your cat gently but firmly at the scruff of the neck where there's loose skin. Put your dog's leash on.

3. Put a cotton ball in each of your pet's ears to protect them from water.

4. Get your pet wet with warm (not hot!) water, making sure the water goes through the water-resistant coat down to the skin.

5. Using a mild shampoo specifically made for dogs, cats, kittens, or puppies, work it into the coat thoroughly.

6. In most cases, healthy dogs and cats don't need a conditioner. However, if your pet has a long coat that tends to tangle, you may want to use a conditioner after the shampoo has been rinsed out. Follow the directions for the conditioner.

7. Begin rinsing at the dog's or cat's head, letting the water run down his or her back, and then finish rinsing the rest of the animal's coat.

8. Rinse again to make sure all of the shampoo is out of the coat.

9. Towel off your pet. Then, with a dry towel, blot away any remaining water.

10. Take the cotton out of the ears and keep your dog or cat warm until the coat is completely dry.

If your pet is cold, use a blow dryer to dry the coat, but do so carefully. Not only will some pets panic when you aim the blow dryer their way, but the hot air can damage the fur and burn the skin. Use a warm (never hot!) setting.

If Your Pet Is Worried

If your pet is worried about the brush, comb, or other grooming tool, stop using the tool for the moment. Teach your pet the tool is a source of good things, and then you can use it again. To teach him or her, have a handful of really good treats at hand. Using treats your pet really likes but may not normally get is important because you want to make an impression. Bits of cheese, leftover chicken, or cooked hamburger should work, depending on your pet.

Call your pet and give a treat. Hold out the brush or other grooming tool and ask in a happy voice, "What's that?" If he or she sniffs the grooming tool, give him or her praise and a treat. Do this two or three times.

If your pet remains leery of the tool, hold the treat close to the tool so your pet has to move toward it to get the treat. Praise your pet when he or she retrieves the treat. Eventually, position the treat behind the tool so your pet has to touch the tool to get the treat. Again, praise your pet when he or she retrieves the treat.

You can try this process with a grooming tool that makes noise or moves, too. Repeat these steps with the tool quiet and still. Then when the pet isn't worried about it, turn it on. Don't touch it to your pet; just let the animal get used to how it sounds when it's turned on.

When he or she gets close to the tool when it's on, offer a treat and then touch the tool to his or her side. Using little training steps such as these will get your pet used to the tool before you use it.

The Least You Need to Know

- A daily massage can help you relax your dog or cat, and it allows you to get to know his or her body so you can identify any changes immediately.

- Brushing and combing your pet every day helps keep him or her looking his or her best and prevents many potential problems.

- Your pet needs help from you to keep his or her nails and claws trimmed and his or her ears and teeth clean.

- Bathe your dog and cat only when he or she needs it. Too many baths dry out the skin and coat.

- Read the labels on shampoos and other grooming products. Choose only natural products when possible, and avoid potentially problematic ingredients.

Play, Exercise, and Time with You

In This Chapter

- The value of playtime with your pet
- Ideas for feline play
- Laying the foundation with dog training
- Everyday activities you can do with your dog
- Agility and other canine sports
- Quiet time counts, too

Dogs and cats are called companion animals for a reason; they're awesome friends. They're intelligent and responsive, and they love to spend time by our side. When you add in the facts that they ignore our flaws and vices and they never judge us, it's easy to see why we love them so much.

There is one problem, though: today, dogs and cats need our companionship to remain physically and mentally healthy. Dogs and cats who spend too much time alone tend to develop behavior problems; dogs bark too much, and both dogs and cats can become destructive. Pets who spend too much time alone can also fail to thrive physically.

Our pets need us as much as we need them. The most natural thing we can do for them to maintain their mental and physical health is to spend time with them. After all, companionship is a two-way street.

Feline Fun

Cats have the reputation for being aloof and independent, and they certainly can be. As any cat owner will tell you, however, the more time you spend interacting with your cat, the less independent that cat is. Most cats—especially inside-only cats—could easily spend most of their time asleep. While this is natural for cats, it's not good for them to sleep all the time.

Although your cat may enjoy just hanging on the back of your chair, laying on your lap, or plastering himself or herself up against your leg at night, your cat also needs interactive, fun playtime with you. After all, you want to be more to your cat than simply the food supplier, litter box changer, and hand that pets.

Play is also good exercise for your cat. Exercise, combined with play, is great fun. It gets the heart pumping and the muscles moving and keeps the internal organs working as they should. After all, we know a sedentary lifestyle is not good for us; the same applies to our pets. Plus, when you play with your cat, you laugh, have a good time, and enjoy your pet even more. Playtime is a great bonding experience.

I've found one of the best toys for cats is a fishing pole toy. A fishing pole with a catnip toy dangling from the end of it will amuse you and your cat for hours; maybe not consecutive hours, mind you, but total hours. About 10 to 15 minutes of daily play is usually enough for most adult cats. Kittens may play for longer time periods. Most cats will stop when they've had enough, but kittens may not. If your kitten or cat is panting or breathing heavy, stop the play. A kitten may be ready to go again after several minutes of rest, and that's fine. Just don't overdo the play.

CAT CHAT

My cat, Xena, loves to play fishing pole games. I periodically change the toy on the end of the string to create a whole new game. Even at 10 years old, she runs, jumps, stalks, and pounces on the toy. It's great fun for both of us, and it's good exercise for her.

Try different types of toys with your cat. If your cat likes catnip—and not all do—just about any toy can be scented with fresh or dried catnip to make it more attractive. A new toy is more likely to gain your cat's attention simply because it's new and unfamiliar. You can make even older toys new again by putting them away for a few weeks and then re-introducing them.

You don't have to go shopping for new toys; a paper bag or cardboard box makes a great toy. Your cat doesn't care if you spend a lot of money on toys—he or she just enjoys playing with you. Place the cardboard box in the middle of the living room floor and drop some catnip, a few bits of cheese, or cat treats inside. Then, wait for the fun to begin. Here's another cardboard box trick: Close the box and cut some holes on different sides, just big enough for the cat's paw to fit through. Then, place the catnip or treats inside the box. Fun in a box—literally!

Environmental enrichment is also good for cats. Hide some treats, toys, and catnip in different places throughout a room or the house. Then, encourage your cat to find them. Start by calling your cat. When he or she approaches you, point to a hidden stash. Then point to another one. Your cat will get the idea soon enough and begin searching on her own.

PET ALERT

Cats are curious and will play with things that can potentially harm them. Put away anything that might cause a problem: rubber bands, string, yarn, feathers, and plastic grocery bags. When not playing with Xena, I put away the fishing pole toy. I don't want to risk her trying to play with it herself and potentially getting the string wrapped around her neck.

Canine Play

Dogs like to play just as much as cats do, if not more. They certainly have more stamina than cats! Whereas 15 minutes will tire out most cats, dogs are still going strong well past that time period.

Playing with your dog can encompass a number of different games. Throwing a ball or toy for the dog to retrieve is one of the most popular games, but not all dogs like to retrieve. Other games are great fun, too, including hide and seek, find the toy squirrel, and anything else you and your dog enjoys.

> **DOG TALK**
>
> To play hide and seek, one person should have a few tasty dog treats. That person hides while another person holds the dog. The hiding person can then call the dog. When the dog finds the hidden person, the hider should reward the dog with the treats.

Canine versatility allows dogs to be involved in many dog sports and activities, which I'll discuss later in the chapter. These can be great fun for both you and your dog.

Improving Your Relationship with Training

Dogs have been, for most of their history, bred to work alongside mankind, helping herd livestock, protecting property and people, and performing a number of different occupations. Although many of these occupations no longer exist, there are a number of activities and sports you can participate in with your dog. All of those activities begin with a strong foundation of training.

Basic Obedience Training

One of the best ways to bond with your dog is to go through obedience training together. A group class is inexpensive, and the class will teach you how to teach your dog. Because each dog is different, this is important—even if you're a long-time dog owner.

When you learn how to train your dog, you also learn how to communicate with him or her. When you can communicate with each other, you can better understand each other. Fewer misunderstandings will help you develop a better relationship.

GO NATURAL

Before enrolling in a dog training class, ask to watch one of the sessions first. Leave your dog at home and just go to observe. Make sure this is going to be the right class for you and your dog.

When you know how to teach your dog and your dog enjoys learning, there are many things you can do together. Without training, most dog sports and activities are off limits—or, if not off limits, definitely not enjoyable.

If you don't know of a good trainer in your area, ask for some referrals. If a neighbor has a well-behaved dog, ask where they went for training. You can also ask your veterinarian—and several other vets—for referrals. If a couple of trainers' names are mentioned, contact them and ask if you can watch one of their classes. Choose the trainer whose personality and method will work best for you and your dog.

The AKC STAR Puppy Program

The American Kennel Club (AKC) has introduced a wonderful new program for all puppies—not just purebred or AKC-registered puppies. It's called the AKC STAR Puppy program; STAR stands for Socialization, Training, Activity, and Responsibility. This program is for young puppies and is designed so the owner learns what the puppy needs, the puppy gets a healthy start in life, and you and your new friend address behavioral problems as early as possible.

There are 20 steps in the STAR Puppy program. To graduate, the puppy must pass all 20 steps and attend six weeks of a group puppy class. There's a reason for all these training and behavior steps: for example, a puppy who allows hugging and petting is easier to groom than a puppy who doesn't accept handling.

Several steps are directed toward the puppy's owner:

- The puppy is healthy and has been started on a vaccination program (as determined by the owner and their veterinarian).

- The owner is actively involved with the puppy, including daily play and exercise.

- The owner picks up after his or her puppy and has a bag or other tools to do so.

- The puppy is wearing identification.

There are several steps for the puppy, too:

- The puppy doesn't show aggression toward people in the group class.

- The puppy isn't aggressive toward the other puppies in the class.

- The puppy tolerates and wears the collar or harness and accepts the leash.

- The puppy accepts hugging and petting from the owner.

- The puppy plays with a toy (or treat) and allows the owner to take it away.

The puppy behavior and training includes the following:

- The puppy allows someone other than the owner to pet him or her.

- The owner can groom, touch, and examine the puppy, including the ears and paws.

- The puppy can walk on a leash with the owner without zig-zagging down the sidewalk and without tripping the owner.

- At the owner's command, the puppy sits, lies down, and comes on leash.

- The puppy doesn't panic at visual or sound distractions, such as a flapping trash bag or an opened umbrella.

Many dog trainers are now incorporating this into their puppy classes. If you have a puppy, call around to local trainers and ask if they offer it, or go to the AKC's website (www.akc.org) for a list of trainers in your area.

The Canine Good Citizen Program

I've been a fan of the AKC's Canine Good Citizen (CGC) program since it began more than 20 years ago. At the time, my husband and I had German Shepherds and a Papillon, and we were all too familiar with breed discrimination. People prejudged our German Shepherds, assuming they were aggressive and potentially dangerous simply because of their breed.

The CGC program was designed to recognize responsible dog owners and well-behaved dogs. When the dog passes all 10 exercises, he or she receives the title "Canine Good Citizen," and the owner can then list CGC after the dog's name. The program is open to all dogs—purebred or mixed breed, registered with the AKC or not.

> **DOG TALK**
>
> Nationwide Insurance and the Hartford Financial Services Group are just two insurance companies now recognizing the value of the AKC CGC. Although the programs vary, some insurance companies offer a discount on homeowner's insurance upon proof of the CGC. Talk to your insurance company and ask if it offers a discount.

The exercises include:

- When with the owner, the dog allows a friendly, unfamiliar person to walk up and greet the owner.

- When with the owner, the dog allows a friendly, unfamiliar person to approach and pet him or her.

- The owner shows responsibility by making sure the dog is clean, healthy, and well-groomed.

- The dog is under control when the owner and the dog go for a walk.

- The dog is under control and doesn't pull or wrap the leash around people's legs when the dog and the owner walk through a crowd.

- The dog and the owner can demonstrate that the dog will sit, lie down, and stay when the owner commands.

- The dog comes when the owner calls.

- The dog behaves politely around other dogs and doesn't lunge or bark at other dogs.

- The dog doesn't panic in response to a visual or sound stimulus, such as a jogger or a flapping trash bag.

- The dog can be left with another person for three minutes. For example, perhaps you need to use the restroom while out on a walk and your neighbor holds the leash. (Note that this exercise isn't to encourage people to leave dogs unattended when out in public. Instead, it's to ensure you can leave your dog with another responsible person while you take care of something.)

The CGC has become so popular many landlords now require it as a condition for allowing a dog in a rental home. Some insurance companies offer discounts for dog owners with homeowner's insurance for dogs who have passed the CGC (see the previous Dog Talk sidebar), and many therapy dog organizations use the CGC as a test for potential therapy dogs. To find a CGC evaluator in your area, go to the AKC's website (www.akc.org).

Trick Training

Dog training is more than simple obedience—it's one of the most enjoyable ways to practice training skills. Although many people think trick training is teaching your dog to shake hands or roll over, there's much more to it than that. The tricks can range from very simple (shake hands) to much more difficult (a routine with several tricks performed one after another).

A few years ago my husband and I had a German Shepherd named Michi. Michi was tall, handsome, and very regal. One day, he and I were out in the front yard, and I was talking to a neighbor. Her son had just graduated from the local police academy and was coming by to show his mother his new uniform. When he showed up I congratulated him, but I also wanted to tease him a little because I'd known him since he was a young teenager. I turned to Michi and said, "Michi, would you rather be a police officer or a dead dog?" Michi dropped to the ground and rolled over to his side with his head down, looking like a very dead dog. The young man sputtered, stammered, and then began to laugh!

This trick worked because Michi's cue was "dead dog," and I had taught him to pay attention to those words when they were embedded in a sentence or conversation. I could then ask if he wanted to be anything or a dead dog and he would react. It made a great trick that always got people to laugh.

Trick training is dog training; you're working with your dog to teach him or her to perform some behaviors he or she might not otherwise do. The primary difference between obedience training and trick training is that people tend to take obedience training more seriously. If your dog doesn't come when called, for example, he or she could run away and become lost.

Trick training is fun and often silly, and that's good! You'll laugh, have fun, and maybe even spend more time teaching your dog new things. As you teach your dog some tricks, use food treats as lures (to guide your dog) and as rewards. Choose treats he or she really likes; after all, if they are going to work as lures and rewards, your dog has to like them. Remember to cheer your dog on as he or she tries new things and to praise your dog when he or she succeeds.

GO NATURAL

Some really good—and healthy!—dog treats are right in your refrigerator. Give your dog some cheese (cut into small pieces), diced baby carrots, bits of sliced apple, or leftover meat from last night's dinner. All are good foods that your dog will love.

A good foundation of basic obedience is always a good idea for trick training. With this, you and your dog already know how to work together, so adding trick training will be easy. You can start trick training with puppies or with older dogs; just tailor the tricks to the dog's skill level.

Begin trick training at home with just you and your dog; there are many good books available that can take you step by step through trick training. Many dog trainers also offer trick training classes. I think my book, *The Complete Idiot's Guide to Dog Tricks* (Alpha Books, 2005), is a wonderful guide for teaching your dog some tricks. But then again, I'm biased.

Dog Activities

Once your dog has a foundation of obedience, and you and your dog are communicating with each other well, there are many activities you can do together. Some are easy, like going for a walk. Others, like volunteer therapy dog work, require more training. There's something for every dog and owner.

Walking and Hiking

Dog ownership and going for regular walks seem to go hand in hand. Walking your dog is good socialization—your dog gets to see, smell, and hear the world around him or her—but it's also a nice time you and your dog can spend together.

A walk really shouldn't be considered exercise for young, healthy dogs. Although going for a nice brisk walk may be exercise for you, and is good exercise for a young puppy or a senior dog, it's not really daily exercise for a healthy adult dog. For these dogs, a walk is just a nice outing.

For more exercise, consider leaving the sidewalk and going hiking with your dog. Many local, regional, and state parks allow dogs on the hiking trails. Fit your medium- or large-sized dog with a back-pack and he or she can carry a couple bottles of water for both of you, as well as a foldable bowl for the dog's water, some pick-up bags, sunscreen, and more.

For both walking and hiking, begin slowly so your dog's muscles can get stronger and his or her pads can toughen up. Let the dog get used to the backpack, too, before you add any weight.

Walking and hiking with your dog can be a pleasant outing if your dog walks nicely with you. If the dog pulls on the leash, charges at other dogs, barks at people, or lifts a leg to mark every vertical object, the walk won't be any fun. If your dog has any of these behaviors, contact a dog trainer for some help.

GO NATURAL

A good foundation of basic obedience training is a good idea for all dogs. In fact, it's natural for dogs to have rules for correct behavior. After all, mother dogs begin training their puppies in social behavior when they're just babies.

Going for a Run

Most dogs are athletic and bred to run. Many, like Doberman Pinschers and Greyhounds, are very fast. Others, like Border Collies and Australian Shepherds, aren't quite as quick but are certainly faster than people. For a few breeds, like Basset Hounds, slow and steady wins the race.

If you're athletic and you like to go jogging or running, you'll probably enjoy having a canine running partner. Not only will both of you get your daily exercise, but also your dog will provide companionship (and perhaps motivation) as you exercise. As with any exercise program, start slowly so your dog can build some muscle strength and cardio fitness. If your dog has any health challenges, talk to your veterinarian before beginning a running program.

Your dog should be on leash as you run. Teach your dog to run by your left side in the heel position. If his neck is next to your left leg, you can pick up speed, slow down, and make turns, and your dog can see you and react with you. If the dog's too far ahead of you, he or she can't see you and you'll end up tripping over him or her. You may want to refresh his or her obedience training before starting a running program.

A variety of collars, head halters, and chest harnesses is available for dogs. For walking and jogging, I prefer a well-padded buckle collar. A regular nylon buckle collar with a lining of fleece also works really well. However, if your dog tends to pull, you might want to use a chest harness. Choose one that has a fleece lining to keep him or her from being rubbed raw.

> ! **PET ALERT**
>
> Be sure to watch your dog closely for signs of fatigue or stress, such as panting, wide eyes, or flattened ears. Stop, give the dog a break, give him or her some water, and let the dog relax. Take your time getting your dog used to running; sore muscles are just as uncomfortable for dogs as they are for people.

Running Alongside Your Bicycle

If you have a very active and athletic medium- to large-sized dog, you may want to teach him or her to run alongside your bicycle. There are several commercially made hook-ups for this purpose. The one I use every day fastens to the bar under the bicycle seat and positions the dog to my side, basically in the heel position. The dog is to the side behind the front wheel so there's no risk of running into the dog, but the dog is up far enough so I can watch him for any problems.

You can introduce the dog to the bike by walking the dog and the bike together for a few minutes for several days. Bounce the bicycle, roll it forward, and move it from side to side, so your dog gets used to those movements. Then, hook your dog up to the bike and begin some slow rides back and forth in front of your house. Let the dog get used to the bike, and at the same time, give the dog's paw pads a chance to get tougher. Gradually increase the time and distance you and your dog ride, making sure to stop and take a break if your dog seems tired or stressed.

Camping

My friends and I enjoy camping with our dogs, and we've done so in tents, cabins, and RVs. We like to be outside so we can enjoy the trees, the sounds of the surf, and the birds singing. We also enjoy hiking in the forest and just hanging out at the campground. In fact, I choose a campsite by looking for two trees from which I can hang a hammock. We usually introduce our dogs to camping during late puppyhood or adolescence so they get used to it. Watching a puppy explore and discover all these new sights, sounds, and smells is great fun.

It's important to keep your dog on leash while camping, not only because it's usually required by the campground or park department, but also for the dog's safety. Should your dog decide to chase a squirrel or deer, he or she could be out of sight and hearing in a flash. Even the best-trained dog could easily become lost. Plus, chasing wildlife is illegal in many places.

Make sure your dog doesn't disturb the other campers. Not everyone loves dogs as much as we do. This means no barking; no running loose; and no chasing other dogs, kids, or wildlife. And this should go without saying: always pick up after your dog.

Before going on a camping trip, give your veterinarian a call. Make sure your dog is up to date on vaccinations, especially the special ones for the region where you will be camping. Talk to the vet about heartworm, flea, or tick preventives in case your dog will need those for camping, too.

GO NATURAL

When camping with several dogs who are used to daily wrestling matches and playtime, make a point to take them away from the camping area for playtime so they won't disturb the other campers.

Therapy Dogs

Therapy dog work can be one of the most rewarding volunteer activities out there. When you take your dog to a nursing home or hospital to visit people, and those people smile, laugh, or even cry when they pet and hug your dog, you'll know you're making a difference in someone's life. There's nothing better than that.

Therapy dogs are privately owned pet dogs who go with their owners to visit people in assisted living homes, nursing homes, hospitals, and retirement homes. The dogs may go to daycare centers or elementary schools to teach kids how to be safe around dogs. Dogs can visit physical therapy facilities to help motivate people to do their therapy. Many dogs participate in reading programs for children. After all, it's a lot more fun to read to a dog than to a teacher.

> **PET ALERT**
>
> Therapy dogs must be healthy. They can't visit while ill, especially with anything that can be transmitted to people. They must be free of fleas, ticks, and any other internal or external parasites.

The first requirement for therapy dogs is that the dog likes people. He or she doesn't have to be gushingly affectionate to everyone, but the dog must be willing to walk up to strangers and allow petting. If the dog is standoffish or aloof, he or she won't provide effective therapy.

The dog can be any size, tiny or giant, and any breed or mixtures of breeds. The dog can have short hair or long hair or a length in between.

The dog must be well trained in all the basic obedience exercises. He or she can't jump on people, paw or scratch them, and the dog can't put his or her mouth (and teeth) on people. There are certain other unacceptable behaviors. He or she can't bark or growl; can't lift a leg or have other house-training lapses; and can't steal food, socks, shoes, or other items from the people the dog is visiting.

Many dog trainers offer therapy dog training to get the dog used to wheelchairs, walkers, and other equipment the dog may encounter on a visit. The classes also teach visiting skills. Talk to your local trainer and ask if the trainer offers therapy dog training, evaluation, and certification.

Canine Sports

There are a variety of canine sports that dogs can excel at because dogs' athletic abilities and intelligence make them wonderful competitors. Most of these sports are for dogs who are both mentally and physically sound and who have a good foundation of basic obedience. In years past, many of the following sports were limited to purebred dogs. Many organizations, including the AKC, now offer programs that allow mixed breeds to compete:

- **Agility:** Many agility competitors have said agility is a combination of a military working dog's obstacles course, an equine Grand Prix jumping contest, and a thoroughbred race course. To compete in agility, the dog and the owner must maneuver through a course where the dog jumps and crosses over or through a variety of obstacles, all while moving quickly and accurately. The dog can earn a variety of titles, including agility championships.

- **Conformation dog shows:** At a conformation dog show, each dog competes against the other dogs and against the written description of the perfect dog of that breed. This description is called the breed standard, and its purpose is to help the judge find the dog who most closely measures up to the standard of perfection for the breed. This competition serves two purposes: First, the best dog of the day wins, and winning a "Best of Breed" or "Best in Show" title is an amazing accomplishment. Second, in conformation competition, breeders can compare their dogs to those of other breeders.

- **Flyball:** This is a fast-paced, exciting team relay sport. Two teams compete against each other as the dogs run from their owners, jump a series of hurdles, bounce on a wall that pops out a tennis ball, and turn and race back over the hurdles to their owners. The team that finishes first wins. Any breed or mixture of breeds can participate in flyball.

- **Freestyle:** Freestyle, also called dancing with dogs, is exactly that. The dog and owner perform dancing, obedience, and trick-type movements with music. It's challenging, but it's great fun. Any dog can compete in these competitions.

- **Obedience trials:** In obedience competitions, dogs and their owners compete in different classes with varying requirements. The class may ask the dog to heel on and off leash; to come when called off leash; to retrieve a dumbbell, glove, or scented article; or to obey the owner's hand signals. As the dog and the owner progress from simple to more difficult exercises, the dog can earn obedience titles. Any dog can compete.

- **Schutzhund:** Schutzhund and other working dog competitions arose from the jobs German Shepherds, Doberman Pinschers, Rottweilers, and other protective working dogs were bred historically to do. It encompasses protection work, obedience, tracking, endurance, and more.

- **Search and rescue:** Search and rescue (SAR) is an intense and rewarding form of volunteer work. The training is for both dog and owner, and it can include air scenting, tracking, scenting in urban obstacle piles (rubble), scenting in rural settings, orienteering, map and compass and GPS work, and much more. Dogs have excelled at SAR work. Medium-sized dogs are best. The dog must have athletic abilities, good stamina, and a great nose.

If you're interested in any of these sports, talk to your local trainer. He or she may be able to help you get started in the necessary training, or can refer you to someone locally who can.

Spending Time Together

Far too often, pet owners feel they have to be doing something to spend time with their pets. Although activities are great and definitely important, just being together is good for all concerned. Your pet loves spending time with you just relaxing. Your cat can snooze on the sofa while you watch television or read a book. Your dog can look out the window while you spend time at the computer or play video games.

You can encourage quiet time together by talking softly to your pet, petting him or her calmly, or just making eye contact as you walk past your pet. Eye contact is an acknowledgment: "Hi! I see you!"

If your pet follows you from room to room, don't get irritated if he or she gets in the way. Instead, pet him or her, smile, and touch the dog or cat gently as you walk by. Enjoy the company.

The Least You Need to Know

- Our pets need us for good mental and physical health as much as we need them.
- Playing with your cat is good for your relationship. At the same time, it keeps the cat's body moving and healthy.
- Most dog activities and sports require at least basic obedience training.
- There's a canine sport or activity to suit the interests of every dog and dog owner.
- Even with all of the activities and dog sports available for dogs and owners, don't forget you can also just spend some quiet time together enjoying each other's company.

Good Food for Better Natural Health

Food is life. Although your pet can survive on a low-quality food or diet, most dogs and cats need a high-quality diet to thrive. A good diet means the correct ingredients from safe sources and in the right amounts.

In the following chapters, you learn what good nutrition means to your pet. You discover a variety of foods and diets, from commercial foods to raw and home-cooked diets—and I give you some tasty recipes you can make for your pet (all taste-tested by dogs and cats). I also include information on supplementing your pet's diet.

A Lesson in Nutrition

In This Chapter

- Exactly what is good nutrition for your pet?
- The importance of drinking water
- Preventing obesity
- Feeding your pet
- Is your pet a picky eater?

It may seem overly simplistic to say food is life, but it's true. Life on Earth wouldn't exist without food. Every being must consume something to fuel its processes, from a plant pulling in water and nutrients from the soil to a gigantic whale scooping up tiny krill. Food is the most natural thing on the planet, and one of the most important subjects to consider when providing natural care for your pet.

Food provides nutrients for everything that happens within your pet's body, facilitating cell reproduction and supplying energy for play. Defining what good food is, however, is much more complicated than simply saying your pet needs to eat. Feral—that is, wild—dogs and cats can survive by eating whatever they can find, but their survival may be short term because of poor nutrition. Lesser-quality nutrition inhibits growth, healing, reproduction, energy, disease resistance, and longevity. Better foods help your pet not only survive, but also thrive.

Defining Good Nutrition

Dogs are carnivores, meaning they eat meat. They are naturally designed to eat and thrive on animal protein. Even though few dogs today actually have to catch their prey, their nutritional needs remain the same, which means meat is a necessary component of their diet.

To survive, dogs will eat an omnivorous diet—they will eat both meat and plants. Omnivores eat and digest a variety of foods. What this means to all canines is that if a hunt fails, a wolf, coyote, feral dog, or other canine can eat tubers or fallen fruits. The canine can fill his or her stomach, obtain nutrition from those foods, and survive until the next hunt.

By necessity, cats are stricter carnivores than dogs. Cats lack the necessary enzymatic pathways to utilize plant proteins as efficiently as animal proteins. However, good nutrition is much more than just feeding your pet meat. There are many components to nutrition, all of which need to be met if your pet is to thrive. A complete diet must address all your pet's individual needs, from food sensitivities to metabolic needs.

GO NATURAL

"Choosing and feeding the best diet for your pet is such an easy thing to do, yet it is the one area of health care often overlooked by both veterinarians and pet owners. Feeding the best diet is so important for total holistic health that most holistic doctors stress diet when talking to pet owners."

—Shawn Messonnier, DVM, author of *Natural Health Bible for Dogs & Cats*

Proteins, Amino Acids, and Enzymes

Much of an animal's body—including muscles, skin, blood, fur, and internal organs—is made up of proteins. Proteins are necessary for hormone production, fighting disease, growth and reproduction, and many other bodily processes. Proteins are more than just a part of your pet's nutrition; they are necessary for life.

Proteins can be found in animal products such as meat and eggs, as well as in some plants. The proteins found in meat and eggs are complete proteins, meaning they contain a balanced and complete assortment of the *amino acids* necessary for good health. Many plants, including cereal grains and legumes, contain proteins. Plant-based proteins are incomplete proteins because they do not contain all of the needed amino acids.

When an animal consumes proteins, the proteins are broken down into individual amino acids, or *peptides*. The amino acids are then absorbed into the bloodstream, where the body uses them for a variety of purposes.

> **DEFINITION**
>
> When proteins are broken down during the digestion of food, **amino acids** are then released from the protein. **Peptides** are chains of amino acids. Amino acids and peptides both serve a variety of purposes within the body, one of which is hormonal functions.

The body needs 22 amino acids to function. Dogs can synthesize—or manufacture—12 of those amino acids in their bodies; cats can synthesize 11. The amino acids synthesized within the body are called *nonessential amino acids* because they don't need to be present in the food the animal eats. The animal's food must provide the remaining amino acids, called *essential amino acids*. Dogs and cats require the following essential amino acids from their food: arginine, histidine, isoleucine, leucine, lysine, methionine-cystine, phenylalnine-tyrosine, theonine, tryptophan, and valine. Cats must also consume the essential amino acid taurine. Before pet food companies began adding taurine to their cat foods, thousands of cats suffered from blindness and dilated cardiomyopathy, with many dying from the deficiency.

Enzymes are specific proteins (called globular proteins) that act as catalysts in many of the body's functions. Enzymes are needed for healing, cell function, brain activity, and digestion.

Plant proteins should be limited in your pet's diet, though to varying degrees. Some dogs can metabolize plant proteins without difficulty; others can't, and suffer from flatulence and other gastrointestinal upset as a result. Plant proteins in a cat's diet should be avoided entirely.

Plant proteins (one of the most common used in pet foods is soy) are often added to commercial pet food recipes because they're less expensive than animal proteins, and because they boost the food's overall protein levels during laboratory testing. This can be confusing because it can deceive the consumer into thinking the food is of a higher quality—or is more nutritious—than it really is.

Most pet nutrition experts agree that the best protein sources— for both dogs and cats—come from animal products. Muscle meat, organs, cheeses, yogurt, and eggs all provide excellent digestible proteins. If you think about a predator's normal food—a prey animal—and what that prey animal consists of, you can then envision what the predator might eat. It would include muscles, organs, skin, bones, cartilage, and blood.

Carbohydrates

The science of carbohydrates is complicated. Carbohydrates are derived from plants and are found in two forms: simple and complex. Simple carbohydrates are made up of simple sugar molecules—for example, table sugar, brown sugar, honey, and molasses. Complex carbohydrates are made up of several sugar molecules joined together in a chain—for example, vegetables, whole-grain bread, oatmeal, and whole-wheat pasta.

The body breaks down carbohydrates into glucose, and then into long glucose chains called *starches*. The body then uses the glucose as energy to fuel many bodily functions.

Dietary fiber is a complex carbohydrate. The intestinal tract needs fiber to move foods through and to form stools. Without fiber, the animal could easily become constipated. Dogs and cats don't have the enzymes necessary to digest fiber as herbivores—or plant eaters—can. Herbivores' intestinal tracts are different from carnivores and omnivores because plant matter isn't digested the same way as animal products.

There are two classifications of fiber: that which is fermented easily in the intestinal tract and that which is less likely to ferment. Fiber that is more easily fermented allows bacteria to latch on to it in the intestinal tract. As the fiber ferments, nutrients leach out of it and the body absorbs them. The downfall to this process is that the fermenting fiber creates flatulence.

The fiber that ferments is called *soluble fiber*; sources include oatmeal, beans, dried peas, and apples. The fiber that is less likely to ferment is called *insoluble fiber*; sources include carrots, zucchini, and celery.

Carbohydrates make up 15 to 20 percent of your dog's diet. You can supply your dog with carbohydrates by giving him tubers (such as carrots, potatoes, sweet potatoes, and yams) and greens (such as green beans, spinach, broccoli, and collard greens), which he can eat and metabolize properly as long as you chop the food into smaller pieces and cook or steam it. Dogs can also eat some fruits, such as apples, bananas, blueberries, and strawberries.

The intestinal tract of dogs isn't designed to handle too many carbohydrates, so when a dog regularly consumes a lot of them, some health issues can result. Diabetes is, unfortunately, far too common, as are obesity, bladder problems, and allergies.

DOG TALK

William Campbell, a recognized authority on dog behavior, was one of the first to write about the link between carbohydrate consumption and a puppy's inability to learn or concentrate. Many puppies and young dogs have trouble with their training—including learning difficulties— when fed diets high in cereal grains.

Carbohydrates can make up 5 to 10 percent of your cat's food intake. Even though your cat is a true carnivore, some carbohydrates are important for good health. Finely diced and lightly steamed greens such as spinach, sprouts, and wheatgrass are usually okay for most cats. Many will also eat grated and steamed carrots. A few cats accept tiny bits of mashed apple or banana, but limit this to only a small part of the cat's overall diet.

When carbohydrates make up a large part of the cat's diet, the food is potentially wasted and leaves the body via the cat's feces. As a result, the cat can suffer from malnutrition and other potentially serious health problems. Food-related illnesses include diabetes, kidney failure, bladder infections, kidney stones, inflammatory bowel disease, obesity, and more.

Fats and Fatty Acids

Fats have gotten a lot of bad press in recent years, and many people assume eating fats results in obesity. While too much fat can make you or your pet obese, fats also play an important role in your pet's diet.

Fats are vital for the correct absorption of fat-soluble vitamins (more about those in the next section). Fats are also needed for hormone processes, healthy skin and coat, and energy. There are three essential fatty acids: omega-3, omega-6, and arachidonic acid. The body needs these fatty acids for cell structure, development, and function. They also support the immune system and help move oxygen in the bloodstream. You can find omega-3 and arachidonic fatty acids in fish such as salmon, mackerel, herring, and halibut, as well as in flaxseeds and walnuts.

Not all fatty acids are created equal; it's best to provide your dog or cat with a healthy amount of omega-3 fatty acids. Limit the amount of omega-6 in your pet's diet because it has a reputation for promoting inflammation, and is known to cause itching, skin infections, and skin inflammation due to scratching.

Your pet's diet often provides adequate fats, especially from sources such as meat, fish, poultry fat, avocados, and nuts. Commercial pet foods often add fat to the food—in the recipe or sprayed on after cooking—to enhance the food's flavor. Because too much fat can lead to weight gain, be cautious about adding additional fat to your pet's diet.

DOG TALK

One reason why dogs eagerly eat cat foods is because the dry kibble cat foods are sprayed with fat to make them appealing to cats who might not otherwise want to eat them. This makes the food smell even better to dogs.

Vitamins

Vitamins are organic compounds found in foods that perform essential functions in your pet's body. These can range from helping maintain healthy vision to keeping the coat shiny. There are two types of vitamins: fat soluble (which require fats for metabolism) and water soluble (using water for metabolism).

Fat-soluble vitamins are A, D, E, and K. If your pet consumes excess fat-soluble vitamins, they're stored in the body's fat cells until needed. If too much is consumed, these vitamins can create a toxic situation in the body, leading to blood thinning and bleeding and a variety of other undesirable side effects. The water-soluble vitamins include the B vitamins and vitamin C. Excess water-soluble vitamins are excreted in the urine. Here is a rundown on both types:

- **Vitamin A:** This fat-soluble vitamin is important for good vision. It helps maintain healthy mucus membranes in the respiratory and gastrointestinal tracts and works with the immune system. It also is a powerful antioxidant.

PET ALERT

Cats can develop vitamin A toxicity if fed a primarily liver-based diet. Variety is important, even if liver is your cat's favorite food.

- **Vitamin B$_1$ (thiamine):** This water-soluble vitamin aids in nerve cell functions, brain activities, blood formation, muscle tone, and more. You can find this vitamin in egg yolks, fish, liver, poultry, broccoli, Brussels sprouts, kelp, and nuts.

- **Vitamin B₂ (riboflavin):** Another water-soluble vitamin, B₂ assists in metabolizing proteins, carbohydrates, and fats. It's also important for good vision and works with the immune system. You can find it in egg yolks, cheese, fish, kelp, and leafy greens.

- **Vitamin B₃ (niacin):** This water-soluble vitamin helps metabolize food; more than 50 enzymes need B₃ to function within the body. Seeds, nuts, cheese, eggs, fish, and some dark green vegetables all contain niacin.

- **Vitamin B₅ (pantothenic acid):** This water-soluble vitamin is required for the adrenal glands to function, and it is necessary for antibody production. It can be obtained from eggs, beef, saltwater fish, and some vegetables.

- **Vitamin B₆ (pyridoxine):** B₆, a water-soluble vitamin, is used for hormone production, and is vital for maintaining a balance of water in the body. B₆ can be found in eggs, fish, nuts, many seeds, carrots, potatoes, and spinach.

- **Vitamin B₁₂ (cyanocobalamin):** Another water-soluble vitamin, B₁₂ is involved in nerve functions, blood production, food digestion, and more. You can find it in eggs, liver, organ meat, fish, and cheese.

- **Vitamin C and ascorbic acid:** Vitamin C is the vitamin and ascorbic acid is the antioxidant portion of the vitamin that is often used as a food preservative. This water-soluble vitamin is produced in the bodies of both dogs and cats, so most don't need vitamin C supplements. In times of stress (such as recovering from an illness or injury), however, your pet may need more than the body can produce. Toxicity is rare, although too much may cause diarrhea. Vitamin C can be found in green vegetables, fruits, berries, alfalfa, and many herbs.

- **Vitamin D:** This fat-soluble vitamin is often called the sunshine vitamin because it can be obtained through sun exposure. Dogs and cats with a thick coat don't absorb as much as short-haired animals. Vitamin D is vital for calcium and phosphorus absorption in the intestinal tract, and it also works with the immune system, thyroid, and circulatory system. Consuming too much can be toxic. You can also obtain vitamin D from cod liver oil, eggs, dairy products, and sweet potatoes.

- **Vitamin E:** This is a powerful antioxidant, is important for healthy nerves, and assists muscles during exercise. It is also important for healthy skin and hair. Toxicity is rarely a problem, especially when the body obtains the vitamin from whole foods (rather than supplements). This fat-soluble vitamin is found in eggs, fish, and liver.

- **Vitamin K:** This fat-soluble vitamin works with the circulatory system, and is especially important for proper blood clotting. It also helps maintain healthy bones and teeth. Eggs and dark green vegetables such as spinach and green beans all contain vitamin K. When this vitamin is absorbed from whole foods, toxicity is rare.

GO NATURAL

Many pet owners assume dog and cat treats must be commercial treats from a box or bag. The best treats are often tiny bits of apple or carrot, or a blueberry or strawberry.

Minerals

Minerals are originally from the earth but are consumed by dogs and cats via meat (the meat animals ate plants that grew in the soil), bones (which contain zinc, potassium, iron, calcium, and more), and plants. Plants grown in depleted or overused soils often lack minerals. Plants grown hydroponically (in water or growing mediums without soil) are often mineral poor as well.

Minerals are vital for good health. These include:

- **Calcium:** This is one of the most abundant minerals in the body. Most resides in the bones, but calcium is also necessary for nerve function and is a co-enzyme for many bodily functions. Too much calcium can cause constipation. A pet can obtain his or her calcium from bones, cheese, seeds, nuts, and dark green leafy vegetables.

- **Copper:** Copper pairs with iron to make sure there are enough blood cells in the body. It's also vital for other processes in the body, including the formation of connective tissues. Good sources include meat, liver, and water that flows through copper pipes. Copper that's not metabolized is stored in the liver, and excess copper can damage the liver.

- **Iodine:** Iodine helps balance the metabolic rate in the body, is essential for correct thyroid function, and is important for growth. It can be obtained from fish, liver, and kelp.

- **Iron:** Iron's most important function is creating red blood cells. It's also needed for muscle function and energy metabolism. It can be found in meat and vegetables.

- **Magnesium:** This mineral works as a co-enzyme to metabolize carbohydrates and is important for nerve and muscle functions. You can find magnesium in dairy products and vegetables.

- **Manganese:** Manganese works with enzymes to help maintain healthy bones and connective tissue. It's also needed for healthy nerves and enzyme functions. It can be obtained from plants.

- **Phosphorus:** Calcium and phosphorus should be listed as one mineral conjoined—calcium-phosphorus—because one wouldn't be effective without the other. Together, they are vital for strong bones, DNA and RNA structure, and energy. Meat and eggs provide phosphorus.

- **Selenium:** This antioxidant, along with fatty acids, supports the immune system. It is found in fish, meat, and some seeds.

- **Zinc:** This vitally important mineral is a co-enzyme for more than 25 different processes during digestion. It also supports the immune system, is important for healthy skin and coat, and aids in healing. It can be found in meat and eggs.

Adding Vitamins and Minerals

Deciding whether to add vitamins and minerals to your pet's food is not a decision you should make lightly; after all, the fat-soluble vitamins are toxic in excess amounts. In addition, because so many of these work together or with other substances, if one is provided in excess, the process can get out of sync.

Commercial pet foods add vitamins and minerals to the recipes to ensure they are present in the food. The added nutrients appear on the labels as a long list of chemical names following the food ingredients.

> **PET ALERT**
>
> A good homemade diet with varied recipes and ingredients, either raw or cooked, should supply all of the vitamins and minerals your pet needs. A deficiency can negatively affect your pet's health and can even be life-threatening. For this reason, it's a good idea to provide supplements for your pet when providing your cat or dog with a homemade diet. See Chapter 13 for more information.

Because consuming excess vitamins is dangerous, supplementation can be problematic, too. Deciding whether to add a vitamin and mineral supplement depends on what's in your pet's diet, the variety of foods he or she eats, and your pet's overall health. Keep in mind, there is far less danger of toxicity if vitamins and minerals are consumed via whole foods. The body metabolizes the nutrients it needs.

Keeping Everything in Balance

Nutrition is a complicated subject made even more complicated by your pet's individual digestive processes. There are so many interrelated and co-dependent parts that if one thing is out of balance, chaos ensues.

When healthy, your pet's large intestine has a thriving colony of bacteria. These organisms are often called beneficial bacteria because they're necessary for food metabolism, proving wrong the common idea that all bacteria are bad things that cause infections. Illness, a poor diet, or a course of antibiotics can upset the balance of bacteria. The colony of bacteria may die, nonbeneficial bacteria may take over, or beneficial bacteria may grow out of control. Diarrhea is usually the first sign that something is wrong.

Probiotics, found in foods like yogurt, assist in maintaining beneficial bacteria. They can re-establish the colony after a problem or a course of antibiotics. When choosing a yogurt, the label must include "live active cultures."

Don't Forget Water

People tend to forget how important it is to drink plenty of water. It's always there, we drink when we're thirsty, and that's all there is to it. But your pet's body is about 75 percent water, and losing as little as 15 percent can result in dehydration or death.

Dogs gain some water from their food, but they tend to drink water for most of their hydration needs. Dogs and cats that eat dry food don't always make up for the food's dryness and never quite rehydrate themselves. This causes the urine to be quite concentrated and the animal may develop kidney and bladder stones.

Cats fed a high-quality diet with a lot of fresh or canned meat can gain a great deal of their water needs from their food. Cats fed a dry kibble food with a lot of carbohydrates need significantly more water.

You can provide water for your pet in a variety of ways:

- There are contraptions that fasten to an outside faucet that the dog licks; most dogs catch on to these without too much trouble.

- Many dog owners who live in hot climates keep large 10- to 15-gallon galvanized tubs full of water all the time.

- An unspillable bowl is important if you have a pet who likes to play in his water. You may also want to have several water bowls—one outside and one inside is always a good idea.

- Cats will often drink more if their water is moving. There are commercial pet fountains available that keep the water circulating. Check your local pet store or online pet supply store.

Keeping the water fresh is also important. It should be changed daily, as bacteria can build up from saliva and bits of food dropped into the water.

Most people offer their pets tap water, but water quality varies from community to community. Dr. Messonnier says, "For those interested in a natural or holistic approach, you may want to consider offering pure spring water or distilled water to reduce the possibility of contaminants. Unfortunately, published studies haven't proven that one type of water is better than another." Until more definitive studies have been done, it's up to you to decide what is safest for your pet.

> **PET ALERT**
>
> If your pet is suffering from liver disease—especially copper toxicosis—he or she shouldn't drink tap water if it comes through copper pipes. Copper pipes add minute amounts of copper to the water, which could exacerbate liver disease.

Battling Obesity

Just as with people, obesity in pets is becoming a far too common problem today. If a pet weighs 15 percent more than his ideal body weight, he is considered obese.

Some health disorders such as thyroid and metabolic disorders can lead to obesity, as can genetics. Most of the time, however, obesity occurs when the pet eats too much—especially a diet high in carbohydrates and fat—and doesn't get enough exercise. Battling obesity often means changing your pet's diet to a healthier one and increasing your pet's activities. It also means offering your pet healthier snacks. Offer slices of carrots and apple to your dog instead of high-calorie packaged treats. When you want to give your cat a treat, give him or her a bite of freshly cooked chicken. Cut down on snacks in general, too. Give your pet one snack instead of five or six. The hardest thing for most pet owners, though, is saying no when pets turn to them with those begging eyes and plead for treats.

GO NATURAL

A feral canine or feline is rarely obese because food doesn't just appear. The canine or feline has to search and hunt for food, and as such, gets exercise.

Counting Calories for Dogs

Far too many dogs weigh more than they should, and just as obesity presents dangers for people, it does so for pets as well. Counting calories and keeping your pet to a healthy daily caloric intake can prevent obesity.

Commercial pet foods include the number of calories on the label, based on a certain amount of food per serving. This means you need to measure the food before serving it to your pet. If you're going to be feeding your pet a homemade meal—either raw or cooked—you can calculate the calories based on the foods you include in the recipe.

Several organizations, including the National Research Council, have determined suggested calorie amounts for pets. Here are some recommendations for healthy adult dogs with an average activity level:

- A 10-pound dog needs from 400 to 420 calories per day.

- A 20-pound dog needs from 675 to 700 calories per day.

- A 35-pound dog needs from 1,000 to 1,100 calories per day.

- A 50-pound dog needs from 1,300 to 1,400 calories per day.

- A 70-pound dog needs from 1,700 to 1,800 calories per day.

- A 90-pound dog needs from 2,100 to 2,200 calories per day.

- A 120-pound dog needs from 2,600 to 2,750 calories per day.

Active dogs, such as working dogs or dogs involved in performance sports, need more calories than a comparatively sedentary dog. How much more depends on the dog's activity level and on the individual dog.

A working ranch dog who herds sheep or cattle, who helps to chase away pests, and who runs after the rancher who is on horseback may need twice the normal calories. A dog who trains daily but competes only on weekends may need just 25 percent more calories.

DOG TALK

An extremely hard-working dog in tough conditions, like a sled dog in the winter who lives outside, may require three times the calories that an average dog of the same size may need.

Here are some guidelines for active or working dogs:

- A 20-pound dog needs from 750 to 1,000 calories per day.

- A 35-pound dog needs from 1,200 to 1,650 calories per day.

- A 50-pound dog needs from 1,400 to 2,000 calories per day.

- A 70-pound dog needs from 1,800 to 2,300 calories per day.

Actively growing puppies also have special calorie needs. These will vary according to the puppy's weight and age:

- An 8-week-old, 5-pound puppy needs from 350 to 400 calories per day.

- An 8-week-old, 10-pound puppy needs from 700 to 800 calories per day.

- A 10-week-old, 10-pound puppy needs from 625 to 700 calories per day.

- A 10-week-old, 20-pound puppy needs from 1,300 to 1,400 calories per day.

- A 12-week-old, 10-pound puppy needs from 550 to 700 calories per day.

- A 12-week-old, 20-pound puppy needs from 1,100 to 1,200 calories per day.

- A 12-week-old, 30-pound puppy needs from 1,600 to 1,750 calories per day.

Later in puppyhood, when the puppy is about half its adult size, he or she will need one and a half times as many calories as when fully grown. When the puppy has reached three quarters of his or her adult weight, the puppy will need one and a quarter times as many calories when fully grown.

These calorie counts are only guidelines. Each dog is an individual and calorie counts must be adjusted according to each animal's needs. When considering a weight-loss program for your pet, or if you have questions about your pet's calorie needs, talk to your veterinarian. See Chapter 17 for more on obesity.

Counting Calories for Cats

Cats are also facing rising obesity rates, especially as more and more cats live their lives inside. Often, the indoor environment has fewer distractions—fewer things to compel the cat to run, jump, play, and investigate. Indoor cats also tend to sleep more. Life inside is significantly safer, however, and that's why so many owners keep their cats inside.

Here are some recommendations for healthy indoor cats:

- A 4-pound cat needs from 125 to 130 calories per day.

- A 5-pound cat needs from 155 to 160 calories per day.

- A 7-pound cat needs from 220 to 225 calories per day.

- A 9-pound cat needs from 285 to 290 calories per day.

- An 11-pound cat needs from 350 to 355 calories per day.

If your indoor cat weighs more than 11 pounds, talk to your veterinarian about calorie requirements.

The suggested amounts for healthy outdoor cats are slightly more because they tend to be more active than their indoor counterparts:

- A 4-pound cat needs from 140 to 150 calories per day.

- A 7-pound cat needs from 250 to 260 calories per day.

- An 11-pound cat needs from 400 to 410 calories per day.

If your outdoor cat weighs more than 11 pounds, talk to your veterinarian about your cat's calorie needs.

Kittens have special calorie needs, too, because they tend to be quite active. In addition, although kittens don't grow as much as most dogs do, they are still growing, changing, and developing:

- A 1-pound kitten needs from 140 to 145 calories per day.

- A 2-pound kitten needs from 230 to 235 calories per day.

- A 3-pound kitten needs from 280 to 290 calories per day.

- A 4-pound kitten needs from 300 to 310 calories per day.

- A 5-pound kitten needs from 310 to 320 calories per day.

As with dogs, these are only guidelines, and a cat's or kitten's needs may vary. Some will be more active and need extra calories. Adjust your recipes and the amount you feed accordingly. Talk to your veterinarian if you have any concerns or questions.

Where, When, and How to Feed

Feeding is easy, right? You just put some food in a bowl, put it in a convenient place for you and your pet, and leave it out until the bowl needs to be refilled. Not so fast! How you feed your pet can directly affect how well he eats and how easily he digests his food. Your approach to feeding also provides information for your veterinarian, should your pet need veterinary care.

Feed in a Quiet Place

Pets shouldn't eat in a noisy, busy, high-traffic part of the house. This type of feeding environment makes dogs nervous and may make them feel they must gulp down food faster than they might otherwise do. Dogs may get defensive and protective of their food if they have to keep shifting their positions because people walk around the feeding area. If cats are disturbed too much while eating, they may simply walk away from their food. If disturbed too often, they may grab a bite and run away to eat it, or they may stop eating altogether. Cats, even more so than dogs, need a quiet place to eat.

Instead of potentially creating problem behaviors, choose a spot that's near people but not high traffic. A corner of the kitchen, a spot in the family room, or a designated area in the laundry room (with the door open) may work depending on your family's normal activities. In addition, make sure your cat's food dish is nowhere near the litter box.

Feed Two or Three Times per Day

Don't *free feed* your pet. In addition to leading to health problems for your pet, free feeding can attract ants, flies, bees, mice, rats, and other critters. If you have a large or giant breed dog, should your dog decide to eat an entire day's worth of dry kibble at one time, he could easily suffer from bloat.

 DEFINITION

Free feeding is the practice of leaving food available for the pet all the time. It may be convenient, but it leads to poor eating habits and obesity.

If your dog or cat nibbles all day long, it's hard to pinpoint their normal eating habits and schedule. Should your pet get sick and have to go to the veterinarian, one of the first questions she may ask is, "Did your pet eat normally today?" If you free feed, it's hard to answer that question.

Most dogs do well when fed two meals per day: one in the morning and the other in the evening. Puppies and cats may do better with three meals per day. Pick up the food bowls when your pet is done eating rather than leaving them down all day; removing the food bowls after meals discourages constant nibbling. In nature, canines and felines hunt, eat a large meal, and then fast until the next hunt.

How to Feed Your Pet

Most of the time dogs can eat comfortably with the food bowl placed on the floor. If your pet has shoulder, elbow, or back problems, however, you may want to elevate the bowl so he or she can reach it without discomfort. A few years ago, it was suggested that tall and giant breed dogs should eat off elevated feeding tables or platforms to help prevent bloating. The benefits of this are still being debated, and experts don't agree as to whether this is actually beneficial.

GO NATURAL

When you feed your pet, place the food down and then leave him or her alone. Sometimes, pet owners are told to touch their pet's food as the pet is eating to prevent him or her from developing a tendency to guard or protect the food. Unfortunately, just the opposite often occurs. When the food is touched too often, the pet may worry that the owner will take it away. Unless a behaviorist suggests doing this and can explain why, don't do it. Let your pet eat in peace.

If you have a dog or cat who gulps his food so fast he makes himself sick, there are several tricks you can use to slow him down:

- **River rocks:** Find three or four smooth rocks, wash them, and place them in the food bowl on top of your pet's food. Make sure the rocks are big enough the dog or cat can't swallow them. Your pet will then have to move the rocks around to eat. Wash the rocks as you wash the bowl.

- **Bowls with pillars:** Several manufacturers make pet bowls with upright pillars in them. These serve the same purpose as river rocks; the dog or cat has to eat around the pillars.

- **Environmental enrichment:** This technique has been used often with cats. Hide small meals in several places and encourage the cat to find them. Just remember where the food is so you can remove it should the cat not eat it.

- **Food-dispensing toys:** The dog's or cat's food or treats can be placed inside a food dispensing toy. Your pet will then have to move the toy around or manipulate it to get his food.

Feeding a Picky Eater

A picky or fussy eater can be a problem, not just because you will worry about your pet when he isn't eating, but also because it makes feeding your pet difficult. Very few pets will starve themselves, but a pet who isn't eating may suffer from malnutrition, especially if the problem continues. Both dogs and cats can suffer from malnutrition, although it tends to be more common in cats than dogs. Of course, cats have a much shorter list of foods they will accept, too, so that compounds the problem.

The first step to solving this problem is to take your pet to a vet to make sure there aren't any underlying health issues. Allergies and upper respiratory infections can cause a decrease in appetite, especially if the animal is not breathing well. The aroma of food is very important to an animal's appetite, and pets who can't smell the food generally won't eat it.

Gastrointestinal upsets, such as nausea and diarrhea, can affect a pet's desire to eat. These can be caused by many different things. Your vet will likely ask about your pet's bowel habits, any changes in your pet's behavior, and what appeared in your pet's vomit if he or she has thrown up. Ask your vet to check your pet's mouth, too. If your pet has dental disease, a broken or cracked tooth, or an infection, he or she will likely avoid eating.

If your pet comes home with a clean bill of health, ask family members or other people in the household if they have been feeding your pet between meals. If someone is sneaking treats during the day or sharing food after meals, then your pet could very well prefer that food over his own. Check to make sure your dog isn't raiding the cat food or vice versa. And make sure your pet isn't stealing food from the pantry or garbage. Even if you don't think anything like this is occurring, check anyway.

Then, take a look at what you're feeding your pet. Things that make food appealing include aroma, taste, temperature, and texture. If you have been feeding cold food, try warming it slightly. If you have an old pet who has lost some teeth or a puppy or kitten in the midst of teething, try feeding softer foods rather than dry kibble. Dr. Narda Robinson says, "With all of the commercial pet food recalls, if your pet walks away from a previously liked food, it may be bad. It may be contaminated or perhaps the fatty acids have turned rancid."

> **PET ALERT**
>
> Most commercial foods also have an expiration date; always check it before buying the food. Be sure to store the food appropriately. Refrigerate opened moist or canned foods. Store dry kibble food in a container with a tight-fitting lid to keep it fresh and bug free. If the food smells or looks bad, has developed mold, or has been infested with rodents or insects, don't feed it to your pet. Throw it away.

Try hand feeding your pet a little bit of food. Although some people claim this is spoiling the pet, I prefer to think of it as showing your pet that the food you're providing is good food and that you want him or her to have it. It's hard to tell what has put a pet off eating, but it's not natural, it's not healthy, and you certainly don't want it to continue.

The Least You Need to Know

- Good nutrition is comprised of animal protein, carbohydrates, fat, and vitamins and minerals in correct proportions.
- Clean water is vital for good health. Keep fresh water available for your pet at all times.
- Puppies, kittens, and cats need to eat three times per day, while adult dogs do well with two meals per day.

- Obesity is usually the result of too much food, the wrong kind of food, and too little exercise.

- When feeding a picky eater, keep in mind the aroma, smell, temperature, and texture of the food are important to both cats and dogs.

Commercial Pet Food

Chapter 10

In This Chapter

- The convenience of commercial pet food
- The pet food recalls
- Who regulates pet food?
- Understanding what *natural, holistic,* and *organic* really mean
- Listed and unlisted ingredients in pet food
- The best food choices for your pet

For the first 20 years of my pet-owning adult life I fed my dogs and cats commercial pet food. Commercial pet food is easy to purchase and convenient to use. Some of my dogs and cats did very well on commercial brands, while others didn't do quite as well. In fact, health issues with two of my dogs inspired me to learn more about pet food and nutrition.

I learned quickly that pet food is a multi-billion-dollar industry. It encompasses a wide variety of companies, from very small, privately owned companies to huge megacorporations.

In addition, I realized that the pet food industry isn't designed to provide natural food for pets; instead, its focus is to provide mass-produced and primarily relatively inexpensive foods that adequately nourish as many pets as possible. However, if you enjoy the convenience of commercial pet foods, it is possible to feed a more natural—if not completely natural—commercial dog or cat food.

What's Good About Commercial Pet Food

It's important to remember that companies create commercial pet food to feed our pets. Some people have labeled pet food companies as evil; they argue they're in existence only to poison our pets or to shorten their lives. Pet owners can disagree over many aspects of the pet food industry, but the fact is they're in business to feed pets.

The primary benefit of commercial pet food is convenience. As a pet owner, you can buy pet food at the grocery store while shopping for the rest of the family. While cooking for the family, you can place dry kibble or canned food in the pet's bowl. Voilà! You've fed the pet.

Over the years, pet food companies have spent a considerable amount of money on research. As a result, they've created food with unique proteins like duck and rabbit, and unique carbohydrates like sweet potato and barley, so dogs and cats with allergies can eat without problems.

There are also pet food brands with small kibbles for tiny dogs, and special ones formulated for large breed dogs. Weight-loss food is available, as well as prescription diets that veterinarians can sell for dogs and cats with health ailments. The variety of food available today is amazing.

 DOG TALK

Milk Bones were one of the first commercial pet food or treat products made specifically for dogs.

Many pets can live their lives on commercial pet food with no negative side effects or problems. These pets eat their food eagerly, have bright eyes and a shiny coat, and live long lives.

What's Not So Good

Although the idea of commercial pet food providing convenience and good nutrition for our pets is wonderful, there's a fly in the ointment—or a worm in the pet food. The pet food recalls of 2007 showed us that.

Actually, pet food recalls began to increase as far back as the mid-1990s. The recalls were small; a company would announce a problem with one batch or a large number of batches, and that would be it. Most pet owners, if they even heard about the recall at all, seemed to think it was an aberration rather than a way of doing business or a signal that something was really wrong.

But the recalls of 2007 woke up everyone who owned a pet. There were headlines in mainstream publications, as well as news articles on the Internet. Websites and blogs like PetConnection.com updated the news hourly. Thousands of dogs and cats became ill, some very seriously, and many died. Although cats seemed to be struck harder than dogs and more cats died, both dogs and cats died as a result of contamination.

At the time, the known and compiled information pointed to pet food manufacturer Menu Foods—sold under hundreds of labels—as the primary culprit. In March 2007, the federal Food and Drug Administration (FDA) belatedly issued a recall of 60 million packages of dog and cat food produced by Menu Foods. These foods contained wheat gluten, imported from China, which was contaminated with *melamine*.

DEFINITION

Melamine is a compound manufacturers use to make many different items, including dinnerware, shelving, floor tiles, and fireproof fabrics. It has been added to cereal grain glutens because it increases the foods' protein levels in laboratory testing. It also helps processed meat keep its shape.

In the weeks and months that followed, the initial recall turned out to be just the tip of the iceberg. Corn and rice glutens were also found to be contaminated. As testing continued, other contaminants were found in assorted pet foods.

At one point, more than 6,000 pets fell ill and at least 3,000 died as a result of consuming contaminated pet food. These figures include only known instances; they're nowhere near a true count because some pets fell ill prior to the official recall and many veterinarians were so busy treating sick pets they never reported any numbers at all. If anything good could come out of this horrible time, it's that many pet owners learned that complacency isn't a good thing. Pet owners now want to know more about what's in their pets' food.

Who Makes Sure Pet Food Is Safe?

Several organizations oversee pet foods, each with a different goal. Because all of these organizations work independently—and often don't communicate well—many of the problems in the industry aren't addressed. The melamine issue of several years ago is a good example; that never should have happened, and if imported ingredients were inspected, it might have been prevented.

The National Research Council (NRC) used to provide nutritional guidelines for pet food, but that role has been taken over by the Association of American Feed Control Officials (AAFCO). This is the best-known agency working with pet food today. Made up of state and federal regulatory agents, the AAFCO is a private group that sets standards for pet food, including nutritional levels. The AAFCO also provides instructions for feeding tests and defines food ingredients.

The FDA regulates many things in addition to pet food, including drugs, medical instruments, vaccines, blood products, cell phones, and a host of other things that can directly affect health. If a recall is required in any of these areas, the FDA issues it.

The Center for Veterinary Medicine (CVM) regulates the manufacturing and distribution of drugs and food additives for pets and pet food. It also investigates advertising claims, such as when a pet food is labeled "pure and wholesome." They ask the tough questions, like asking the manufacturer to define pure and wholesome.

In addition to all of these agencies, the Federal Trade Commission, U.S. Department of Agriculture, and other agencies all have something to do with pet food, from the ingredients to the shipment of the finished product to stores. Unfortunately, no one agency is in charge of making sure the ingredients in pet food are safe. Nor does one agency oversee the safety of pet food. There are too many organizations involved, and they don't always communicate well with each other.

Testing the Food

Because many, if not most, commercial pet foods are designed to be a pet's sole food source, the pet owner needs some assurance that the food is nutritionally complete. According to the AAFCO, food that has *complete and balanced* nutrition or *for all life stages* on the label must meet the AAFCO feeding trial requirements to make sure it meets the requirements of the pet that is supposed to eat it.

DEFINITION

Complete and balanced means that no additives or supplements need to be added to the food—the food contains everything the pet needs for good nutrition. **For all life stages** means that a food can be fed to all ages of pets of the appropriate species—from weaning through old age.

There are two acceptable ways to test the food: laboratory analysis and feeding trials. Laboratory analysis can check the food's amino acids, fatty acids, sugars, starches, and vitamins (see Chapter 9). Tests can also check for meat contaminants and even the species of meat in the food. The downside to laboratory testing was brought to light during the 2007 pet food recalls. Most consumers learned then that the melamine that was poisoning pets was added to increase the protein levels of the food during laboratory testing.

Another means of testing the food is through feeding trials. Animals in a laboratory setting are fed the food for a period of time and checked regularly for side effects and state of health. This may seem an effective means of testing pet food, even if many people aren't happy about the idea of caged animals living only to determine a food's value.

If a feeding trial brings to mind a huge kennel and cattery with hundreds of animals, think again. The AAFCO mandates that a feeding trial for an adult maintenance food may only include eight dogs or cats, and six of the animals must remain alive and healthy for 26 weeks. A trial for puppies may only be 10 weeks long.

Many times, a feeding trial includes only a couple of breeds of dogs or cats, rather than a wide selection. Because some canine and feline breeds have breed-specific feeding challenges, feeding trials may not be as effective as we'd like to think. Greg Martinez, DVM, says, "Many toy breeds, Labrador Retrievers, and German Shepherds are some examples of dogs who are more sensitive to allergens in their foods. Food allergies may take months to develop and then are life-long maladies. A six-month trial won't help these animals."

All commercial pet food must be tested. Just keep in mind there are limitations to each type of test.

Quality Control

The 2007 pet food recalls highlighted the problems associated with quality control of ingredients in pet foods. Manufacturers in China added melamine to their wheat gluten so laboratory results would show higher protein levels in the food; their product was then imported into the United States. Those higher levels didn't translate into better nutrition for pets; it only made the wheat gluten appear to be a higher-quality ingredient than it really was.

Many large pet food companies buy ingredients in vast bulk shipments. The companies can test samples of each food item, of course, and they do. However, there is no way they can test trainloads of sweet potatoes, for example, to verify that each and every potato is mineral rich and not contaminated with pesticides, insecticides, or other potentially problematic substances. Quality control then becomes voluntary, and that in itself is a problem. Each company or corporation can establish its own guidelines for quality control.

While some dog food companies have set their standards low, that's not true of all. The Honest Kitchen, a San Diego–based, privately owned company, has set higher standards than most. Lucy Postins, the founder and president, says, "We purchase all of our ingredients directly rather than allowing our production facility to purchase on our behalf. That way we know who we're buying from and what we're buying. We taste each and every ingredient ourselves when we're selecting what to purchase. We've bought from many of the same suppliers for the past eight years and know where our crops are grown."

> **GO NATURAL**
>
> The Honest Kitchen is an approved member of Green America, which places a high priority on sustainability, green business, and fair trade. Learn more about Green America at www.greenamerica.org.

The Problems with Heat

Most commercial pet foods, especially dry kibble and canned food, are processed using heat. Heating canned food destroys any bacteria or other organisms within the cans. Manufacturers bake or otherwise process kibbled food at high temperatures to cook the food.

The manufacturing process requires that the food be cooked at a much higher temperature than you would use to cook food at home, thus destroying or reducing many nutrients. For example, when cooking chicken at home, most experts recommend using a meat thermometer to make sure the internal temperature reaches 165°F to 170°F. Canned meat, however, such as canned chicken cat food or dog food, needs to cook at a minimum of 240°F to 250°F.

When food is cooked at high heat, vitamins, minerals, and enzymes are destroyed or significantly reduced. Pet food manufacturers know this, and it can be verified through laboratory analysis of the foods, so the manufacturers add supplements to the food after the cooking process. Often, the body isn't able to metabolize these supplements as easily as the nutrients in the food itself.

Teeming with Terms

It's hard to understand commercial pet food and pick out those that lean toward natural more than others. Doing so is difficult not only because the industry as a whole doesn't tend to focus on natural products, but also because there are so many different terms used.

"Natural"

Several companies use the word *natural* for their pet foods. Their very nature—mass-produced, processed food—seems to contradict what most pet owners think of as natural.

In fact, the AAFCO's definition of *natural* is downright confusing: "A feed or ingredient derived solely from plant, animal or mined sources, either in its unprocessed state or having been subject to physical processing, heat processing, rendering, purification, extraction, hydrolysis, enzymolysis or fermentation, but not having been produced by or subject to a chemically synthetic process and not containing any additives or processing aids that are chemically synthetic except in amounts as might occur unavoidably in good manufacturing practices."

Exceptions to the definition of *natural* include synthetic vitamins, minerals, and other trace elements. This means manufacturers can render the food to a mush, bake it to a crisp kibble, or add synthetic vitamins and minerals, and the food can still be labeled as natural.

The term is made even more confusing when some companies post on their label that the food is natural because they used natural ingredients to make it. If the AAFCO doesn't consider the processing natural by their standards, or the company includes non-natural ingredients in the food, then the term becomes worthless when trying to determine the value of the food.

"Holistic"

There's no legal definition for *holistic* pet food, even though several manufacturers now use this term. In general usage, *holistic* refers to the body as a whole, taking into account all its parts, including the mental, emotional, and spiritual. For pet foods, *holistic* seems to mean the food is of good quality, made with natural ingredients, and nourishing to the animal who eats it. However, even if we as consumers believe that this is true, with no regulations to ensure that the food is what we expect it to be, the term is worthless.

"Organic"

Organic is another word companies use in many different ways, leaving consumers confused. In 1990, Congress adopted the Organic Foods Production Act (OFPA), which began a decade of discussions, arguments, and public input as to what is and isn't organic, as well as what farmers could and couldn't do. Eventually, organic standards were established for growing, producing, and handling crops and livestock.

Products labeled "100% Organic" and displaying the "USDA Organic" seal are exactly that: they contain only organically produced ingredients. Products that contain at least 95 percent organic ingredients—with the other 5 percent being approved by the USDA for use in organic products—may also carry the "USDA Organic" seal. Products containing 70 percent organic ingredients may denote the individual ingredients as such on the package's ingredients listing.

With these guidelines, the labeling of the pet food and the actual ingredients must agree. For example:

- A pet food labeled "100 percent Organic Beef Dog Food" must consist entirely of organic beef with no other ingredients, excluding water and salt. It may contain flavorings and additives only if they're all from approved organic sources.

- A pet food labeled "Organic Chicken Cat (or Dog) Food" must contain 95 percent organic chicken. The other 5 percent must consist of approved ingredients.

- A pet food labeled "Organic Beef Dinner" must be 95 percent organic, and all of the beef must be organic. As a dinner, however, it can contain other nonorganic ingredients.

"Human-Grade" Food and Ingredients

As of this writing, the AAFCO doesn't have a definition for *human-grade* pet food or for ingredients in pet food. Without that definition, the term is not supposed to appear on pet food labels. That's not to say the term doesn't appear in advertising, though—it actually appears quite frequently. Newman's Own Organics uses the term in question-and-answer portions of its advertising, in print, and on its website.

The Honest Kitchen uses the term *human grade*, and even went as far as to go to court and defend its right to use it. The court ruled The Honest Kitchen has a constitutional right to truthful commercial free speech, and because of its business practices, the company can use "human grade" on its labels.

An Overview of Pet Food

The commercial pet food business produces a wide variety of pet food, and the types of food are increasing all the time. Unique ingredients—such as rabbit, bison, and duck—are one aspect of the increase, and so are the types of food. These expansions are occurring to appeal to pet owners whose pets have allergies and need a different type of food, but they're also aimed at the owners trying to supply their pets with healthier food.

Types of Food

The most commonly purchased pet foods are those sold in dry kibble form. These foods are easy to feed, and most dogs and cats eat them with little fuss. Other forms of food include canned, cooked frozen, raw frozen, semi-moist, dehydrated, and freeze-dried.

- Dry kibble foods are packaged in bags or boxes, usually have a shelf life of about six months, and contain 6 to 10 percent moisture by volume. These are often cereal grain–based products (rather than meat based), but many manufacturers are responding to consumer demand and offering grain-free recipes.

CAT CHAT

Lisa Pierson, DVM, of www.catinfo.org, says, "The average dry cat food contains 35 to 50 percent carbohydrates. This is not the diet Mother Nature intended for cats to eat." She says because cats get most of their moisture from their food, they need food higher in moisture content than dry kibble can provide.

- Canned food contains more moisture than dry food and usually higher protein levels (depending on the recipe). Remember to read the label, though, because many canned food products contain grain glutens so the meaty chunks can retain their shape.

- Semi-moist foods are not as popular as they once were, primarily because consumers have become more educated concerning pet food. Semi-moist pet food, the pinnacle of processed pet food, contains salts, sugars, artificial colorings, flavorings, propylene glycol, and preservatives.

- Fresh refrigerated foods are a recent addition to the pet food business. These foods are cooked and then sealed in vacuum packaging. They must be refrigerated, so they can only be sold in stores willing to have a refrigerator in the pet food section. These products are only as good as the recipe used to create them.

- Frozen food products are much like refrigerated food; they require special handling and a freezer. They, too, are only as good as the recipe used for making them. Frozen pet food may contain cooked or raw ingredients. Pet owners must thaw the food prior to serving to pets.

- Dehydrated foods have appeared on the market in the past decade or so. Most of the recipes are quite good, and the foods are advertised to be as good as a raw food diet without the dangers of raw food. Pet owners must rehydrate the food prior to serving to pets.

- Freeze-dried treats have been available for many years, but freeze-dried food is a relatively recent addition. These foods are either cooked and then dried, or they're raw. Each manufacturer has instructions for how the food should be served.

Each type of pet food has its pros and cons. Choosing which food to feed your pet is a personal decision. Not only does it affect your pet's nutrition, but it also has a huge impact on his or her health. It can be a financial decision for you, too; be sure to take into consideration not only the cost of food, but also potential veterinary costs related to your pet's diet.

Definitions of Ingredients

When you look at the label of a particular pet food, you may see something as simple as chicken on the label. Most of us would assume that means the edible meat of the chicken, right? But is that true? Not really.

The AAFCO has established guidelines for what ingredients are allowed in both livestock food and pet food. These guidelines and definitions are confusing at times. For example, here are a few ingredients often included in dog and cat food:

- **Animal digest:** This is the material that comes from processing clean, fresh, animal tissue (that is, it hasn't started the process of decomposition). The animal tissue used must not include hair, horns, teeth, hooves, and feathers, except in the trace amounts that may occur despite good factory practice.

- **Barley:** To list this ingredient, the food must contain at least 80 percent sound barley. It can't contain more than 3 percent heat-damaged kernels, 6 percent foreign matter, 20 percent other grains, or 10 percent wild oats.

- **Beet pulp (beet pulp, dried molasses):** This is the dried residue from sugar beets.

- **Dehydrated eggs:** These whole poultry eggs are dried (that is, the moisture is removed) by cooking. This isn't the equivalent of scrambled eggs, however. The eggs may be dehydrated or cooked in other ways.

- **Dried kelp:** This ingredient is a dried seaweed of the families Laminaricae and Fu-caeae.

- **Lamb meal:** The rendered product from lamb tissue is defined as lamb meal. This does not include blood, hair, hoof, horn, hide, manure, and stomach and rumen contents, except in the trace amounts that may occur despite good factory practice.

As you can see, some of the ingredients sound fine. Dehydrated eggs are just dried eggs, right? Not necessarily. Dehydrated eggs are sometimes comprised of leftover egg parts, remaining after the manufacturer used the other portions for other purposes or recipes—perhaps in recipe preparation for human food.

It doesn't sound like there is an issue with dried kelp, either. There can be, though, because kelp contains iodine, which can upset normal thyroid function. A little kelp is good, but too much is dangerous.

Beet pulp can be a problem. Many pet food brands advertise that beet pulp is added to increase the fiber in the food. These are sugar beets, however, so even after processing to remove the sugar, they are said to still contain low amounts of sugar. Certainly, there are other ways to add fiber, without adding sugar, to the pet food.

When looking at meat, such as animal digest and lamb meal, the definition doesn't absolutely prohibit horns, hooves, feathers, manure, and other leftovers. It simply says only small amounts are allowed. I'm sure I'm not the only one who has wondered how small those amounts really are.

It's important to understand exactly what ingredients actually are when you read the label. It's the only way you can know what is actually in a dog or cat food.

> **PET ALERT**
>
> Many pet food ingredients contain hidden ingredients. Insecticides, fungicides, fertilizers, and other chemicals from the fields can remain on or in plants. Fortunately, the use of these is strictly controlled by the USDA's Organic Trade Association (OTA) for organic plant culture. For more information, go to www.ota.com.

Ingredients Not Listed

Dog food companies are required to list on the label any ingredients they add to their recipe. If they include corn, lamb, dried eggs, or any other ingredient in the recipe, it must be listed. However, they don't have to list any ingredients added prior to becoming a part of the food. So if a bulk shipment of wheat is imported from China and the manufacturers added melamine to it prior to sending it to the United States, the dog food company that uses the wheat doesn't have to include melamine on the ingredients list. The same applies to meat: if a shipment of meat has an added preservative that protects it during shipping, that won't appear on the label.

As we've learned with melamine, what you don't know can hurt your pets. This is why the individual company's quality control is important.

Organic Ingredients

In 2005, the National Organic Standards Board appointed a Pet Food Task Force to study regulations pertaining to pet food, including the ingredients and substances potentially used by manufacturers.

The task force separated pet food from livestock feed; previously, these were lumped together in both regulations and definitions. Pets were defined as dogs and cats, and pet food was defined as any commercial feed prepared and distributed for consumption by said pets. Making such a distinction may seem nitpicky, but it's really important nutritionally for dogs and cats. Livestock have a different purpose than do our pets. We want our pets to live long, happy, healthy lives, and good food is needed for that. Livestock, however, face a different future and their foods reflect that.

The task force also clarified what organic production and handling is—namely, what's allowed and what isn't. Some of the things not allowed according to these regulations are synthetic substances and ingredients, as well as ionizing radiation.

The National Organic Program governs organic pet food ingredients by maintaining a list of what substances can be included in food labeled as organic. For example, boiler chemicals aren't allowed. And yes, they had to consider boiler chemicals; someone actually asked that they be included on the list of acceptable foods, and they were turned down. On the other hand, calcium carbonate (the nonsynthetic form) can be used in organic food. Nonsynthetic bacterial enzymes made from nontoxic plants and nonpathogenic fungi are also allowed.

The various lists can be confusing, making it difficult for pet owners to understand what is and isn't in the pet food. If you read the labels and look for clarification for what you don't understand, however, it's possible to feed your pet a quality commercial pet food.

Choosing a Quality Food

Many pet owners prefer to feed their dog or cat a commercial food. After all, these foods are convenient and reasonably priced. At the same time, they want a healthy food that's as natural as possible. Although these preferences sometimes conflict with each other, it's not impossible.

When considering pet food, take a look at the packaging and label. Don't be fooled by phrases that have no legal meaning, such as holistic. Look for companies that list human-grade ingredients or human-grade processing.

Here are some other things to look for:

- Look for the species name for meat ingredients. You want the label to list the meat as chicken, turkey, or bison. If it simply says meat or poultry, it could be anything that falls under that heading or any combination of meat. The same applies to animal fats. Know what animal the fat comes from.

- Meat meal is acceptable if it's listed by species name. For example, chicken meal is okay, but not meat meal. Chicken meal includes chicken meat, organs, and other digestible parts. Meat meal may be any species or combination of species.

- Avoid by-products meal. Just like meat meal, by-products may indicate any variety of things, and quality could vary from batch to batch.

- Avoid potentially dangerous preservatives. Dry food and refrigerated food should be preserved with tocopherols (natural preservatives) rather than BHA, BHT, or other potentially problematic preservatives.

- Consider avoiding cereal grain glutens. Not only were glutens the focus of the 2007 (and subsequent) recalls, but they're also a poor nutrient for pet food. Additionally, many dogs and cats suffer gastrointestinal upset when fed a diet high in glutens.

- Better-quality food doesn't include sugar in the recipe, whether from beet pulp, corn syrup, or other sweeteners.

CAT CHAT

Cats don't have taste receptors for sugar. Not only do they not need it in their diet, they also can't taste it.

- Avoid cereal grains. Cats don't need cereal grains in their diet at all, and dogs can metabolize carbohydrates from other sources far better.

- Look for a high-protein, moderate-fat, low- to moderate-carbohydrate food for dogs. A high-protein, moderate-fat, low-carbohydrate food is best for cats.

If you have any questions about a specific food, call the manufacturer and ask them specific, detailed questions. Understand they are trying to sell you the food, but they should be able to answer your questions.

Keep in mind, too, there is no one food that's right for every pet. Just because your neighbor's dog or cat is thriving on one particular food doesn't mean it's right for your pet. You may also have different food requirements than your neighbor.

If you decide to change foods, do so gradually. Changing too rapidly can cause diarrhea and other gastrointestinal problems. A good rule of thumb is to first feed the pet one third of the new food and two thirds of the old food for a week. Then, you can adjust the food to half and half for a week. On the third week, feed your dog or cat two thirds of the new food and one third of the old food. If your dog or cat has diarrhea, soft stools, or a bellyache, slow down and make the change even more gradual.

Allow your pet a good six months to adjust to a new food. At the end of the six-month trial, re-evaluate the food by taking a look at your pet's weight, skin and coat, and energy level. If your pet is doing well, looks healthy, and is happy and playing, then stay with that food. If at any time during that six months your pet seems to be having food-related problems, then stop feeding that food.

You may want to feed your pet a bland diet—chicken and rice usually works, or chicken and puréed steamed pumpkin—until the gastrointestinal system goes back to normal. Then rethink your pet's nutritional needs and try a different food.

The Least You Need to Know

- The commercial pet food industry is a multi-billion-dollar industry designed to feed our pets; however, it's not without problems.

- Several organizations oversee the pet food industry, including the Association of American Feed Control Officials and the Food and Drug Administration.

- Natural, holistic, and organic pet food categories are not well identified, consistently labeled, or properly regulated. This makes it difficult to choose a good food.

- Understanding what pet food manufacturers can use in pet food and understanding the labels is important when choosing a good pet food.

- Most dogs should eat a high-protein, moderate-fat, low- to moderate-carbohydrate food. Most cats need a high-protein, moderate-fat, low-carbohydrate food.

The Raw Food Alternative

In This Chapter

- The pros and cons of a raw food diet
- Controlling the ingredients
- Feeding your pet a raw diet safely
- Transitioning your pet to a raw food diet
- Sample recipes for dogs and cats

Raw pet food diets have been fed to pets for many years, but they've become very popular in the last couple of decades. This is due in part to the growing desire of many people to live a more natural lifestyle and to use more natural products. Raw food diets have also become more prevalent with pet owners whose pets aren't thriving on commercial pet food. In addition, the pet food recalls scared many pet owners into avoiding commercial foods altogether.

Raw foods are natural; wild canines and felines eat raw foods. But are our pets still the same as their wild cousins? Many veterinarians have concerns about raw food diets. Yet pet owners feeding raw food diets to their pets often say it's the best thing that could have happened to their pets. There are people on both sides of this issue who have equally strong arguments.

Raw Food Diets Are Not New

One of the first studies concerning the benefits and effects of a raw food diet occurred in the 1930s and 1940s in California. Francis Pottenger Jr., M.D., conducted studies regarding the destruction of nutrients by heat. He used cats in his laboratory studies and fed the cats raw milk, cod liver oil, and cooked meat scraps. He had ongoing problems with the cats not surviving the operations he performed, and many of those who survived the surgeries died soon afterward.

Pottenger continually accepted new cats into his program, and soon the cats exceeded his supply of cooked meat. He ordered raw meat scraps from a local meat packing plant and put some of the new cats on a raw meat diet. Within months he saw that these cats were healthier than the cats fed a cooked diet. They were also better able to survive the surgeries and fewer died afterward.

The difference in the cats was so marked he began a 10-year study that included 900 cats. He fed one group a raw diet and the other group a cooked diet. Throughout the study, he noticed many differences in the cats, especially in successive generations. The most impressive study result was that the cats to whom he fed a raw diet maintained good health, while the cats who ate a cooked meat diet suffered a number of health issues—in fact, by the fourth generation, that entire line of cats had died.

Pottenger admitted that there was something going on in the study or with the food that he didn't recognize. At that time, no one had identified the importance of taurine to feline health. Today, we know that taurine must be added to the cats' food after cooking.

In More Recent Years

Two Australian veterinarians, Ian Billinghurst and Tom Lonsdale, are the biggest proponents of raw food diets. Their feeding programs have caused thousands of pet owners to rethink how they feed their pets.

Dr. Billinghurst introduced the Biologically Appropriate Raw Food diet, also known as BARF. (Many people also refer to raw food diets as *Bones* and *Raw Foods.*) Dr. Billinghurst's diet emphasizes quality raw meat, bones, fruits and vegetables, eggs, and dairy foods.

Dr. Lonsdale's diet also promotes raw foods, but he emphasizes bones with meat on them and whole carcasses, such as chicken or turkey carcasses. His reasoning is that dingoes and feral cats eat these foods and remain healthy, so our pets should, too.

The raw pet food movement has grown significantly in recent years. Many racing greyhounds are fed raw food diets with good results. Sled dog teams eat raw food or a combination of raw and cooked food. Many dog and cat breeders feed their show and breeding animals a raw food diet and suggest their kitten and puppy buyers continue this feeding regimen.

Commercial Raw Foods

The growing interest in raw food has led to the introduction of several commercial raw food brands. Dr. Billinghurst sells raw food patties and supplements based on his recipes and guidelines for raw foods. The Honest Kitchen, Addiction, EasyRaw, and Sojo's all offer dehydrated raw foods. To preserve the nutrients, producers dehydrate these foods at lower temperatures than food is cooked at, but the temperatures are still high enough to ensure no bacteria exist in the food. Healthy Meals Freeze Dried Patties are also raw foods with minimal processing.

Several companies sell frozen raw pet foods. Some are recipes with vegetables, grains, and meat, while others don't include cereal grains. Other companies just sell meat and organs for use as pet food. As pet owners continue to ask for high-quality food and more feeding options for their pets, this field is bound to continue to grow. These diets are available at pet food supply stores that have freezers. (The foods are frozen to prevent spoilage.)

The Benefits Are Many

Pet owners often consider raw food diets because they have concerns about commercial pet food. The dog or cat may not be thriving on the commercial food, or the pet may actually have some health problems from or related to the food (see Chapter 10 for more on commercial pet food). The pet owner may be worried about quality control or the ingredients in the food.

> **GO NATURAL**
>
> Juliette de Bairacli Levy of Manchester, England, was called the grandmother of herbal medicine. An Afghan hound breeder, she started the holistic pet care movement in the 1930s, and preached that dogs and cats require a natural diet of raw foods.

Carol Bennett of Tulsa, Oklahoma, has been raising American Shorthair cats for more than 20 years. She switched all of her cats to a raw food diet about 10 years ago, when she was seeing a difference in her cats: "I can't explain exactly what I was seeing at the time except that the cats just weren't doing as well as they had in the past. Coats weren't as shiny, the kittens were quieter and there was less play, and there were fewer kittens per litter. My cats weren't sick; they just weren't as well as they could be."

About three to four weeks after changing the cattery over to the raw food diet, she saw a visible difference. The cats' coats were shiny and soft, all of the cats appeared more alert, and the younger ones were playing more. After a year on the new diet, she said litters had an average of two kittens more per litter, the mother cats appeared to have more milk, and the kittens were thriving.

Many pet owners who feed their pets raw food diets mention the same benefits. Raw food diets help keep the skin and coat healthy, shiny, and soft. The dog or cat seems to be eager to play, and dog owners have mentioned a better attitude toward training. Those who feed their pets a raw diet that includes bones also mention their pets' teeth are cleaner due to the scraping action of teeth against bone.

Smaller stools are an added benefit of a raw food diet. Because the food is metabolized more completely, and because there is no filler and less fiber in the diet, stool size is decreased. Basically, there is less waste.

Dogs and cats who are picky eaters often lose that tendency when fed a raw food diet. Although it takes a while for many to make the transition—most likely because raw foods are so different from commercial kibble food—most dogs and cats eat the food eagerly once they're used to it.

Legitimate Concerns

Although many pet food experts agree that a raw food diet is more natural for dogs and cats than other diets, they still have some concerns. The first is that dogs and cats are no longer wild canines and felines; they've been domesticated for thousands of years. In addition, wild carnivores don't tend to live long lives. Pets cracking open bones and eating them is certainly a danger, as is the bacterial contamination and parasites in scavenged meat and wild prey animals. Certainly, these are legitimate concerns that need to be considered.

The bacteria in much of today's commercially produced raw meat are also an obvious concern. Feedlots and slaughterhouses are not the cleanest of facilities. Although most raw food advocates say carnivores were designed to cope with those bacteria, some veterinarians have concerns. Most veterinarians have treated more than one pet in their practice who has developed a bacterial infection from raw food diets. Several veterinarians interviewed for this book could name several pets each—dogs and cats—who died. That isn't taking into consideration the pets who developed parasitic infestations.

Take care when introducing a raw food diet to a dog or cat with health problems. Alfred Plechner, DVM, author of *Pets at Risk*, says, "Dogs and cats, of course, evolved on raw meat. Many veterinarians, particularly in the alternative medicine field, recommend raw meat." He adds that dogs with health issues, however, especially those with compromised endocrine-immune systems, shouldn't eat raw meat.

"I fear they do not have the resources to wage an effective defense when exposed to harmful bacteria such as salmonella and E. coli that is present in raw meat. The bacteria could spread rapidly and put the animal into crisis."

Many raw food diets emphasize adding bones to the diet, as with both Dr. Lonsdale's and Dr. Billinghurst's diets, for which bones are the pillar. However, bones can be dangerous. Bone shards can lodge in the throat or between the teeth. Bone shards that are swallowed can puncture organs or create an intestinal obstruction.

Joan Weiskopf, MS, a Veterinary Clinical Nutritionist, says, "Raw food diets have failed." She blames its promoters' overzealousness for a good part of the failure. Many raw food diets are so strict and set up so many rules that pet owners either can't or don't want to follow them. In addition, handling raw meat on a daily basis can be a little disgusting.

These are all legitimate concerns. If you decide to feed your pet a raw food diet, do so with knowledge and care, and keep safety in mind.

GO NATURAL

"The arguments about raw and commercial foods are at the very heart of nutritional debate. Raw food proponents have a multitude of testimonials to its success, including that of treating and curing chronic medical problems. The potential cost of raw foods and the threat of bacterial contamination keep this diet from becoming more popular. Hearing the success stories over 10 years ago was one of the reasons I began relearning veterinary nutrition."

—Greg Martinez, DVM

Finding, Storing, and Safe Handling

One of the benefits to any homemade diet, whether raw or cooked, is that you can control the quality of the ingredients in your pet's diet. Because the foods won't be cooked, it's vital to choose foods that are as clean and safe as possible.

To find quality ingredients, you may have to explore new shopping habits. But that's not bad, right? Here are some possible ingredients for your pet's foods and some suggestions on where to find them:

- **Eggs:** Eggs provide excellent nutrition and contain all the amino acids necessary for good health. Because commercial eggs have been the focus of several contamination recalls, especially in late 2010, see if you can find a local grower from whom to buy eggs rather than buying mass-produced commercial eggs.

- **Fish:** Many experts recommend that fish be a part of a nutritional raw diet. If you have a local fish market, or if you can find frozen fresh fish caught locally, these should be clean and healthy. Of course, if you enjoy fishing, you may want to share your catch with your dog or cat.

> **PET ALERT**
>
> Be cautious of frozen fish not caught locally; most will have ethoxyquin added on board the fishing boat. Ethoxyquin is used as a preservative in pet food. It's also a pesticide that has been linked to several health problems in pets. Although studies are ongoing, most pet owners avoid foods containing ethoxyquin.

- **Meat:** Most raw food diets emphasize meat as the primary food. If at all possible, find a butcher in your community who finds, buys, and butchers local meat animals. Perhaps he purchases high school kids' Future Farmers project animals or those from local farmers. Ask the butcher if he chooses animals with no or minimal growth hormone and antibiotic use. The local butcher can also ensure that the butchering and storage of the meat is clean and careful. If you can ensure you will buy so much meat—muscle meat, organs, and meat cuttings—on a regular basis, he may be able to give you a good price.

- **Vegetables and fruits:** Although most raw food diet recipes emphasize that meat is the foundation of the diet, some fruits and vegetables are necessary for good health. Cats need significantly less than dogs do, but some carbohydrates and fiber are needed. During growing season in your region, you can grow a garden, and it's amazing how much food even a small garden can produce. Your local farmers' market is also a good source of clean food.

Sales, Deals, and Barter

If you're feeding more than one dog or cat, or if you're like so many other people today and are keeping an eye on your budget, watch for sales and other good deals. Not only can you come up with some good food for your pets, but you may also be able to save some money on both your pet's and your family's food. After all, many of the foods are the same.

Here are some tips for finding some good deals on foods for your pet:

- Sales at the local store can be great, as long as the food is of good quality. If the sale is for produce grown out of the country that has been sprayed with insecticides, herbicides, and/ or wax, then it's not a natural food anymore. However, if the food is locally grown and clean, then it can be a great deal.

- If there are local farms that sell food on their properties, in stands, or from the fields, you may be able to get some really good deals. Picking your own berries, strawberries, apples, and other produce requires some physical labor on your part, but just think of it as exercise instead of work.

- At the local farmers' market, look for someone who has a table overloaded with produce. The grower might be willing to offer a deal if you buy a large quantity of his or her squash, pumpkin, zucchini, or other vegetables. When the day is almost over and the farmer's produce is unsold, make an offer. Chances are, the farmer will accept it.

- If you have a friend who has backyard chickens, ask if she'll add several more chickens to her flock and offer to barter for eggs. Bring over any leftover produce to feed her chickens or plant a garden and share produce from your garden in exchange for the eggs.

Once you begin thinking outside of the box, it's amazing how creative you can be. Not only will you find good food for your pets and your family, but you'll save money, too.

GO NATURAL

Freeze any excess ingredients or food. Newer freezers are energy efficient, and freezing most foods is easy. You don't need to cook most of them prior to freezing, you don't need to add preservatives or other ingredients, and you can use the foods quite easily once you've thawed them.

Storing the Food

Once you've found good-quality foods for your dog and cat, keeping those foods clean, healthy, and well-preserved is important. Dog and cat owners feeding their pets raw food diets have found a variety of ways to do this:

- Use a cooler to bring home meat and fish. If you put a cooler with ice in your car, you can load it up with meat and fish on the way home from the store. This is particularly important on hot summer days or if you have a long drive. Of course, this is a good idea for the meat you feed your family, too.

- Package or repackage the food once you get home. You can cut up meat into meal-sized sections, wrap the sections individually, and either refrigerate or freeze them.

- Wash, cut up (if needed), and freeze your vegetables and fruits, too, if you got more than you and your pet can eat in a few days.

- Home vacuum packing products for foods are very useful for those who feed their pets raw foods, primarily because they can greatly extend the shelf life of many foods in the refrigerator and freezer. If you already have one you use for your family's foods, think about using it for your pet's foods, too.

Many pet owners take advantage of sales and seasonal produce, and will buy large quantities of raw foods when they're available. That might mean preparing and freezing quantities of zucchini at the height of growing season, or buying a half a butchered cow. This can save a great deal of money over time, but it does require significant room in the freezer. Investing in a freezer is often a good idea.

Practice Safe Handling

Many detractors of raw food diets for pets speak of the dangers of raw meat, especially the possibility of contamination. Although there are some safety procedures you should follow, there isn't anything you need to do when preparing your pet's food that you don't already do when preparing meat for your family.

You should take care when handling raw meat. Be sure to clean the counter or cutting board, knife, and any other tools immediately after preparing meat. Don't leave the tools out thinking you will take care of them later because someone could use the kitchen after you and not realize raw meat was on the counter or cutting board. Bleach is an excellent disinfectant to use after preparing raw meat.

Clean the cat's or dog's dish with bleach after each feeding. Make sure to rinse the bowl well and let it air dry.

If the cat or dog eats in the house (and hopefully he or she does), and he or she lifts food out of the dish to chew and swallow, then run an antibacterial wipe over that spot and toss the wipe in the trash. Don't use it anywhere else.

With some basic precautions and common sense, a raw food diet isn't going to cause any more problems than any other means of feeding your pet. In fact, it may lead to fewer issues. If you feed your dog or cat a dry kibble food and leave it out so your pet can nibble all day, that food can easily attract ants, cockroaches, and flies. A raw food diet isn't going to sit out long enough to attract anything; your pet is going to immediately eat it.

Raw Food Basics

There are several schools of thought regarding raw food diets, and each considers itself the best. Without weighing judgment on any of them, here is what a raw food diet can be:

- **Bones:** This includes the bones of meat animals, raw, with meat on them and marrow inside.

- **Carcasses:** Dr. Lonsdale recommends feeding dogs and cats whole carcasses of small animals such as chickens or rabbits. He also suggests pet owners give them portions of larger animals, such as calves, deer, sheep, or goats.

- **Carrots, potatoes, sweet potatoes, and yams:** Dogs more easily digest these foods when their owner cooks them first.

- **Dairy:** Goat's milk, goat cheese, aged cow's milk cheese, yogurt with live active cultures, and cottage cheese are all good foods.

- **Dark green vegetables:** Greens such as spinach, broccoli, collard greens, and kale are full of vitamins and minerals. These can be served chopped finely and raw or lightly steamed.

GO NATURAL

To steam grated vegetables or greens, place ¼ cup of them on a paper towel in the microwave. Place another paper towel on top of the food. Cook for 15 seconds on high. Doing so ensures the food remains raw, but the slight cooking breaks the cell walls, making the vegetables more digestible.

- **Eggs:** Many raw food proponents offer their pets raw eggs, shells and all. Others cook the eggs, grind them up, and bake the shells. Then they offer their pet the baked, ground shells as a powdered supplement in another meal.

- **Fish:** Fish meat, or whole fish or fish heads.

- **Fruits:** These include apples, bananas, blueberries, strawberries, pears, melons, and mangos.

- **Grains:** Most dogs and cats don't need cereal grains. If for some reason your dog or cat does, perhaps for additional energy or fiber, offer some cooked oatmeal.

- **Meat:** This includes muscle meat and organs of beef, bison, elk, venison, chicken, turkey, duck, goose, and rabbit.

- **Organ meat:** Liver, lungs, heart, trachea, and other organs.

- **Pumpkin and squash:** Raw grated pumpkin and squash (such as butternut, zucchini, summer, acorn, and spaghetti squash) provide carbohydrates and fiber.

Most raw food diets and recipes are very simple; it's definitely one of the appeals to this method of feeding. To provide a balanced diet, however, it's important to vary the foods and ingredients. See the recipes at the end of this chapter, and see Appendix C for a few additional recipes.

Raw Bone Safety

Although many raw food diet proponents advocate giving dogs and cats raw bones as a part of the diet, this must be undertaken with care. Even though eating bones is natural for carnivores, bones can cause some problems:

- When feeding bones, offer raw ones. Cooked bones can shatter.

- Offer either large bones, such as beef femur bones, or significantly smaller ones, such as those in a chicken neck. Although some raw food experts say small bones are okay, most veterinarians say for safety's sake they should be avoided.

- Watch your pet—dog or cat—while he or she is eating bones. If your pet breaks off shards of the bone, take the bone away. Swallowing shards or chunks can cause a perforation in the intestinal tract or a blockage.

You can provide your pet the nutritional advantage of bones without the danger by using a meat grinder to grind the bones into a powder. The powder can be frozen until used as a supplement with the meal.

DOG CHAT

For a good raw treat, buy a piece of raw beef femur from the butcher. (A 3- to 4-inch piece is great for small dogs; get proportionately larger portions for bigger dogs.) Using a knife, scrape the marrow out of the bone and mix it with 1 tablespoon of flaxseed meal and 1 teaspoon of peanut butter. Stuff the mixture back into the hollow of the bone. Remember to take the bone away if your dog begins to break off shards of bone.

Transitioning to a Raw Food Diet

As when making any major food change, do so gradually so your pet can get used to the new foods. Changing too rapidly can cause gastrointestinal upset, which can range from an upset tummy to diarrhea. A good rule of thumb is to provide one third of the new diet and two thirds of the old diet for a week, and then offer your pet half and half for a week. On the third week, offer two thirds of the new diet and one third of the old diet. This is just a basic recommendation; many pets need more time.

When my husband and I adopted one of our dogs, he'd been eating a very poor grade commercial food, and it took him two months to switch over to a better diet. When we tried to make the change more quickly, he had horrible diarrhea. So take your time.

You may also want to talk to your veterinarian prior to making a change to raw foods. Many are hesitant because they've seen some problems with raw food diets. Other veterinarians understand the benefits but may have some cautions for you. In addition, if your pet has some chronic health problems, you'll want some guidance during this transition.

Cats Can Be Resistant to Food Changes

Cats who have eaten dry kibble foods from kittenhood can become addicted to dry food. Often, these cats will eat nothing else— whether it's a canned food, a homemade diet, a frozen raw diet, or an entirely raw diet. Some experts feel kittens can imprint on specific types of food and then, as adults, refuse adamantly to try anything new.

For these cats, making a change requires patience. Don't try to starve your cat (or make your cat fast) to accomplish this. This is a bad idea, particularly because some cats can develop potentially life-threatening liver disease if they fast for more than a day.

Try adding a tiny bit of food that appeals to many cats to your cat's kibble. You might try canned or cooked salmon, tuna, mackerel, chicken, or beef. Cooked food is often better at this point because cooking releases the smell of the meat and its juices. Over several weeks, transition from cooked meat to tiny bits of raw meat—perhaps just a sliver of raw fish. Try some lightly steamed, finely grated squash or pumpkin, as well as some freshly grown wheatgrass.

By offering a variety of foods with different smells, tastes, and textures, you can help your cat become a little more adventurous with his or her eating habits. Through this process, you can also discover which foods your cat prefers.

CAT CHAT

For a great cat treat, cut a ½ inch × 1 inch slice of raw fish of any kind into slivers. Mix it with a few drops of cod liver oil and a pinch of finely diced wheatgrass. Watch your cat enjoy it!

Introduce kittens to a variety of foods early. A pinch of flaxseed meal, a couple pieces of lightly steamed and grated carrot, some finely diced wheatgrass, and some slivers of fish can get your kitten used to eating a variety of foods.

Watching for Problems

Most pets will change over to the new diet with few problems. In fact, most owners immediately begin noticing the change in their animal's coat. Some pets, however, may have trouble adjusting to a raw food diet. The gastrointestinal system may not calm down, and vomiting and diarrhea can result. If you find this to be the case, put your dog or cat back on his or her original diet, at least for the time being. Once your pet's system has calmed down and returned to normal, you can try adding small amounts of raw food treats—just a teaspoonful for a small dog or cat and a tablespoonful for a larger dog—to see if he or she can adjust to smaller amounts.

If you find your pet just can't seem to adjust to a raw food diet, you may want to try a home-cooked diet instead (see Chapter 12).

Creating Recipes for Your Pet

It's going to take some practice with a variety of ingredients to determine what foods, ingredients, and recipes your pet likes best. For example, all four of my dogs and my one cat like fish, especially fish with a strong odor (like mackerel). All five of my pets also like beef, although I don't feed them much of it because one of my dogs has had allergy problems. All of my dogs like eggs, but Xena, my cat, doesn't. You just have to try a variety of foods and see what happens.

It can also be a little scary to let go of commercial foods and begin developing recipes on your own. If you're concerned about this, make the transition easier by feeding the commercial food for one meal per day and a raw food recipe for the other meal.

Many owners have switched their pets over to raw food diets, though, and you can, too. Here are some tips:

- Proteins are the foundation of raw food diets. It's important to vary the proteins—meat, fish, eggs, and dairy. By using a variety of protein sources, you change the recipe's nutritional value. Your pet then gets a selection of amino acids, enzymes, vitamins, and minerals.

- Steam many of the vegetables. Because carnivores—especially cats—have a hard time digesting many carbohydrate foods, it's important to make the foods as digestible as possible. Steaming breaks the cell walls and makes the nutrition more readily available.

- Use appropriate supplements to fill in the nutritional gaps in a recipe. See Chapter 13 for more on supplements.

Until you get used to preparing a raw food diet, it's a good idea to keep track of the calories in the foods you're feeding your pet. There are many foods available that can help you do this, as well as a variety of websites that make it easy. Check out the BARF diet at www.barfworld.com and raw feeding at www.rawlearning.com. You may also want to do some research ahead of time, and jot down the calorie counts of some foods you plan to use on a regular basis. Although this may be annoying at first, once you get used to these foods, you'll learn how much of what to feed your pet.

For Dogs

Bashir's Favorite

This recipe is one of Bashir's favorites. It provides 1,200 calories and is one day's ration for Bashir, a 50-pound Australian Shepherd.

1 cup fresh spinach, finely chopped

½ cup fresh yam, finely chopped

3 cups raw rabbit meat, ground or finely chopped

2 TB. cod liver oil

1 TB. flaxseed meal

1 TB. molasses

1 cup plain yogurt

1. Lightly steam spinach and yam. Place in a bowl.

2. Add rabbit meat, cod liver oil, flaxseed meal, and molasses. Mix well.

3. If you plan to add supplements, add them now and mix well.

4. Store in an airtight container in the refrigerator. When serving, divide into as many meals as you normally feed. Add a portion of yogurt when serving, dividing into equal amounts per each meal.

Variation: Use sweet potato instead of yam, honey instead of molasses, kefir instead of yogurt, or other greens in place of spinach.

bone appétit!

Beef and Greens

This is a tasty recipe that supplies 1,200 calories, or one day's ration, for a 40- to 50-pound dog.

> ¼ cup raw carrots, finely grated
> ¼ cup raw broccoli florets, finely chopped
> ¼ cup fresh spinach, finely chopped
> 2 cups raw beef, ground or cut into small pieces
> 1 raw chicken, duck, or goose egg
> 1 TB. flaxseed meal
> ½ cup plain yogurt

1. Place carrots, broccoli, and spinach on a paper towel, cover with another paper towel, and steam for 15 seconds. Place in a bowl.

2. Add beef, egg, and flaxseed meal. Mix well.

3. If you plan to add supplements, add them now and mix well.

4. Store in an airtight container in the refrigerator. When serving, divide into as many meals as you normally feed. Add a portion of yogurt when serving.

Variation: Change the nutritional value of the food for subsequent meals by using bison, elk, or venison instead of beef. You can also use other dark green vegetables instead of spinach or broccoli, and grated squash instead of carrots.

For Cats

Seafood Delight

This recipe provides 350 calories, which is a daily ration for a 10-pound indoor cat.

> 2 TB. carrots, grated
>
> 2 TB. broccoli florets, finely diced
>
> 1 cup raw oysters
>
> ¼ cup fresh tuna (not canned), cut into fine pieces
>
> 1 chicken egg, hardboiled, shelled, and crumbled
>
> 1 tsp. salmon oil (or fish or cod liver oil)

1. Lightly steam carrots and broccoli. Place in a bowl.

2. In a food processor, liquefy oysters, tuna, egg, and salmon oil until the mixture becomes a thick paste.

3. Add paste mixture to vegetables in the bowl. Stir well.

4. Store in an airtight container in the refrigerator. When serving, divide into small meals throughout the day, depending on your cat's schedule. Add supplements, including taurine, when serving.

Turkey and Pumpkin

This recipe is acceptable for most cats, even those who haven't tried many raw foods. It provides about 350 calories, a daily ration for a 10-pound indoor cat.

> 1 raw chicken neck
>
> ¼ cup fresh pumpkin, or canned without spices
>
> 1 cup raw turkey meat or ground turkey
>
> 1 TB. cod liver oil

1. Chop chicken neck into quarters, bones and all. Freeze three pieces for subsequent meals or recipes. Retain one quarter for this recipe, and set aside.

2. Grate pumpkin and then lightly steam it. Place in a bowl.

3. Cut turkey meat into slivers. In a food processor, liquefy turkey meat, chicken neck, pumpkin, and cod liver oil until the mixture becomes a thick paste. If needed for processing, add a small amount of water or chicken broth.

4. Store in an airtight container in the refrigerator. When serving, divide into small meals throughout the day, depending on your cat's schedule. Add supplements, including taurine, when serving.

Variation: Use a turkey neck instead of chicken or chicken meat instead of turkey. You can also use squash or zucchini instead of pumpkin.

meow, love, eat

Feeding Them Right

It's very difficult to know how to feed your pet. Although raw foods are obviously the most natural foods, our pets are no longer wild animals. It can be scary to assume the responsibility of developing recipes and feeding routines, but if this is something you feel is best for your pet, you can do it. Just watch your pet as you make changes to his or her diet. Keep an eye on your pet's skin and coat, energy levels, and overall health. Don't hesitate to talk to your veterinarian if you notice a problem.

The Least You Need to Know

- A raw food diet is good for pets when fed with care and knowledge, but it's not without some concerns.
- A varied diet using different meat and a variety of other ingredients, including supplements, is important to provide complete nutrition.
- Choose the best ingredients you can find from trusted sources because cooking will not be used to kill any bacteria.
- If your pet has been eating a commercial food, change to a raw food diet must be gradual. Realize not all pets will like the diet change.
- Try a variety of different ingredients as you make the change so you can find out what foods your pet likes best.

Cooking for Your Pet

In This Chapter

- The benefits and concerns of a home-cooked diet
- What you need to know to cook for your pet
- Ingredients to avoid
- Transitioning your pet to a home-cooked diet
- Sample recipes for dogs and cats

Researchers can't tell us exactly how and when dogs and cats became domesticated. We do know that when dogs and cats joined with us, what we ate affected their natural diet. A natural diet for wild canines would have included animals they hunted and caught, portions of the gut that contained the food the prey animal ate, and tubers and fallen fruits. Wild felines are hunters, so their diet would have included the animals they caught, as well as that animal's internal organs.

Over time, dogs and cats became more dependent on humans, and people usually fed them leftovers. These leftovers may have been from their food preparation or from food that was not eaten during a meal. After all, refrigeration is a relatively recent invention in our history. People often preferred to feed the dog who helped herd the livestock or the cat who helped control mice than let the food spoil.

Coming Full Circle with Home Cooking

The "leftover" method of feeding domestic dogs and cats continued until the introduction of commercial pet food. These became popular because they're convenient, just as the prepared frozen dinners became popular with busy people. (See Chapter 10 for more on commercial pet food.)

Not everyone made the switch to commercial pet food, though. My grandfather owned dogs all his life, up to his death in the early 1990s. He grew up on the family farm in Michigan, and the dogs ate leftovers from the family meals, as well as leftovers from cheese making, broken eggs from the chickens, and scraps from butchered animals. When he left the family farm and began his own family, he and my grandmother continued to feed their dogs a home-cooked diet. It consisted primarily of animal proteins—meat, eggs, cheese, and yogurt—but they also fed the dogs fruits and vegetables. As long as I can remember, their dogs always looked wonderful—they had shiny coats, bright eyes, and plenty of energy for play. Their dogs also lived long lives; their last dog—a Miniature Poodle named Fifi—lived to be 15 years old.

Today, many dog owners are taking another look at feeding their pets a home-cooked diet. Not only are many pet owners worried about the many recalls for commercial pet foods, but they also want to be more involved in determining exactly what their pets eat.

Some pet owners prefer to feed a raw food diet (see Chapter 11), saying that's the most natural type of food for carnivores. However, Joan Weiskopf, an MS veterinary clinical nutritionist, says, "I am against raw food in general, because the risk of bacterial infection is too high, and the consequences too dire, not to cook the meat." A home-cooked diet can provide the benefits of healthy food without the risk of possible contamination from raw food.

Providing a homemade diet for your pets allows you to control the quality and source of the ingredients, just as with a raw food diet. However, cooking kills any parasites or bacteria that might be in the raw foods.

GO NATURAL

The word *natural* doesn't mean a food must be raw; instead, it pertains to how the food is grown, processed, and handled.

The Benefits Show

The benefits of a quality home-cooked diet appear quickly. When my dogs and cats ate a good-quality commercial kibble, they looked good—their coats were shiny and they loved to play. But I was always complaining about their shedding and tendency toward rapid weight gain, and one of my dogs even suffered from allergy symptoms (resulting from an allergy to an ingredient in the food).

Once they were switched over to a home-cooked diet, however, their coats were even better—they were shiny, bright, and soft, and they didn't shed as much. My allergy-prone dog's symptoms disappeared completely. They had bright eyes and were more eager to play, and the dogs did better in their training.

I also saw a change in the dogs' and cats' bodies; they didn't get fat as easily, and they appeared to have more lean muscle. Injuries healed more quickly, too. Most importantly to me, my pets appeared to feel good. The puppies grew at a slow, even pace without any problems, and the older dogs aged well with fewer infirmities.

You Control the Quality

The primary benefit of a home-cooked diet for your dog or cat is that you can control the quality of everything you feed your pet. You can also choose the ingredients you want your pet to eat and oversee the quality and freshness of those ingredients. If you want your dog to have more meat and your cat to have fewer cereal grains, that's totally up to you.

Of course, as with most things, this isn't as easy as it sounds. You need to do some footwork to find quality ingredients:

- **Farm-fresh eggs:** Eggs are an excellent food, and free-range, farm-fresh eggs taste much better and are potentially safer than commercially produced eggs. You can often find these at a farmers' market, or look for a farmer who raises free-range chickens.

- **Farmers' markets:** You can often find locally grown, good-quality vegetables and fruits at local farmers' markets, though the variety will vary depending upon where you live. Farmers' markets in southern California, for example, are stocked with locally grown avocados, while those in New England often have a wide assortment of apples. You can also choose good foods that are not perfect; blemished or overripe fruits and meat that is fresh and clean but not pretty enough to sell to people is still good food.

- **Fish markets:** If you live near the ocean or a large lake, you may have a nearby fish market. Freshly caught fish can easily be a part of a home-cooked diet for both dogs and cats.

- **Garden:** I have a large garden every year, and I plant all kinds of vegetables, from tomatoes to squash to pumpkins. The produce is for both my family and our pets.

- **Local butcher:** I buy much of the meat my family and pets consume from a local butcher. He ensures the animals he processes are not fed antibiotics, growth hormones, or any other potentially problematic chemicals. Because he controls the entire process, he makes sure the animals are killed and butchered humanely and cleanly.

- **Specialty markets:** You may be able to find quality ingredients at health food, natural food, or organic food stores. Many small groceries provide quality ingredients not found large chain grocery stores.

One additional benefit of a home-cooked diet is that you have control over the preparation of the food. You can know not only that you're using high-quality ingredients, but also that you're preparing the food in a clean, safe manner.

It's Not Always Easy

Implementing a home-cooked diet for your dog or cat isn't nearly as easy as feeding them a commercial kibble or canned food that can simply be poured into a bowl. And although dogs and cats used to eat leftovers from our ancestors' meals, that shouldn't be the basis of their meals today—we don't eat the same way our ancestors did!

Far too many of us don't eat just meat, dairy, fresh vegetables, and fruit. Instead, our diet includes too much sugar; salt; and processed, take-out, and fast foods. We also use preservatives, additives, spices, and flavorings that our pets don't need or that can even make them sick.

Some leftover unseasoned or lightly seasoned meat is okay for both dogs and cats. Fresh vegetables and fruits are great for your dog. But otherwise, your pet's home-cooked diet needs to be formulated with your pet's needs in mind.

Home-cooked meals can be more difficult than using commercial pet foods in other ways:

- **Food preparation:** It takes seconds to pour kibble food into your pet's bowl. A home-cooked diet requires more time; not only do you need to go shop for the ingredients, but you also need to prepare, cook, and store the food. Fortunately, you can slow cook the food in a Crock-Pot, an easy and often cost-effective approach.

- **Price:** Quality ingredients can cost more, but keep in mind your pet may eat less of a quality home-cooked diet than he or she eats of the average kibble food. So the cost may even out.

- **Travel and vacation:** If your pet normally travels with you or stays at a boarding kennel, a home-cooked diet can be a challenge. You can cook ahead of time, however, and then freeze the food in meal-sized containers. You do need to plan ahead, though, to make it work.

GO NATURAL

I keep several meals for both dogs and cats in the freezer. On mornings when I know I'm going to be busy, I can put them in the refrigerator to thaw, or I can thaw them in the microwave if I run out of time.

Nutritional Content

Inspectors routinely test commercial pet foods—or their ingredients—to determine their nutritional content. This includes identifying the foods' protein, fat, and carbohydrate levels, and measuring its moisture content, vitamins, and minerals. It's very difficult, if not impossible, for pet owners to do the same thing for their pets' home-cooked meals. You would need to test each recipe, and the ingredients can vary from batch to batch. The cost of testing would most certainly be prohibitive.

It's important for pet owners to vary the recipes they feed their pet. Varying the recipes and ingredients on a regular basis ensures that your dog or cat is able to consume all the necessary elements for good nutrition. For example, you can routinely change your pet's protein sources. In one batch of food, you could provide beef; then, in subsequent batches, you could provide turkey, chicken, fish, or bison. The vegetables could be alternated in the same fashion, as could the fruits, eggs, and other ingredients.

Add a vitamin and mineral supplement to your dog's or cat's food on a daily basis. This, too, ensures your pet is getting the best nutrition. See Chapter 13 for more on supplements.

The Concerns

By buying quality ingredients, pet owners ensure their pets get the best foods. When they cook the foods, that process eliminates the dangers of bacterial contamination. Still, some people—particularly some veterinarians—are concerned about home-cooked diets.

Dr. Greg Martinez says, "Most veterinarians are concerned because we weren't taught much about ingredients. We were warned to stick to commercial foods that are complete and balanced. I've come to realize that commercial diets are tragically unbalanced for some dogs and cats. For some these diets have too many carbohydrates, and too little fat, protein, and moisture for optimal health. Dogs will thrive on homemade diets that consist of at least 30 percent protein and over 15 percent fat with a varied mixture of meat, vegetables, and fruits." He adds that cats need more protein and fewer vegetables and fat.

The predominant concern among critics is that the pet is getting all of the needed vitamins, minerals, fiber, and other nutrients needed for good health. Cats especially must have taurine. A taurine deficiency can result in serious illnesses and even death.

CAT CHAT

Taurine is an essential amino acid that's easily destroyed by heat, so even if it's in a raw food, the cooking process can greatly deplete or even destroy a food's taurine levels. A taurine deficiency can lead to vision and heart problems. Cats should have 1 gram of taurine per 2.2 pounds of food.

Another concern is that pet owners will choose to feed the wrong foods. Foods too high in meat fats, for example, can cause pancreatic problems for some dogs. Pet owners should avoid many spices and seasonings, not because they themselves are problems, but simply because our pets aren't used to them.

Obviously, you should acknowledge and take into consideration veterinary concerns when choosing the right foods for your pet. After all, your pets' health is their primary concern, too. If you have any doubts or concerns, talk to your veterinarian. Tell her about your worries for your pet on a commercial food and your hopes for a new type of feeding regimen. An open discussion can only be beneficial to your pet.

The Basics of a Home-Cooked Diet for Dogs

If you decide a home-cooked diet is the best feeding choice for your dog or cat, there are some things you need to keep in mind. After all, there are some valid concerns regarding creating your pet's diet, and you want to make the best choices possible.

As I discussed in Chapter 9, dogs are scientifically considered carnivores (meat eaters), but behaviorally they are omnivores. That means when hungry they will eat a variety of foods. Therefore, the ingredients of a home-cooked diet can include the following:

- **Dairy:** Goat's milk, fresh goat cheeses, cottage cheese, and yogurt. Avoid cow's milk for most dogs because it causes gastrointestinal upset. Aged cheeses from cow's milk are usually fine.

- **Eggs:** Chicken, duck, goose, turkey, and quail eggs.

- **Fish:** Just about any deboned fish is acceptable, including trout, bass, catfish, mackerel, salmon, tuna, and herring. Clams, oysters, shrimp, and lobster are also fine. Leave the tails on the shrimp because they're a natural source of glucosamine and chondroitin.

- **Fruits:** Apple, banana, pears, melons, mango, strawberry, raspberry, and blueberry. Offer very little citrus.

- **Meat:** Chicken, turkey, duck, goose, lamb, beef, bison, elk, and rabbit.

- **Vegetables:** Carrots, celery, zucchini, broccoli, squash, pumpkin, green beans, peas, chickpeas, kidney beans, sweet potatoes, yams, and potatoes.

Many commercial dog foods use a significant amount of cereal grains in their recipes. The grains boost the laboratory analysis of proteins, plus cereal grains are inexpensive. However, dogs don't necessarily need cereal grains. Plus, they can potentially cause several health and behavioral problems. See Chapter 10 for more information.

The Basics of a Home-Cooked Diet for Cats

Just as for dogs, a home-cooked diet for cats is dependent upon high-quality ingredients. As an obligate carnivore, however, cats have a limited food selection. A home-cooked diet for cats can include the following:

- **Dairy:** Goat's milk, fresh goat cheese, cottage cheese, and yogurt. Avoid cow's milk, which can cause gastrointestinal upset. Aged cheeses from cow's milk are usually fine.

- **Eggs:** Chicken, duck, goose, turkey, and quail eggs.

- **Fish:** Just about any deboned fish, including trout, bass, catfish, mackerel, salmon, tuna, and herring. Clams, oysters, sardines, shrimp (with or without the tails), and lobster are also fine.

- **Meat:** Chicken, turkey, duck, goose, lamb, beef, bison, elk, venison, and other meat.

PET ALERT

Although most cats absolutely love tuna, limit this ingredient to no more than three times per week. That includes all tuna—commercial cat food, canned tuna, or fresh tuna. Many cats like it so much they can actually become addicted to it, avoiding other foods.

Although cats are primarily meat eaters, they still need some fiber to help the gastrointestinal system function properly. They also need some carbohydrates for the body's processes. Small amounts of finely chopped or grated and lightly steamed (to make the food more digestible) carrots, spinach, squash, pumpkin, green beans, sweet potatoes, yams, and potatoes are good additions to the diet. Limit the amount of vegetables to about 1 tablespoon daily for a 10-pound cat.

Cats don't have the ability to digest cereal grains correctly, so don't add these to the homemade diet. Cereal grains in cats' diets have been linked to many feline health problems, including diabetes. Although research on this subject is ongoing, avoid cereal grains as much as possible. See Chapter 10 for more information.

Ingredients to Avoid

It would be much easier to feed our pets a home-cooked diet if dogs and cats could safely consume all of the same foods we do. Unfortunately, it's not that easy. Here are some foods your pet should *not* eat:

- **Alcohol:** Don't share your beverage with either your dog or your cat.

- **Avocado:** Thousands of dogs in southern California eat avocados off the trees every day. They may get fat from the fruit's high fat content, but few get sick. Unfortunately, the pits, skin, leaves, and stems are toxic, and the pits, if swallowed, can cause an obstruction.

- **Caffeine:** Don't share your coffee, tea, or other caffeinated products. A dog's or cat's much smaller body size can quickly lead to toxicity and even death, as the caffeine affects on them are fast and strong, which can lead to heart problems.

- **Chocolate:** Chocolate contains theobromine. A small amount will cause your pet to be restless, but depending upon how much he or she consumes and the pet's size, toxicity and death can occur. Dark chocolate, including baker's chocolate, is the most concentrated and the most dangerous. Cats don't have the taste receptors for sweets like dogs and people do, and so usually aren't attracted to chocolate.

- **Citrus oils:** Dogs and cats, but especially cats, are sensitive to citrus oils. In sensitive animals, exposure can even lead to death.

- **Cow's milk:** Most dogs and cats can't digest cow's milk correctly and will suffer gastrointestinal upsets if they consume even a small amount. Luckily dogs and cats can tolerate aged, fermented, and soured dairy products such as cheese, cottage cheese, and yogurt, and these provide good nutrition.

- **Grapes and raisins:** Don't give your pet grapes or raisins, even if they want them. Grapes and raisins can cause toxicity that can lead to kidney failure.

- **Grease:** Leftover grease (from meat or other cooking) can lead to gastrointestinal upset. Some dogs may suffer pancreatic upsets after ingesting grease.

- **Macadamia nuts:** Although cats usually aren't attracted to them, dogs seem to like macadamia nuts. Unfortunately, these nuts are toxic and potentially lethal to dogs.

- **Spices:** Very few dogs and cats are attracted to spices, so you don't need to include these in their diets. Many can cause an upset stomach.

- **Sugar:** Cats don't taste sweets like dogs and people do, so they have no need for sugar. Dogs, like people, can become addicted to sweet foods. Because sugar has no nutritional value, it's usually a good idea to avoid it.

- **Xylitol:** This sweetener is used in more and more of today's products, from baked goods to cough syrups. Although it tastes good, it can be deadly to pets. Read the labels of any products before offering it to your pet to ensure that this sweetener is not included in the ingredients.

Preparing a Home-Cooked Diet

You'll find that cooking for your pet is much like cooking for you and your family. Your family probably has a few favorite recipes, and you'll likely find there are a few recipes you enjoy preparing for your pet that your pet enjoys as well. Having a few recipes to choose from, with varied ingredients, will ensure your pet is well-nourished. (See the recipes at the end of the chapter and in Appendix C.)

Most pet recipes call for boiling, baking, or cooking the food in a slow cooker. You should include in the food any juices you use or produce while cooking, rather than draining them off; these juices contain nutrients from the food.

When the recipe calls for steamed vegetables, that is to help break down cell walls so the food becomes more digestible for your pet. You can place a tablespoon or so of finely chopped or grated food on a damp paper towel, cover that with another paper towel, and warm it in the microwave on high power for 15 to 40 seconds, depending on how much food there is and the power of your microwave. For example, you can adequately heat a tablespoon of grated carrots in a 1,000-watt microwave for 15 seconds.

Be sure to cook all meat until well done to ensure that all bacteria is destroyed. It's usually fine to feed your pet raw fruits.

Store your leftovers in airtight containers, and keep them in the refrigerator or freezer. Most foods remain safe in the refrigerator for three to four days. Many pet owners make several days' worth of food at one time, and then store premeasured amounts for each meal. You can also keep large batches in the freezer, and thaw them as needed.

Transitioning to a Home-Cooked Diet

Changing what your pet eats can be difficult because rapid changes in a diet can cause gastrointestinal upset, such as upset stomach, flatulence, and diarrhea. All changes should be made gradually over several weeks. Dogs and cats who've been eating dry kibble food may have trouble getting used to a home-cooked diet. They may have soft stools and some flatulence. Just keep the transition slow, adding a tiny bit of the new food to the old food each day. If we ate a diet of fast-food or processed foods and then changed to a better-quality, natural-food diet, we'd have a hard time initially, too. Our pets are much like us in that respect.

An easy way to help your pet make the transition to a home-cooked diet is to begin adding side dishes or treats to the old diet. With small tasty bits of home-cooked food, you can find out whether you really want to continue cooking for your pet. You may discover it's more work than you anticipated, or you may find you really enjoy it. Plus, by adding tidbits of new foods, you help your dog or cat discover new tastes and textures. Most dogs willingly try new things. Cats, on the other hand, tend to be wary of new foods.

Ideally, puppies and kittens should be exposed to a variety of foods when young. Not only can this help them avoid food allergy problems later in life, but it can also help you provide them with a healthier and more varied diet. When your pet will accept different foods, and isn't worried about trying new foods, you can use different recipes.

DOG TALK

Many dogs really enjoy the home-cooked diet; the foods smell better and taste wonderful, especially compared to a dry kibble diet. Don't allow your dog to beg for more, and don't keep adding more food to your dog's meals just because he or she asks for it.

Developing Recipes for Your Pet

Everyone—human, canine, and feline—has unique nutritional needs. My 10-pound cat, Xena, may be more active than your 10-pound cat, so Xena may need to eat more food than your cat. My Australian Shepherds, Bashir and Sisko, each weigh 50 pounds, so you might think they need to eat the same food and the same amount. However, that's not true. Sisko is very active, while Bashir is not quite as active. Plus, Bashir tends to gain weight easily and Sisko doesn't. I feed Bashir less food than Sisko so I can help Bashir control his weight.

Kittens, puppies, pregnant animals, lactating animals, and those recovering from illness or injuries need more calories or special diets. Talk to your veterinarian about your pet's special needs prior to switching foods or recipes.

Individual dogs and cats may have food allergies or sensitivities. My oldest Australian Shepherd, Riker, will itch and itch and itch if he eats wheat or beef. My other dogs are fine with either ingredient. Other allergy symptoms include paw licking, chewing at the base of the tail, red and flushed skin, and hair loss. Food sensitivities often appear as flatulence.

It's easy to avoid certain ingredients if you already know your dog has problems with them. But if you begin feeding your pet a different food and your dog begins itching, scratching, chewing, or has any other reaction, stop offering that food and call your veterinarian. Allergy tests are always an option, but let your veterinarian guide you as to what to do next.

Some Easy Steps

Letting commercial foods go and taking on the responsibility of formulating a home-cooked diet for your pet can be tough. Your pet's well-being rests on your shoulders. You can do it, however, just as many other pet owners have. Here are the main points to keep in mind:

- **Add supplements:** Just as many people add nutritional supplements to their daily diet, so should you for your pet. After all, commercial pet foods add vitamins and minerals to their recipes to ensure better nutrition.

- **Steam the vegetables:** Lightly steam vegetables and other plant products (other than fruits) so your pet can easily digest them.

- **Vary the proteins:** When you vary the protein—the meat, eggs, and dairy—you not only change the taste of the food, but you also change the food's nutritional value. Different proteins offer a variety of amino acids, enzymes, vitamins, and minerals (discussed in Chapter 9).

Determining the Calorie Counts

It's easy to determine the calorie counts for your home-cooked pet food recipes. Several sources on the Internet (for example, www.thecaloriecounter.com and www.nutritiondata.self.com) offer easy methods for determining the nutritional value of foods and ingredients, including the calorie counts. Here are a few examples of foods and their nutritional values:

- Ground beef, 95 percent lean: A 3-ounce serving has 145 calories, 0 carbohydrates, 6 grams of fat, 0 fiber, and 22 grams of protein.

- Roasted chicken, dark meat, no skin: A 3-ounce serving has 174 calories, 0 carbohydrates, 8 grams of fat, 0 fiber, and 23 grams of protein.

You aren't going to have to look up every ingredient forever; after a while, you'll learn how much your dog or cat needs, and it will become second nature. Just look things up for a while so you don't over- or underfeed your pet.

Keeping Track

As you begin cooking for your dog or cat, you will find that there will be some ingredients and recipes your pet loves and some he or she doesn't like. Some picky dogs or cats may turn up their noses at a few foods. It's a good idea to make note of what you feed your pet, how much you serve, how well it was eaten, and whether you observed any problems (flatulence or soft stools) afterward. A calendar, journal, or daily planner should work. Pay particular attention to ingredients your pet doesn't like, and any ingredients that cause a bad reaction. Count calories in your journal as well, until you have a better idea of how many calories are in what foods.

By keeping track of everything, you can easily make changes to your pet's menu. Also, if your veterinarian asks about your pet's diet, you can answer in detail.

For Dogs

Bison and Broccoli Side Dish

You can mix this tasty and nutritious side dish with your dog's normal meal. The entire recipe is about 700 calories, so to determine the calories, divide by how many servings this makes for your individual dog.

> 1 cup ground bison, well cooked, sautéed with just enough water to cover the bottom of the pan (so meat doesn't dry out)
>
> 1 cup broccoli florets, finely diced, steamed for 15 seconds
>
> ¼ cup unflavored oatmeal, cooked according to package directions

1. In a large bowl, mix cooked bison, steamed broccoli, and cooked oatmeal.

2. Store in an airtight container in the refrigerator.

Slow Cooker Stew

This recipe makes a full day's worth of food for a 50-pound dog—about 1,300 calories of food—and should be split into two meals. If you have a small dog or a dog who needs fewer calories, split the recipe into additional servings.

> 1 lb. ground turkey
>
> 2 cups potato, chopped into ½-inch cubes
>
> ½ cup raw carrots, grated
>
> ½ cup fresh spinach, finely chopped
>
> ¼ cup celery, finely chopped
>
> ¼ cup fresh parsley, finely chopped
>
> 2 TB. flaxseed meal

1. In a large saucepan, brown ground turkey. Transfer to a slow cooker.

2. Add potato, carrots, spinach, celery, parsley, and flaxseed meal to the slow cooker. Add just enough water to cover all ingredients.

3. Set the slow cooker to low heat. Cook all day.

4. Divide mixture into two (or more) servings. Serve warm (but not hot) with a vitamin and mineral supplement made specifically for dogs.

5. Store remaining food in an airtight container in the refrigerator.

Variation: Use ground chicken, duck, or goose instead of turkey. You can use sweet potatoes or yams instead of potatoes. You can also use wheatgrass, collard greens, kale, or broccoli florets instead of spinach, celery, and parsley. Keep in mind the calorie counts will change depending upon the substitutions, so check those out prior to serving the food.

For Cats

Sardine Side Dish

This tasty treat can be mixed in with your cat's normal food.

> 1 (6-oz.) can sardines in water or oil (not in tomato sauce)
>
> 1 egg, hardboiled and crumbled finely, with shell (the shell is a good source of minerals)
>
> ¼ cup grated summer squash, lightly steamed for 15 seconds
>
> ¼ cup plain yogurt

1. In a blender, liquefy sardines, egg, summer squash, and yogurt in a blender. Periodically, stop the blender and stir the contents to ensure all ingredients (especially the eggshell) are finely ground and well mixed.

2. Store in an airtight container in the refrigerator.

meow, love, eat

Savory Salmon

This recipe makes one day's worth of food, about 350 calories, for an adult 11-pound cat. Split this recipe into three meals, fed throughout the day. You can also split it into several smaller meals if your cat needs fewer calories.

> 4 oz. fresh salmon, cooked (or use canned salmon, drained)
>
> 1 large egg, hardboiled and crumbled, with shell
>
> 2 TB. raw carrots, grated and steamed
>
> 1 TB. pumpkin, canned, without spices (not pumpkin pie mix)

1. In a small bowl, shred salmon with a fork until it's in small pieces.

2. Add egg, carrots, and pumpkin and stir gently, but do not allow mixture to become a purée.

3. Store in an airtight container in the refrigerator. Offer servings three times per day. When serving, add a vitamin and mineral supplement with taurine made specifically for cats.

Variation: Use catfish, trout, tuna, mackerel, or another fish instead of salmon. You could also use puréed, cooked squash instead of pumpkin. Finely chopped wheatgrass, lightly steamed, can be used instead of carrots. The calorie count will change depending upon the ingredients, so make sure you check that out before serving.

meow, love, eat

Feeding Them Right

The world has changed significantly since our pets were first domesticated, and they can no longer fend for themselves and supply themselves with food. Plus, we know wild carnivores live tough, often hungry, and short lives. Our pets deserve better. By feeding them the best we can, we can only hope to give them longer, healthier lives.

The Least You Need to Know

- Feeding home-cooked meals can provide your pet with better nutrition, but make sure your pet is getting all of the needed vitamins, minerals, fiber, and other nutrients he or she needs.
- Keep track of the changes you make to your pet's diet, including the recipes you use, calorie counts, and ingredients so you can refer back to your notes if you need to make changes.
- Protect your pet from harmful foods, including alcohol, caffeine, chocolate, and cow's milk.
- It may take a minimum of several weeks for your pet to transition to a home-cooked diet. Introduce the new diet gradually so your pet's system can adjust.

Supplements Add Nutrition

Chapter 13

In This Chapter

- Exactly what are supplements?
- Choosing supplements for the right reasons
- Food supplements from A to Z
- Herbal and commercial supplements
- Don't forget about treats!
- Cats love catnip

You can add natural supplements, such as high-quality whole foods and herbs, to your pet's diet, or synthetic supplements, such as commercial vitamin and mineral supplements. For pets eating a cooked or raw homemade diet, you can use supplements to fill in any nutritional gaps.

Advertisers often tout supplements as miracle foods or additives. Many people feel they are highly beneficial and totally harmless, but that isn't necessarily so. For example, if you are feeding a commercial food, a supplement could upset the nutritional balance of that food. Take great care when adding anything to your pet's diet, and remember that supplements aren't cure-alls. Learning what supplements are and where they come from will help you decide which ones are best for your pet.

Defining Food Supplements

A supplement is anything you add to your dog's or cat's regular diet. This means it can be any number of things. For example, you might decide to add flaxseed meal to your dog's food to provide omega fatty acids. Doing so makes the flaxseed meal a supplement.

To make things more confusing, some whole foods can be both a supplement and an ingredient in a recipe. To continue with the flaxseed meal example, if a recipe calls for it because of its nutritional value as well as its nutty taste, then it's a food ingredient.

A supplement can be a vitamin or a mineral as well. If you add something to your pet's food in hopes of adding nutritional or medicinal benefits, then that addition is a supplement.

Food supplements can be natural—that is, made from natural whole foods or ingredients—or they can be synthetic.

Because of the variety of supplement types, as well as the blurred definitions, understanding this subject matter can be difficult.

Choose with Care

Although supplements can provide benefits with very little risk, others have a less than beneficial side. Plain yogurt, for example, is great for most pets. But other items have side effects. For example, adding anything containing beef can trigger a reaction in a dog with allergies to beef. There are also some supplements that are safe to use with dogs but not with cats. Never assume using a supplement is risk free.

The field of supplements has very few regulations, and many companies have made unproven or downright false claims about their products. If the advertising sounds too good to be true, it probably is.

Supplement manufacturing and labeling is also unregulated, causing potential problems for users. The ingredients in a packaged supplement can vary widely. For example, a ginseng supplement may be derived from one of three different plants: Siberian ginseng

(*Eleutherococcus senticosus*), American ginseng (*Panax quinquefolius*), or Asian or Korean ginseng (*Panax ginseng*). Ideally, the manufacturer would put the plant species on the label.

> **GO NATURAL**
>
> Every dog and cat is a unique individual, just as every person is. There is no one supplement that's right for every dog and cat.

Some Supplements to Consider

There are several types of supplements that veterinarians, nutritionists, and other pet nutrition experts commonly recommend. Supplements such as these can be found in pet supply stores or online pet supply stores as well as health food stores. Here are just a few:

- **Bone meal:** Meat is high in phosphorus, but not as high in calcium as bones. By adding a bone meal supplement to your pet's diet, you can achieve a better balance of these minerals. When feeding bone meal, add a fish oil supplement at the same time so the bone meal is properly metabolized.

- **Enzymes:** Dr. Shawn Messonnier, a holistic veterinarian, recommends several supplements for dogs and cats, one of which is an enzyme supplement. He says, "The major function of enzymes is to help digest and absorb food. This is critical for the vital nutrients contained in the food to be absorbed by the body." When you give your pet an enzyme supplement, the food's value is potentially increased because the enzymes allow more of the nutrients to be absorbed into the body. There are several commercial enzyme supplements available, but yogurt with live active cultures (read the label to make sure it contains them) is an excellent source of digestive enzymes.

- **Fatty acids:** These are necessary for several functions throughout the body. Although manufacturers often add fatty acids to commercial foods after processing, and raw and home-cooked diets usually provide good quantities in significant amounts of meat, a fatty acid supplement can still be a good addition to the diet. Fish and fish oils are also good additions because they're rich in omega-3 essential fatty acids and act as anti-inflammatory agents.

- **Vitamin and mineral supplements:** Joan Weiskopf, a veterinary clinical nutritionist, recommends a vitamin and mineral supplement for pets eating homemade diets (see Chapter 12) to fill any nutritional gaps in the diet. These supplements must be specific to the species being fed. In other words, don't give your cat a dog vitamin, because it wouldn't have sufficient taurine. Buy vitamins formulated for cats or dogs; don't give your pet vitamins made for people.

> **CAT CHAT**
>
> Taurine is an amino acid found in meat, eggs, dairy products, and fish. A deficiency produces blindness and potentially fatal heart disease. Cats need taurine in their diet on a daily basis. Commercial cat foods are required to have taurine added, so don't supplement those. However, supplement any homemade recipes for cats.

If you have any doubts about adding a supplement to your pet's diet, talk to your veterinarian. It's better to ask questions first than to worry about your pet if the supplement causes a problem.

Food Supplements

People have used whole foods and food remedies for thousands of years to help people and their domestic animals stay healthy. If you use food as a source of vitamins, minerals, and other nutrients, over-supplementation isn't usually a problem because the body expels unneeded nutrients.

With whole food supplements, keep in mind cats need to eat diets very high in meat, and any plants and plant matter should be a small part of the diet. If you wish to supplement your cat's diet with some apple, for example, offer only a tiny bit of apple the size of a pencil eraser.

- **Alfalfa:** Although farmers most commonly feed alfalfa to livestock, this supplement has nutrients that are also beneficial to dogs and cats. It contains proteins, vitamins, minerals, and *phytonutrients*. It is thought to have cancer-fighting properties, and it's good for mental health. Although cats rarely like dried alfalfa, they'll often nibble on fresh stalks.

> **DEFINITION**
>
> **Phytonutrients** are organic compounds in plants. They include carotene, lutein, and lycopene. They're not considered essential, but they contribute to good health.

- **Apple cider vinegar:** Apple cider vinegar is high in many minerals, has antibacterial qualities, and may help boost the immune system. Unfortunately, vinegar tastes bad, and most dogs and cats won't drink it. Some will consume food or special treats that contain just a tiny amount of apple cider vinegar.

- **Apples:** Apples contain many vitamins and minerals, are good for healthy skin, and promote good liver health. They also add fiber to the diet.

- **Bananas:** Bananas are an excellent food. They're high in potassium, fiber, and B complex. They also contain several minerals, including zinc. Dogs usually eat them eagerly, but cats aren't normally attracted to them. Sometimes, you can mix a tiny bit into a cat food recipe.

- **Bee pollen:** This whole food supplement contains a number of enzymes, antioxidants, and other essential nutrients. You only need to provide a small amount as a supplement, and most dogs and cats will eat it without a problem.

- **Bilberries:** This fruit is related to blueberries. It's good for eye health and aids the circulatory system. Dogs usually eat the berries. Cats will consume a small amount of bilberry juice if you mix it with their food.

- **Blue-green algae:** Spirulina is a blue-green, freshwater algae. It's an antioxidant, a good source of B complex vitamins and several minerals, and an excellent phytonutrient. Both dogs and cats will usually eat this readily. Beware, it often stains their stools blue-green. This isn't a problem, but it can be startling.

- **Blueberries:** These are full of antioxidants, vitamins, and minerals. Dogs will gobble blueberries down like candy, while you need only squeeze a few berries for their juice and add that to your cat's food.

- **Carrots:** These root vegetables are high in antioxidants and vitamins A, C, and E. They're also good sources of enzymes and minerals. To be readily metabolized by the body, carrots should be finely grated or chopped and lightly steamed.

- **Cottage cheese:** This dairy food is often overlooked, but it provides really good nutrition. It's a good source of protein, and it contains fatty acids and vitamins A, C, D, E, and K. Both dogs and cats eat it without issue.

- **Cranberries:** Cranberries are good medicine for bladder health. Although researchers admit these claims are true, studies haven't yet shown how or why cranberries work to improve bladder health—they just do! Dogs will sometimes eat cranberries, but cats won't. If you feel they can help your pet and your pet won't eat the berries, use a commercial capsule supplement.

- **Dandelions:** Dandelion leaves and flowers are rich in vitamins, minerals, and phytonutrients. Dandelion is also helpful for liver function and healing. Cats often nibble on shredded flowers. You can add finely diced greens to your dog's food.

- **Eggs:** Nutritionists often call eggs a biologically complete food because they contain all the essential amino acids. They are also rich in B complex vitamins, minerals, and vitamins A and E. The shells are also a good source of calcium. If you have a good source of clean eggs, you can feed your pet the yolks either cooked or raw. Don't feed your cat or dog raw egg whites too often because they bind up the B vitamins, preventing their absorption.

- **Fish:** Fish meat, whole fish, and fish oils are a good source of essential fatty acids.

- **Flaxseed meal:** Flaxseeds are high in fatty acids, B vitamins, and phytonutrients. They're also high in fiber. Of special interest for cats, flaxseeds are low in carbohydrates. Use flaxseed meal rather than oil because the oil can cause diarrhea. The meal is also more digestible for pets than oil. It has a nutty flavor, and both dogs and cats usually eat it quite readily.

- **Green beans:** These are a great source of fiber and full of vitamins and minerals. They're excellent for dogs on a weight-loss diet because they make the dog feel fuller. They can also be good dog treats. For cats, dice them finely before adding to the food. For both dogs and cats, steam the green beans before feeding to make them digestible.

- **Honey:** Honey is very nutritious, and it's high in protein; carbohydrates; minerals; B complex; and vitamins C, D, and E. Dogs love it because they have a sweet tooth just like people. Cats aren't attracted to sweets, but they'll readily eat a tiny bit of honey mixed in with food.

- **Kefir:** This is a cultivated, enzyme-rich food filled with friendly microorganisms, much like yogurt. It's made from grains, and it stimulates the digestive enzymes, thereby making the intestinal tract function better. Dogs can digest it well, but cats may do better with yogurt.

- **Kelp:** This seaweed, when dried, is an excellent source of iodine. It's rich in many minerals. When you mix it in with food, both dogs and cats will eat it. Use only a tiny bit—a pinch—as a supplement. Kelp is high in iodine; when given in excess, this can affect the thyroid gland function.

- **Molasses:** This is high in potassium and B complex vitamins. Dogs usually like it, but cats don't. If you mix a few drops in with food, however, most cats will eat it.

- **Nutritional yeast:** This is grown on molasses. It's a nonactive yeast, which means it won't raise bread. It's full of B vitamins, protein, and trace minerals. Dogs will eat it eagerly and digest it well; don't give it to cats because it can cause gastrointestinal upsets.

- **Papaya:** This fruit is very important for good intestinal health. Not only does it help calm the intestinal tract and prevent infections in the colon, it contains papain, an effective digestive enzyme that can help your pet's intestinal tract function better. Dogs will eat ripe papaya raw when added to their food. Some cats may nibble on small pieces.

- **Pineapples:** Pineapple and pineapple juice contain bromelain, a digestive enzyme that assists the body in digesting and metabolizing foods. Not many dogs and cats like the taste, so be sure to mix it very well into the food.

- **Pumpkin:** This very nutritious vine fruit from the squash family is high in fiber, so much so that many use it to calm an overactive bowel. Pumpkin is also a good source of minerals, especially calcium, potassium, and zinc, and it's high in antioxidants. To feed your pet pumpkin, offer it cooked and mashed or grated and steamed. Dogs usually like it so much they will gnaw on raw rinds, but the rinds aren't easily digested.

- **Squash:** There are several kinds of squash, all containing high levels of fiber, minerals, and assorted vitamins. To serve squash to your cat or dog, grate it into fine pieces and steam.

- **Sweet potatoes:** These need to be cooked well prior to feeding them to your pet because the nutrition isn't as readily available—less digestible—to carnivores when raw. They're high in beta carotene, antioxidants, and fiber.

- **Vegetables:** Many dark green vegetables, especially spinach, broccoli, and collard greens, are excellent sources of vitamins and minerals. They also provide fiber. Finely chop or dice and lightly steam greens before serving them to your pet.

- **Wheat germ:** Wheat germ is very nutritious, containing vitamin E, B complex, and a variety of minerals. It's a great food for helping active dogs maintain energy and endurance. Avoid all wheat products if your dog or cat is allergic to wheat. Cats may have trouble digesting it.

- **Yogurt:** When a yogurt container's label indicates the yogurt contains live active cultures, then it's a good source of beneficial bacteria needed by the intestinal tract for optimal digestion. Yogurt is also a good source of protein, B_2, and calcium. Always get plain, unflavored yogurt.

- **Zucchini:** This summer squash is high in many minerals, as well as vitamins A, C, and K. It's a good source of fiber and is low in calories. Finely grate and lightly steam the zucchini for your dog or cat.

Many other foods also provide good nutrition. Most cheeses, for example, are high in protein and calcium, and pets who are otherwise lactose intolerant can eat and digest them without problems.

If you would like to add another food to your pet's diet, as an ingredient or as a supplement, first do some research to make sure the food is safe and beneficial for your dog or cat. You can easily research this information on the Internet.

GO NATURAL

Keep your pet's food and water bowls clean to prevent bacterial contamination from one meal to the next. Wash the dishes in the dishwasher daily, or wash them in hot soap and water, rinse them well, and let them air dry. Stainless-steel, glass, or porcelain bowls are the easiest to keep clean. Plastic bowls often harbor bacteria, even when washed frequently. Many pets will also develop chin acne when eating from plastic bowls.

Other Nutrients to Consider

Although foods are often the best choice for adding nutrients to your pet's food, there are some beneficial nutrients that are difficult to supply as foods. Here are some other supplements to consider:

- **Chondroitin:** This is found in animal cartilage and helps inhibit the enzymes that are destructive to joint tissue. Most chondroitin supplements also contain glucosamine. It is usually available in tablet form.

- **Cod liver oil:** While fish is a great ingredient to include in many pets' diets, cod liver oil is easier to use and it's a more concentrated supplement. It's rich in fat-soluble vitamins, including A and D. It's also a good source of essential fatty acids. It's usually sold in liquid or capsule form, and you can mix either into your pet's food.

- **Nuts:** These aren't normally considered a pet food, but nuts are very nutritious. Peanuts, for example, are good sources of B_3, B_6, vitamin E, and minerals. Almonds are good sources of potassium and calcium. Nuts also contain plant proteins and fatty acids. Dogs and cats don't easily digest whole nuts, so be sure to liquefy or purée them first. Plain peanut butter with no added ingredients is also great.

Your veterinarian may also have ideas about additional ingredients or supplements to try, especially if your pet has specific health problems. During the conversation with your vet, be sure to let him or her know everything you give your pet. This is particularly important with homemade diets because your vet may need to know what you're feeding your dog or cat.

A Recipe Supplement for Dogs and Cats

Dog and cat breeders often use a recipe called "Glop" for incidences in which a dog or cat needs supplemental nutrition. Perhaps a mother dog or cat had a hard time giving birth or doesn't have enough milk, or a puppy or kitten just needs a little extra. Glop is also a good supplement for a hard-working dog who needs a boost or a cat recovering from an illness. Glop is not a daily food; instead, it's a supplement designed to boost an animal's appetite or provide extra nutrition.

> 1 cup water
>
> 1 cup unsalted chicken broth
>
> 2 (¼-oz.) envelopes unflavored gelatin
>
> 1 cup goat's milk, fresh or canned
>
> 1 cup cooked chicken, finely shredded

1. Pour water and chicken broth into a microwave-safe bowl and add gelatin. Stir well.

2. Microwave mixture for 1 to 2 minutes, or until bubbling.

3. Add goat's milk and chicken. Stir well.

4. Refrigerate until gelatin has set.

5. Store in a refrigerator in an airtight container. Give cats and small dogs 1 teaspoon, medium-sized dogs 1 tablespoon, and large dogs 2 tablespoons. You can serve Glop alone or mixed in with regular food.

bone appétit!

How Much to Add?

When you're adding supplements to your pet's diet, keep in mind it doesn't take much to affect your pet's nutrition. A small cat or dog may need only 300 to 500 calories per day. Adding supplements to the diet can affect the diet very quickly.

Most nutritionists agree that supplements—all combined—should never add up to more than 10 percent of the animal's total dietary intake. Include whole foods, herbs, and even treats when calculating the percentage of supplements.

Herbal Supplements

Herbal supplements (or remedies) are plants thought to have nutritional or medicinal benefits. Plants have been used as medicine for as long as we know—definitely as far back as 5,000 years in ancient China. Native Americans and Europeans have been using plants for hundreds, if not thousands, of years.

The recent surge in using traditional remedies has come about because many people are concerned about the side effects that many modern drugs have, for both people and pets. Many people are also looking for more natural approaches to both nutrition and medicine.

With many herbs, the nutritional and medicinal benefits are hard to separate because many herbs are used for both. Consider ginger as an example. It's a good source of fiber, has vitamins E and B_6, and like many root vegetables, it contains a variety of minerals. In addition, it's great for digestive health. Ginger is also effective in reducing inflammation—and it's tasty!

PET ALERT

Always inform your veterinarian about the supplements you're giving your pet. For example, your vet needs to know if your dog is receiving ginger because if she or he is undergoing chemotherapy treatments, the ginger may conflict with the drug's cancer-fighting abilities.

In this section, I've listed herbs only by their nutritional and digestive benefits. I'll address their use as remedies for other conditions in Part 4.

- **Chamomile:** This herb is calming for both the body and the intestinal tract. Pet owners have used it for car sickness in pets. You can find it in teas, which many dogs will drink, but it's also available in capsule form.

- **Ginger:** This root's primary use, other than as a flavor in food, is to calm an upset intestinal tract. You can find it as a food, as a powdered spice, and in capsule form.

- **Ginseng:** Ginseng can help animals with diabetes because it helps keep blood sugar stable. It's usually found in capsule form.

- **Goldenseal:** This herb works as an antibacterial in the intestinal tract. Find it in capsule form.

- **Peppermint:** This mint is calming for the stomach and intestinal tract, and pet owners often use it for car sickness. You can usually find it in teas, but plants will grow readily in the garden, and you can feed fresh leaves and flowers to your pet. Cats often enjoy the leaves and flowers.

Don't assume a natural product is safe simply because it comes from nature. There are many substances that are natural that are also deadly. Choose any product, natural or not, with care. If you have any concerns or questions about adding herbal supplements or remedies, talk to your veterinarian. If your vet's not familiar with herbs, ask for a referral to a local holistic veterinarian for guidance.

Commercial Supplements

The field of commercial supplements for pets is growing tremendously, fueled primarily by pet owners looking for more natural solutions to their pet's needs. The quality of these supplements varies widely because of a lack of regulatory control. The products vary by type, too. Some are nutritional, adding nutrients to the foods. Some tout benefits for certain pets, either cats or dogs, or growing puppies, or older animals. Some are made of whole foods while others contain synthetic ingredients.

Consumers need to do their homework before using these products. Check into the company and find out how much research they do. Do an Internet search and see what reviews look like for the products. Then ask your holistic veterinarian what she knows about the products. Commercial supplements can be found at pet stores and online pet supply stores.

Some well-known supplements that have been on the market for quite a while, and have good reviews, include the following:

- **Canine Bladder Control** is designed to help dogs, especially older ones, who suffer from incontinence. It contains pumpkin seed powder, rehmannia glutinosa, wild yam, soy protein extract, corn silk, saw palmetto extract, olive leaf extract, and vitamin B_6.

- **Dr. Billinghurst's BARF Plus Supplement** is made to supplement Dr. Billinghurst's raw food diet, called BARF (see Chapter 11). The supplement contains organic dried kelp, organic dried alfalfa meal, ground flaxseed, dried yeast, organic dried ground barley grass, organic dried ground wheatgrass, oat bran, organic apple pumice, and a long list of other foods.

- **Longevity,** by Springtime Inc., is a whole food supplement for dogs. It is based on the supernutrient spirulina, a blue-green algae. Other ingredients include bee pollen, beef or pork liver, yeast, chondroitin sulfate, glucosamine, ascorbic acid, citrus bioflavonoids, kelp, sea salts, and biotin.

- **Only Natural Pet's Super Daily Multi-Vitamin & Mineral Formula** is for dogs and cats of all ages and breeds. It contains not only vitamins and minerals, but also amino acids, enzymes, and essential fatty acids.

- **Only Natural Pet's Vital Digest** is for both dogs and cats. It adds digestive enzymes to increase digestive health and improve food metabolism.

- **Tri-Natural's Missing Link Supplement for Cats** is a whole food supplement designed to fill in the nutritional gaps in a cat's diet. Ingredients include flaxseed, blackstrap molasses, rice bran, dried yeast, freeze-dried liver, sunflower seeds, alfalfa, carrot, freeze-dried bone, fish meal, oyster, sprouted green barley, kelp, lecithin, and yucca extract.

Determining your pet's needs can be difficult. It's critical to ensure that your dog or cat is eating the best diet possible, whether that is a commercial food, a homemade raw food diet, or a home-cooked one. If you're feeding a homemade diet, most veterinarians recommend adding a vitamin and mineral supplement, but again that depends on the recipes you're using. If in doubt, talk to a pet nutritionist and/or your veterinarian.

Choosing Commercial Supplements

Ideally, any supplement you choose to add to your pet's diet will have an obvious benefit. It's usually a bad idea to add something just because it sounds great or because your neighbor is giving it to his or her dog. Have a definite reason for adding a supplement and choose the one that addresses that reason. Again, don't hesitate to talk to your veterinarian about any supplements you would like to use, especially if your pet is being treated for any health issues. Some supplements can interfere with medications, so it's important to check with your vet before starting a supplement.

If you're considering using a commercial supplement, the company name should be familiar to you or your vet. Although smaller companies and off brands may be fine, they could be a problem, too. Do some research, find out where the company is located, see what products they produce, and take a look at their website. Look for reviews on the Internet. Only use the product if you feel comfortable with the company.

Does the company have proof the supplement is effective? Nancy Kay, DVM, says, "Companies that support clinical research and have their products used in clinical trials with results published in peer-reviewed journals are more likely to have a quality product." The product label should list all the ingredients in the supplement— active and inactive. The active ingredients may be the vitamin, mineral, or herb. The inactive may be the ingredients that form the tablet or capsule.

Look for other instructions, too. Is the supplement safe for both dogs and cats? What is the dosage? How much should you give your pet and how often?

Make sure any supplements you plan to use are cost-effective. It would be a shame to begin a supplement, see it begin to work for your pet, and then not be able to continue it because it's too expensive.

It may actually seem like a small thing, but it's important that you can give the supplement to your pet. If it tastes bad, or it smells awful, and your pet doesn't want to eat it, it's going to be difficult to make sure your pet gets it.

Let's Talk Treats

Let's face it, treats are often more important to pet owners than they are to our pets. Sure, dogs and cats love the extra food, but treats are a way for pet owners to show their love to their pets. Too many treats, however, can result in weight gain and even obesity. Too many treats given when the pet demands them can also lead to behavioral problems. It's important that you give treats sparingly and that you take great care when choosing treats.

DOG TALK

Puppies and dogs who are participating in training with their owners often consume quite a few treats. It's important to choose good-quality treats so your dog's diet isn't upset and so he's not eating a lot of junk food. Try dicing some cheese or meat into small pieces and putting the pieces in a small plastic bag in the freezer; you can use these as a training treat. Because it's frozen, it's easier to handle. Your dog then gets good food for training treats, rather than junk.

For dogs, treats can be small chunks of carrots or apples, bits of cheese, or pieces of meat. Most cats enjoy small pieces of meat, but many also enjoy tiny bits of aged cheese (such as cheddar). These treats are, for the most part, better choices than most commercial treats because commercial brands are often cereal grain recipes; often contain wheat; and usually contain artificial colors, flavorings, and preservatives.

You can make homemade treats for your dog or cat. When you do this, you control the quality, just as you can do with your pet's daily diet.

Turkey Treats for Dogs and Cats

This treat is good food, but is just that—a treat—and is not a daily diet.

> 2 eggs, hardboiled and shelled
> 1 cup cooked turkey, finely chopped
> 1 cup cooked sweet potato, finely chopped

1. Crumble hardboiled eggs into a bowl. Mash with a large fork until yolks and whites are mixed well.

2. Add turkey and sweet potato to eggs and mix lightly.

3. Store in a refrigerator in an airtight container. Offer cats and small dogs 1 teaspoon of the mixture as a treat. Medium-sized dogs can have 1 tablespoon; large dogs can have 2 tablespoons. You can also add the same amount to your pet's daily food as a side dish or supplement.

meow, love, eat

Catnip and Cats

Cats and catnip seem to go hand in paw, or flower in paw to be more correct. Catnip has a mild stimulating effect on many (but not all) cats, who like to eat it and roll around in it. Older cats may even rediscover their inner kitten.

CAT CHAT

Catnip is in the mint family, is an attractive herb, and is easy to grow. In mild climates, you can grow catnip outside. In colder climates, it grows well inside at a sunny window with a ledge. When the plant blossoms, pick the flowers, buds, and the top soft parts of the stems. These are the parts cats like best. And by only removing those parts, you ensure the plant will regrow and reblossom in a few weeks. Check with your local nursery. Your cat will love it!

You can give some of the fresh catnip to your cat, but dry most of it so you can use it after the growing season is over. There are several ways to dry the catnip. If you have a food dehydrator, place the entire stem—with leaves, buds, and flowers—on the racks. Spread the stems out so they don't overlap. Dry for two to three hours or until the thickest stem is completely dry.

If you don't have a food dehydrator, you can hang the catnip to dry. Gather the thick part of the stems as if you're making a bouquet. Use a string to tie the stems together tightly. Then, turn the bouquet upside down (flowers down) and hang the catnip in a cool, dry location (such as your garage or pantry). Drying time will vary according to temperature and ambient humidity.

Dried catnip can be stored in a plastic bag for months. Just keep it dry and store it in a cool place. However, if the catnip is fresh or not thoroughly dry, freeze or refrigerate it in an airtight container to prevent mold.

You can use catnip as a treat during playtime; just drop some on the carpet and watch your cat have fun. You can stuff your cat's toys with fresh catnip, or make some new toys. Or, if you get a new scratching post for your cat, rub catnip into the post's covering so your cat will be attracted to it.

The Least You Need to Know

- Supplements are anything you add to your dog's or cat's daily diet, and can include foods, vitamins and minerals, herbs, and treats.

- Whole foods can be nutritious supplements, and many dogs and cats will eat them eagerly.

- Herbs carry with them medicinal properties, and can be beneficial to digestive processes and the intestinal tract.

- Treats, when given on a daily basis, must be considered a supplement.

- Supplements should not exceed 10 percent of your dog's or cat's daily diet.

- Most cats enjoy catnip. This herb from the mint family is easy to grow, and it provides a stimulating treat for cats.

Your Pet's Health from A to Z

This part includes an extensive list of health concerns, presented in alphabetical order for ease of use. With each health concern, I provide some natural health remedies or therapies and explain how you might use them.

It's important to remember that every dog and cat reacts differently to each remedy, so always keep an eye on your pet, especially when you first introduce it to him or her. If you have any doubts or concerns about your approach to care, talk to your veterinarian.

In the last chapter, I discuss aging pets. It's hard to watch our pets grow older and become frail, but thanks to natural remedies and therapies, you can help your dog or cat cope with the inevitable challenges that come with this stage in life.

Allergies to Conjunctivitis

14

In This Chapter

- Allergies irritate many pets
- Caring for a pet with cancer
- Other pet ailments
- Understanding causes and prevention
- Natural remedies that can help
- Knowing when to call your veterinarian

The first few letters of the alphabet contain some interesting yet potentially heartbreaking health and behavioral issues. In this chapter, I'll identify each dog and cat problem, provide a list of symptoms, and describe potential ways to prevent the problem.

There are a variety of natural remedies available to help your dog's or cat's health issues, ranging from changing your pet's diet to increasing exercise, as well as herbal remedies, homeopathic medicine, acupuncture, and chiropractic care. Keep in mind that every pet is an individual; how much exercise your pet needs, and dosages for homeopathic medications and herbal remedies, will vary. If you have questions or concerns, talk to your veterinarian, a holistic veterinarian, an acupuncturist, or another natural remedies professional.

Allergies

Both dogs and cats can develop allergies, although they're more common in dogs. Some dog breeds are more prone to allergies than others; those include Golden Retrievers, Labrador Retrievers, German Shepherds, Boxers, Shar Peis, Dalmatians, and many of the small terrier breeds.

An allergic response is the immune system responding to a substance to which your dog or cat is allergic. An allergic response can develop into inflammation and infections. In the worst cases, it can cause life-threatening *anaphylactic shock*. A food allergy can trigger itching, scratching, chewing (on paws and tail), hives, and even hair loss. An allergic response can result from contact with something, too, like molds, mildews, and even grass. A pet can also inhale something (like pollen) that triggers an allergic response.

DEFINITION

Anaphylactic shock is an immediate, serious allergic response. Symptoms of anaphylaxis include swelling, itching, pain, redness, pale gums, agitation, pacing, vomiting, diarrhea, and difficulty breathing. If allowed to continue, the animal will go into anaphylactic shock. In this situation, your pet needs immediate emergency veterinary care to prevent death.

You may find it difficult to identify the substance causing the allergic response. If you suspect a food allergy, your vet will likely recommend a food elimination diet. Switch your pet to a diet with a unique protein he or she hasn't eaten previously—such as rabbit, venison, or elk—as well as a unique carbohydrate like yams. Feed your pet this diet until the allergy symptoms cease and then add in one food ingredient per week that he or she has previously eaten—beef, for example, or cheese. When the symptoms reappear, you can confirm a food that causes an allergic response in your pet. Don't stop the test, though, as more than one food may be triggering the response.

It's not easy to pinpoint inhalant and contact allergies. You can't see what your dog inhaled, and the thing causing an allergic response may no longer be around your pet by the time the reaction occurs.

Allergy tests are available through your vet, although their effectiveness varies depending on the allergy involved. If you're at a loss as to what might be causing the allergic response, talk to your veterinarian about allergy tests.

Causes

A tendency toward pets developing allergies appears to be an inherited trait, although the experts don't yet know why or how. The specific allergies pets develop aren't necessarily inherited, just the potential to develop allergies. So if a mother dog is allergic to flea bites, her offspring may not have that specific allergy, but they may develop other allergies later.

GO NATURAL

It's easy to pinpoint an allergic response to fleas. If your dog or cat has fleas and is scratching, biting at his or her skin, and your pet's skin is red and inflamed, your pet is allergic to flea bites. This reaction can easily turn into skin infections. NaturVet makes Herbal Flea Powder that you can use on puppies, dogs, kittens, and cats. You can also use it on the pet's bedding or anywhere the pet rests or sleeps. It contains rosemary, an herb, and cedar oil. For details, go to www.naturvet.com.

Prevention

You must identify an allergy before you can prevent future allergic responses. When you know what the substance is, you can often prevent your pet from coming in contact with it. An allergy to beef or wheat, for example, is easy to prevent. Just read labels carefully and never allow your pet to eat beef or wheat.

Inhalant and contact allergies are a little more difficult. When possible, help your pet avoid the substances that cause a reaction. If your pet is allergic to grass, for example, keep him off the grass. But just as with people, avoiding inhalant allergies can be difficult; we can't see what's in the air we breathe.

Remedies

If your pet has one or more food allergies, managing the diet is your most important task. You may find commercial foods without those ingredients, or you can develop a raw food or home-cooked diet that doesn't use those ingredients. (See Chapters 11 and 12 for more on raw food and home-cooked diets, respectively.)

For pets with allergies, veterinarians often recommend increasing the pet's intake of whole foods containing antioxidants. Foods such as carrots, blueberries, spinach, and broccoli are high in antioxidants and provide good nutrition to boot. In whole-food form, your pet's digestive system can more easily metabolize the antioxidants, and the risk of an overdose is significantly less than if you gave your pet a commercial supplement.

Arsenicum albus and formica rufe are both homeopathic remedies for allergies. The herbal remedies alfalfa, burdock root, chamomile, dandelion, echinacea, gingko, licorice root, red clover, and sarsaparilla are also good for allergies.

The Honest Kitchen's tea, Invigor, is designed to support the immune systems of dogs and cats. It contains kelp, astragalus, hawthorne berries, olive leaf, spirulina, and watercress.

Make sure your pet is getting a good variety of foods with essential fatty acids, too. Research has shown that many pets—especially cats—who are not eating sufficient fatty acids are prone to allergic responses. Fish, fish oils, and flaxseed meal all contain good amounts of fatty acids.

A dog or cat with itching allergic skin may benefit from an oatmeal bath. Put ½ cup of oatmeal and ½ cup of warm water in a blender and blend until you've created a paste. Using this paste in place of shampoo, work it into the skin of a wet dog or cat, massage for a few minutes to let it calm the skin, and then rinse. After rinsing, pour white vinegar or apple cider vinegar over your pet's fur, work it into the coat, and then rinse again. Vinegar also calms and soothes irritated skin.

> **GO NATURAL**
>
> Chamomile tea is calming for the mind and body. You can give it to your pet if he or she will drink it, or you can mix the tea in with your pet's food. The tea can also be applied to irritated skin.

Ginkgo biloba inhibits histamine production. The body produces histamines as a part of the allergic response. You can give your pet ginkgo biloba in capsule form.

Talk to Your Veterinarian

Consult your veterinarian about allergies if you feel your pet needs tests to identify the particular allergen. Call your vet if you feel your natural remedies aren't helping your pet, or if the allergic response is continuing. Always call your veterinarian if the allergy symptoms suddenly get worse because your pet may be developing an anaphylactic reaction.

Sometimes your pet needs modern medicine. One of the most common ways to calm an allergic response is with a corticosteroid, either through an injection or a pill. Although these are powerful medications with some potential side effects (depending on the animal, the problem, and the dosage), they're life savers when it comes to stopping an allergic response.

Arthritis

Osteoarthritis and degenerative arthritis are two disorders that tend to both be called arthritis. They are debilitating chronic conditions that can make an animal's life miserable.

When the cartilage that cushions a joint breaks down, inflammation occurs. Arthritis can affect any joint, but it's more common in the hip and elbow joints. Experts believe more than 25 percent of all dogs will suffer from arthritis as they age. Cats, however, are not nearly as prone to this as dogs.

Arthritis tends to begin gradually, and changes in the pet's behavior are often the first signs of it. The dog or cat may begin moving slower, especially when getting up from a nap. The pet may not want to jump, may not run as much, or may be reluctant to walk as far as he or she once did. Some pets will become grumpy and show soreness when you touch them. The joint may also be swollen and warm.

> **DOG TALK**
>
> Warmth feels good on arthritic bones and joints. If your older dog wants to lie outside in the sun, let him. On cold days, offer him a warm blanket to curl up in or a sweater to wear.

Your veterinarian can diagnose arthritis. He or she will first examine your pet, test your pet's reactions to range of motion tests, and will watch your pet walk and, if possible, run. Your vet may also recommend x-rays.

Causes

Arthritis is apparently inherited in people, or the tendency toward it is, because it tends to run in families. However, we don't know why this is the case. The same is true of dogs and cats; it's apparently inherited, but research hasn't identified how and why.

Injuries can also cause arthritis. Traumatic arthritis can occur after an injury, such as a strain or sprain, in the same leg as the injury, but it may develop years after the accident occurred. Athletic dogs and cats who push themselves hard and dogs who work hard are more prone to this than dogs and cats who are less active.

Prevention

Because arthritis is inherited, breeders should take care when choosing the animals they will use in their breeding program. Unfortunately, this is difficult because arthritis doesn't usually show up until later in life, after the animal has already had offspring.

A good diet that includes antioxidants and fatty acids may slow the disease's progression. Unfortunately, research hasn't provided any answers for how to prevent the disease definitively.

Remedies

One of the best ways to keep arthritis from crippling your pet is to keep him or her moving. If your pet stops moving and becomes inactive, the joints may become even stiffer and more painful. Although your pet may move slowly when he or she first gets up from a nap, the joints will loosen up once he or she stretches and begins walking.

For dogs who like to swim (and those rare cats who like water), swimming is an excellent exercise. There's no weight on the joints during swimming, but the body is moving. If you have or can find a heated pool, that is even better because cold tightens arthritic joints.

Weight control is very important to controlling arthritis symptoms. Too much weight can put more stress on painful joints. A lean cat or dog is going to be more comfortable than an overweight animal.

Glucosamine, either as glucosamine chondroitin or glucosamine sulfate, is highly recommended by veterinarians for arthritis. It helps the body repair damaged cartilage, and it has anti-inflammatory properties.

Several foods have natural anti-inflammatory properties. These include kelp, salmon, papaya, blueberries, broccoli, and sweet potatoes. Although these rarely relieve all of the inflammation for a pet with arthritis, they certainly can help.

The herb boswellia is an anti-inflammatory that pet owners have used effectively for pets with arthritis. A 2004 study on dogs with joint pain showed significant improvement in the dogs taking boswellia. Large doses can cause nausea and diarrhea. Other supplements with anti-inflammatory properties include yucca, nettle, licorice root, alfalfa, and parsley. Homeopathic remedies include belladonna and silicea.

The Honest Kitchen's Lithe Tea is designed to support normal joint health and movement. It has received rave reviews from pet owners who are using the tea for their dogs. It contains alfalfa, white willow bark, yucca, ginger, red clover, and boswellia.

Acupuncture and chiropractic therapies can reduce the discomfort of arthritis in your pet. Treatment regimens and schedules vary depending on the animal's condition and response to the treatment. A daily massage from you will also help keep the body warm and soft and help prevent some stiffness.

Managing the pet's environment can be a huge help for the arthritic pet. Many manufacturers have created ramps and stairs of various kinds to help pets get in and out of the car or up and down on the furniture. Something as simple as a hot water bottle or a heated pet bed can also help ease sore muscles and joints. Be careful using electric heating pads, though, as not all have temperature controls. Test the heated pad with your hand to make sure it's a comfortable heat, then check it often to make sure it doesn't get too hot.

Talk to Your Veterinarian

If your dog or cat is limping, talk to your veterinarian. After all, you want to know exactly what the problem is. Don't assume it is arthritis; it may be an issue with a tendon or ligament in the knee, hip or elbow dysplasia, or some other injury.

After your veterinarian has diagnosed the issue, talk to him or her about natural remedies you wish to use. Your vet may recommend an anti-inflammatory—usually a corticosteroid—to reduce inflammation. He or she could prescribe it as a short-term treatment while you begin natural remedies. If the situation changes, however, and your pet becomes more stiff, experiences more pain, or appears unhappy, contact your veterinarian again.

Bladder Infections

A bladder infection, or cystitis, is an infection of the lining of the bladder. Pets with diabetes are more prone to this, as are older animals, pets on certain medications, and those who tend to go for long hours without urinating. Often, a urethral infection occurs first, and then the bacteria moves up the urethra and into the bladder.

A dog or cat with a bladder infection may lick at the genitals more than normal, urinate more frequently, and cry when urinating. There may be blood in the urine.

Your veterinarian can make a diagnosis by conducting a urinalysis test to look for bacteria, white blood cells, and red blood cells in your pet's urine.

Causes

Bladder infections are caused by bacteria. Although the bladder is normally sterile, bacteria can move up the urethra into the bladder, thereby causing an infection.

PET ALERT

Dogs and cats must relieve themselves on a regular basis. Asking a pet to go for long time periods without relieving himself or herself is very unfair. If your pet must stay home alone for long hours each day, make sure there's a litter box, doggy door, or some other means available to your pet, so he or she can go outside and relieve the bladder.

Prevention

Female dogs who squat very low to urinate can actually touch the ground when doing so, potentially picking up bacteria in the process. Dogs and cats who don't groom themselves well can build up bacteria on the genitals. Wash these pets often with a mild soap and water to help prevent infections.

Pets with highly alkaline urine (urine with a high pH) are more apt to develop bladder infections than pets with highly acidic urine (urine with a low pH). Feeding your pets diets high in animal proteins can help create acidic urine. Diets high in cereal grains tend to produce alkaline urine.

Remedies

Cranberries have been the standard remedy for anyone with a bladder infection—be they human, feline, or canine—for a very long time. Even people who don't use any other natural remedies know about cranberry's benefits. Cranberry makes the urine more acidic, and it helps the lining of the bladder resist bacteria.

Blackberries and raspberries seem to have a similar action, although researchers haven't studied them nearly as much as cranberries. They will lower the urine's pH, just like cranberries.

Dandelion can help the body flush toxins from its system, including the bladder. Echinacea and goldenseal help fight inflammation and strengthen the immune system. You can use them in conjunction with cranberries. Other herbs that benefit the immune system include dandelion leaf, gingko, marshmallow (the herb, not the candy), plaintain, and yarrow.

Keeping the immune system strong is important. The Honest Kitchen's Invigor tea is designed to support the immune system of dogs and cats. It contains kelp, astragalus, hawthorne berries, olive leaf, spirulina, and watercress.

Glucosamine chondroitin, which pet owners normally use to treat their pets' arthritis and sore joints, has been effective in treating bladder infections in cats. So far, it hasn't shown the same benefit in dogs.

CAT CHAT

Cats can be reluctant to try new things, herbs included. If the herbs are diced or crumbled very small, you can mix them in with a favorite food, such as crumbled cheese, a hardboiled egg, or tuna.

Talk to Your Veterinarian

If your pet has trouble urinating or you see blood in the urine, call your veterinarian immediately so he or she can make a diagnosis. Then, talk to your vet about using natural remedies. She may wish to prescribe a round of antibiotics and have you follow up with cranberries, diet changes, and other natural remedies.

If your dog or cat is straining to urinate but isn't passing any urine, call your veterinarian immediately. This could be a blockage, which is potentially fatal if not treated right away. See Chapter 17 for more information.

Cancer

Cancer is one of the most dreaded diseases on the planet because it's so often fatal. Although researchers continue to explore cancer treatments, and the survivability for many cancers is also increasing, the diagnosis is still frightening.

Cancer is the unlimited, unrestrained reproduction of cells in the body. When a cell reproduces and divides, each new cell lives a normal lifetime (for that particular type of cell) and then dies. Cancer cells continue to reproduce more quickly and often live longer than normal cells. Problems occur when these rapidly reproducing cells spread and inhibit organ function.

Symptoms of cancer vary depending on the type of cancer and the organs involved. Some potential symptoms include appetite loss, weight loss, abnormal lumps or masses, and limping. The pet may also have difficulty performing a normal bodily function, such as eating, urinating, or defecating.

In many cases, the pet owner or veterinarian finds cancer when he or she feels a new lump or bump on the pet's body. A biopsy can then confirm the diagnosis.

GO NATURAL

Giving your pet a daily massage is a wonderful way to bond with your dog or cat. At the same time, you can tend to his or her grooming needs. As you massage, you can also learn what your pet's body feels like so you can detect any changes, including lumps or masses.

Causes

A cat or dog can inherit the tendency to develop cancer, especially certain types, just as humans can. Environmental toxins have been linked to cancer, as has secondhand smoke from cigarettes. Some viruses cause cancer, especially the feline leukemia virus and feline sarcoma virus. Some believe vaccines—or more correctly, too many vaccinations—are linked to increased incidences of cancer. Cancer is more common in aging pets than in younger ones.

Some dog breeds, unfortunately, are more prone to cancer than others. Bernese Mountain Dogs, Flat Coated Retrievers, Golden Retrievers, and Rottweilers appear to have a genetic tendency toward developing cancer at some point during their lifetime. The Morris Animal Foundation has just funded a $25 million research project to follow 2,500 Golden Retrievers throughout their lifetimes. They will be watching the dogs' diet, where the dogs live, their vaccinations, and everything else the dogs do, so hopefully they can identify some of the causes of cancer.

Prevention

The research and studies for how to prevent cancer are ongoing, for both people and pets. We have no idea what will develop in the future. Currently, several factors have been linked to cancer. First, limit—or better yet, eliminate—your pet's exposure to secondhand cigarette smoke. Cats and dogs aren't prone to lung cancer, but those living with smokers do develop it.

Consider not using pesticides, herbicides, and insecticides in your home and yard. Obviously, if your pet is infested with fleas or your house is being eaten by termites, you're going to need to do something. But use natural or nontoxic products whenever possible.

Be cautious about feeding your pets any commercial foods containing BHA, BHT, or ethoxyquin. Many pet owners are also avoiding the synthetic colors and flavorings found in many commercial pet foods. A healthy, high-quality diet, with all the essential fatty acids and high in antioxidants, is also important. (See Chapter 10 for a review of commercial pet food.)

Discuss your pet's vaccination schedule with your veterinarian. Vaccines are important and have saved thousands of pets' lives, but more isn't necessarily better. Today, even veterinary organizations are rethinking vaccination protocols.

Dog and cat breeders may be able to slow the advance of cancer simply by breeding only animals who are descended from long-lived ancestors who didn't die of cancer. Because some cancers are inheritable, this alone could make a difference.

Remedies

Although natural remedies can't cure cancer, they do have some benefits when used in conjunction with modern medicine's cancer-killing techniques. One of the most effective natural remedies is diet. The most success related to cancer treatment seems to result from a diet high in antioxidants and essential fatty acids, with higher amounts of animal protein, moderate amounts of complex carbohydrates, and no simple sugars. Proponents say this diet feeds the body, but not the rapidly growing cancer cells.

Herbal remedies that can help strengthen the immune system include echinacea and milk thistle. Astragalus, ashwagandha, and Reishi mushrooms have a beneficial effect on the immune system and may also slow cancerous cell growth. Red clover, burdock root, and alfalfa are also very good for strengthening the immune system.

There are a few commercial remedies companies have designed to help the immune system. One is made by Thorne Research, and is called Immugen. It contains vitamins, minerals, amino acids, botanicals, and other nutrients, including Reishi mushrooms. C-Caps from PetAlive uses a combination of herbal remedies known for their antitumor properties. These products don't kill the cancer cells, but they slow them down (in theory).

The Honest Kitchen's Invigor tea supports the immune system of dogs and cats. It contains kelp, astragalus, hawthorne berries, olive leaf, spirulina, and watercress.

Acupuncture is helpful in suppressing pain from cancer. Veterinarians often recommend pet owners give it to their pets in conjunction with natural remedies and conventional cancer treatments.

> **CAT CHAT**
>
> Although cats are more sensitive to many substances than dogs, they tend to handle chemotherapy fairly well. The type of cancer and chemotherapy treatment obviously affect the end result, but chemotherapy can usually give the cat at least several more months of life.

Talk to Your Veterinarian

A veterinarian must make the initial cancer diagnosis. Even if you feel the lump or mass first, your vet will have to determine exactly what the mass is.

Modern medical treatments for cancer vary depending on the type of cancer. A surgeon might be able to remove the cancer entirely, or at least reduce its size. Radiation works by damaging the cancer cells so they can't reproduce. Chemotherapy entails a vet administering drugs of different kinds, depending on the cancer, to damage the cancer cells. What your veterinarian recommends will vary due to the type of cancer, your pet's age, his or her state of health, and the potential for success.

Cataracts

A cataract is an opaque spot on the eye's lens. The spot may be small or large, and slightly cloudy or completely opaque. Essentially, a cataract is the loss of the normal transparency of the eye's lens. These are more common in dogs and are quite rare in cats.

As cataracts develop, they're quite noticeable. The lens will develop a milky or bluish color, rather than having the clear appearance it normally has. The dog may begin to bump into things, signaling he's not seeing well. He may squint or try hard to see things. The dog may become reluctant to do activities he's done before or to try anything new.

Although cataracts are visible, your veterinarian should examine your pet so he or she can determine whether it's caused by an eye injury. In addition, your vet can see whether the eye is otherwise healthy.

Causes

Unfortunately, the tendency to develop cataracts is a far too commonly inherited disorder in dogs. Many breeds are prone to them, including Cocker Spaniels, Bichon Frises, Fox Terriers, Standard Poodles, Golden Retrievers, and Labrador Retrievers. Although most cataracts appear in dogs as they grow older, juvenile cataracts can appear in dogs less than 6 years old.

Cataracts can be caused by nutritional deficiencies, especially diets lacking in beta-carotenes and antioxidants. Puppies fed a milk replacement formula delinquent in arginine may develop cataracts. Eye injuries can also cause cataracts to form. Unlike inherited cataracts, these often disappear with treatment.

Cats can develop cataracts, especially those caused by eye injuries. They aren't as prone to inherited or old-age type cataracts.

Prevention

Feeding your pet a good-quality diet can help prevent cataracts caused by poor nutrition. Trying to protect the eyes from injuries may also help. For example, don't let your dog ride in the car with his head hanging out the opened window. Not only is this unsafe should you have to brake or swerve, but also the wind, dust, and flying insects can injure your dog's eyes.

The most important prevention, however, is for breeders to have all their breeding animals checked for inherited eye disorders. A veterinary ophthalmologist can perform an eye exam prior to the breeder selecting animals for breeding.

 DOG TALK

The Canine Eye Registry Foundation (CERF) has a website at www.vmdb. org/cerf.html, which maintains a database of dogs whose eyes have been examined by veterinary ophthalmologists for inherited eye diseases. The goal is to breed healthier dogs in the future.

Remedies

Inherited disorders can't be corrected with natural remedies, but they can prevent cataracts caused by poor nutrition. Blueberries are high in antioxidants and carrots are good sources of beta-carotenes. Dark green vegetables contain nutrients for healthy vision, including zinc and other minerals, and lutein. Vitamins A, C, and E also promote good eye health.

Talk to Your Veterinarian

If your pet is able to see enough to get around and doesn't seem anxious about his or her vision, your pet may not need after-diagnosis veterinary care. If your dog becomes completely blind, however, and isn't adjusting well to blindness, talk to your veterinarian about surgical removal of the cataracts. If your pet's eyes are otherwise healthy, and your dog is healthy enough to undergo surgery, this may be a viable treatment.

Cognitive Disorder

Cognitive disorder, often also called senile cognitive disorder or cognitive dysfunction syndrome, generally affects older pets and is often compared to Alzheimer's disease. Dogs may be 11 years old or older when it develops, while most cats won't develop the disorder until their mid-teens.

Symptoms generally include wandering aimlessly, as if the pet doesn't remember where he is, as well as exhibiting a feeling of being lost. Your pet may display a lack of energy as well as no desire to do familiar things, like going for a walk, playing, or interacting with the owner. Some pets may not recognize their owners. In addition, housetraining skills may lapse, there may be changes in the day and night cycles, and the pet may even forget to eat or drink.

CAT CHAT

Older cats with cognitive disorder tend to become significantly more vocal than normal, crying and yowling when they feel lost or disoriented.

Many older pets may develop one or two of these symptoms during the aging process, but the diagnosis is usually pretty clear-cut when several are present in the animal. A visit to the veterinarian is usually in order, even if only to confirm your thoughts or to see if any other health problems exist.

Causes

Researchers are currently working to identify causes of this disorder. We don't even know if this is one disorder or the symptoms of several health problems. A lack of oxygen going to the older pet's brain may be one cause; plaque in the brain, much like with Alzheimer's disease, may be another.

Prevention

Because we know so little about cognitive disorder, we know little about preventing it. Some experts recommend providing the best diet and health care possible during the pet's early life.

Remedies

One of the best things you can do for a pet with cognitive disorder is to remain calm in your pet's presence. If you're upset, stressed, or emotional, and—worse yet—if you get angry with your pet over housetraining lapses, your pet will sense this and become even more confused and upset. Maintain a calm environment for your pet as much as possible.

If your pet's housetraining lapses increase, limit your pet's access to the entire house, just as you did when your pet was a puppy or kitten. Take the dog outside often, or set up multiple cat litter boxes. Gingko biloba is often good for incontinence.

Protect your pet. A confused pet won't recognize dangers, such as rosebushes with thorns. Your pet will need the same supervision and protection that a puppy or kitten would need. In addition, don't let your cat outside where he could wander off and get lost, and keep your dog on a leash.

The B complex vitamins are important for a healthy brain. Pets with cognitive disorder function better when they consume more foods high in the B complex vitamins. These foods include liver, tuna, turkey, bananas, and kefir.

Herbal remedies that can assist with brain functions include alfalfa, gingko biloba, ginseng, horsetail, and CoQ10.

The Honest Kitchen has two teas that are good for older pets. Invigor is made from ingredients that support a healthy immune system, including kelp, astragalus, hawthorne berries, olive leaf, spriulina, and watercress. Lithe Tea is made to support normal joint health and movement, but it has also shown to be helpful to elderly dogs in many ways, including alleviating depression. It's made with alfalfa, white willow bark, yucca, ginger, red clover, and boswellia.

Talk to Your Veterinarian

If you suspect your pet is developing a cognitive disorder, talk to your veterinarian to eliminate any other health problems that could cause problems in the brain. Your vet may prescribe the medication Anipryl, which has been shown to be effective in slowing the disease in dogs.

Conjunctivitis

Conjunctivitis is the inflammation of the conjunctiva, the membranes lining the eyelids. These tissues work as barriers, trapping dust and debris, to protect the eyes. The first sign of conjunctivitis is usually a discharge, sometimes clear, but often it's yellow or green. Your pet's eyes may become watery and teary, with the hair and skin under the eye remaining wet. Sometimes, the pet will act uncomfortable, blinking or squinting frequently. He or she may also rub his or her face or paw at the eyes.

Causes

Most cases of mild conjunctivitis are caused by an eye irritant, such as dust or dirt. These cases don't last long and don't often require veterinary treatment. Allergies can also cause eye irritation, as can viruses. Blocked tear ducts, cornea irritation or injuries, and eyelashes irritating the eyes can all cause eye inflammation.

Prevention

Most dogs and cats will have a case or two of conjunctivitis at some point during their lives, if for no other reason than that their eyes are delicate. Many different things can irritate them, including dust, strong winds, and allergies.

GO NATURAL

Several manufacturers make eye protection for dogs and cats. These are goggles with tinted lenses that are held in place with elastic that goes behind your pet's head. Although most dogs can, with some praise and treats, learn to accept them, cats aren't always so tolerant. Introduce the goggles slowly to your cat, give her a special treat, and tell her how special she is to wear them. You can find pet goggles at pet stores or at online pet supply stores.

Remedies

If you feel your pet's conjunctivitis is caused by an allergy, wash out the eyes with saline solution. Then, concentrate on helping your pet deal with the cause of the problem—the allergies.

If the eyes are tearing or have matter in them, rinse the eyes with a saline solution and then gently wash around the eye to remove any dried matter. A soft soap that won't sting the eyes or some baby shampoo will work.

PetAlive Eye-Heal is a commercial formula created to help the eyes recover from infections and injuries. It contains meadowsweet, burdock, and rosemary.

Talk to Your Veterinarian

If your pet rubs at the eyes, squints, or won't open his or her eyes, call your veterinarian. If the discharge is green, the discharge increases, or the eyes are heavily crusted with matter, call your veterinarian

The Least You Need to Know

- Cat and dog breeders can reduce some health problems by choosing breeding animals wisely.
- Although looking at the means of preventing health problems is a good practice, unfortunately not all are preventable.
- Natural remedies can include nutritional supplements, herbal remedies, acupuncture, and other techniques.
- Work with your veterinarian and make sure he or she knows what natural remedies you're giving your pet.

Constipation to Feline Urinary Tract Disease

Chapter 15

In This Chapter

- Understanding the damage caused by dental disease
- Identifying contagious and serious feline diseases
- Understanding causes and prevention
- Tips for using natural remedies
- Knowing when to talk to your veterinarian

Generally, some health problems aren't the subject of polite dinner conversation, and constipation is one of those. Constipation can make your pet extremely uncomfortable, however, and sick if he or she doesn't find relief. Dental disease is a similar problem; it's unpleasant to think about, but it's very important to address.

In this chapter, for each of the health problems listed, I suggest a number of natural remedies. They range from a change in food or nutritional supplements to the use of herbal remedies, acupuncture, and more. As with all remedies, there's the potential for side effects, so watch your pet carefully when using any remedy.

It's important to remember that your veterinarian is an important part of this process. Even if you prefer to emphasize natural healing techniques, these often can be combined with modern veterinary medicine to provide the best care for your pet.

Constipation

Constipation occurs when a dog or cat is unable to pass feces or is having difficulty having a bowel movement. Every dog and cat has his or her own normal bowel habits; most pass feces twice a day. If an animal goes for more than two days without passing any feces, the stools become dry and hard, making it even more difficult to pass them.

The first sign of constipation, besides the lack of feces in the backyard or litter box, is straining. The animal may try to walk or move while in the arched position, or it may cry while straining. Other symptoms include a bloated abdomen and abdominal discomfort (signaled by anxiety, whining, and pacing). Your pet may also lose his or her appetite. Any feces passed are hard and dry.

CAT CHAT

If a cat is having a hard time passing feces and is clearly becoming uncomfortable, he or she may avoid the litter box; it's as if your cat's blaming the litter box for the discomfort. You may need to provide a new litter box in a new location after solving the constipation issue.

Causes

Dogs may develop constipation from eating trash, sticks, and other nonfood items. A poor-quality diet can also cause constipation, as can ingesting too much bone or bone meal.

Cats can develop a disorder called megacolon, in which the colon loses its ability to contract, and is therefore unable to move feces through the colon. Because cats are naturally designed to get most of the water they need from their food, eating dry kibble food can lead to dehydration, followed closely by constipation.

Prevention

Preventing puppies and young dogs from raiding the trash can or otherwise getting into stuff they shouldn't helps make sure they don't eat nonfood items.

Feeding your pet a high-quality diet, commercial or homemade, with adequate amounts of fiber is also important. Feed cats who are prone to constipation moist foods rather than dry kibble.

Remedies

Fiber keeps the bowel working as it should by helping the intestinal tract move the food, then the feces, along. Because fiber also absorbs water, it helps keep water in the stool, thus making it easier to move. You can add fiber to the food by adding cooked pumpkin or lightly steamed greens to the dog's or cat's daily diet. Herbal remedies often effective for constipation include chickweed, dandelion root, slippery elm, and yellow dock.

Talk to Your Veterinarian

If your pet doesn't pass a stool in two days, or if your pet appears very uncomfortable, call your veterinarian. Call, too, if you see any blood in the stools that have been passed.

> **PET ALERT**
>
> Don't try to treat constipation on your own by giving your pet a laxative. This doesn't always work; plus, if there's something else going on in the intestinal tract (such as an obstruction), the laxative may cause more problems.

Cushing's Disease

Cushing's disease, or Cushing's syndrome, is found in middle-aged and older dogs, and every once in a while in cats. Some breeds are more prone to it than others, like Boston Terriers, Boxers, Dachshunds, and Poodles.

One symptom of the disease is hair loss over the body in a symmetrical pattern, with the remaining hair coat looking dry and unhealthy. The animal's abdomen will look pendulous and distended, and his or her skin may darken. The dog will be lethargic and lack energy, and will be excessively thirsty. In addition, the dog will lose muscle tone. Ultimately, the dog may develop heart failure, diabetes, seizures, and blood clots.

Blood tests will confirm a diagnosis. Even with veterinary treatment the prognosis is not good; some pets live only two to three more years after the onset of symptoms.

Causes

Cushing's disease is caused by long-term exposure to glucocorti-costeroids, either from medication or from those produced by the body's adrenal glands. Tumors on the pituitary gland can cause the adrenal glands to overproduce natural steroids.

Prevention

There is no known means of preventing this disease.

Remedies

Although there isn't a known cure for Cushing's disease, either with natural remedies or with conventional medicine, a few natural remedies can help your pet cope. These can at least help you manage the disease and perhaps give your pet a little more quality time.

Dandelion, either as fresh greens or as a tea, helps liver and kidneys function. It can also help normalize adrenal gland function. Burdock is a cleansing herb, a diuretic, and helps the body flush toxins from the body.

Dr. Shawn Messonnier says, "The most common therapy is glandular therapy, which uses whole animal tissues or extracts of the adrenal gland. Current research supports this concept that the glandular supplements contain active substances." Glandular supplements also provide nutrients to the body, including hormones, and function as a source of enzymes.

PetAlive formulated its commercial remedy PetAlive Cushex drops specifically for pets with Cushing's disease. It contains both herbal and homeopathic remedies, and it helps the body balance adrenal gland function.

Acupuncture has also been used successfully in pets with Cushing's disease. Acupuncture won't cure the disease, but it can help your pet have a longer life and a better quality of life.

Talk to Your Veterinarian

Your veterinarian must diagnose Cushing's disease. After the diagnosis, your vet will guide you through your pet's care. Your vet will likely prescribe the medications Lysodren and Anipryl. Talk to your vet about your desire to combine natural remedies with any medical care.

Dental Disease

Dental disease in dogs and cats can include several things, including cracked or broken teeth, bad breath, mouth abscesses, and periodontal disease. Healthy dogs' and cats' teeth should be white. The gums should be light pink, except in pets who have dark colored skin, like Chow Chows.

When the pet's gums and mouth become inflamed, infected, or diseased, it can affect much more than just his or her teeth and mouth. An infection in the mouth can spread bacteria throughout the body; in fact, it can lead to heart disease. According to recent estimates, anywhere between 50 and 80 percent of all dogs and cats over the age of 3 have some form of dental disease.

One of the first signs of dental disease is bad breath. If your pet's breath smells disgusting, take a look inside his or her mouth. If the teeth have *plaque* and *tartar* on them, the gums are red and inflamed, or there is some swelling in the mouth, your pet has dental disease.

DEFINITION

Plaque is a film of saliva and proteins that forms on the teeth. If you don't remove it, it will harden into **tartar,** that brown stuff caked on a dog's or cat's teeth.

Causes

Many different things can cause dental disease. Chewing on hard objects such as rocks or cooked bones can crack a tooth, but some dogs are such powerful chewers that even chewing on a raw bone can crack some teeth. Small pieces of bones can also become lodged between teeth.

Some dogs and cats inherit less-than-healthy teeth. Poodles, Papillons, Pugs, Chihuahuas, and several other small breeds often have poor teeth. Some cats are the same way; my husband and I had a tortoiseshell short-haired cat who had terrible teeth. We spent a lot of time and money on her mouth, and she still ended up toothless before she was 12 years old.

An incorrect diet can also lead to poor dental hygiene. Many dogs and cats, when eating a cereal grain–based dry food, will end up with pieces of dry food stuck between the teeth. These foods, which are high in carbohydrates, attract bacteria, resulting in an infection.

A lack of dental care, both at home and at the veterinarian's office, can also lead to dental disease. Although many owners can take care of their pet's teeth at home, at some point many pets will need a professional dental cleaning to remove what the owner couldn't keep up with.

Prevention

Feeding your pet a high-quality diet is one of the first steps toward good dental care. Many veterinarians highly recommend a diet based on meat rather than carbohydrates. Providing safe items for your pet to chew on helps as well.

CAT CHAT

Because cats don't chew on toys like dogs do, getting a cat to chew to clean her teeth can be tough. Many cats will chew on a chicken or turkey neck, and these are tough enough to scrape the teeth.

Caring for the teeth at home is important. Teach your pet to accept brushing. For cats, do so with the smallest-sized child's tooth brush;

for dogs, use a child's or adult's toothbrush. Use baking soda mixed with water to form a paste, or use commercial pet toothpaste (don't use toothpaste made for people). Although your pet may never love the process, he or she can learn to tolerate brushing if you do so regularly (daily is best).

Remedies

Although there are several herbal remedies for dental health, none are effective if the pet's mouth isn't clean. Therefore, daily brushing is the best remedy. When the animal's mouth is clean and the pet is eating a good food, then a vitamin and mineral supplement can support good mouth health. Calcium, phosphorus, and zinc are especially important for strong teeth.

Dr. Greg Martinez says, "Teddy's Pride is a natural oral culture of peroxide producing bacteria that fights tartar and cleans teeth. It is added to the pet's food." He adds, "I also offer my Poodle mix, Reggie, frozen chicken wings on a weekly basis. Reggie's teeth are scraped clean while chewing." You can find out more about Teddy's Pride at https://www.buyteddyspridesite.com.

Probiotics and other digestive enzymes—including those found in yogurt, papaya, and pineapple—will also help keep the mouth healthy. Again, these only help if the teeth are already clean.

Dr. Shawn Messonnier recommends Coenzyme Q-10 (often called CoQ10), an antioxidant, for good dental health. He says, "While CoQ10 is often recommended for pets with heart disease, anecdotal studies suggest that by acting as an antioxidant it may also help pets with dental disease." Other sources suggest CoQ10 may improve dental health by reducing inflammation in the gums as well as bleeding and pain in the gums.

It's easier to keep a clean mouth healthy if the immune system is also healthy. Thorne Research has created a formula called Immugen. It contains CoQ10, vitamins, minerals, and several botanicals known to support the immune system. PetAlive has a supplement called Gumz-n-Teeth that combines several herbal and homeopathic ingredients, including spirulina, horsetail, and silica.

Talk to Your Veterinarian

If your pet already has bad breath and tartar buildup on the teeth, call your veterinarian and schedule an appointment. Your pet will probably need a professional dental cleaning to get all of the tartar off the teeth because natural remedies can't do that. Your vet may also recommend a course of antibiotics, depending on the state of the mouth.

Then, after the mouth is clean and healthy, you can begin daily brushing and mouth care. You can also begin some natural remedies to keep the mouth healthy.

Diabetes

Diabetes—or, more correctly, diabetes mellitus—is a far too common disease in our pets. It is estimated that 1 in 400 cats and 1 in 500 dogs suffer from diabetes.

Diabetes is a disease of the pancreas that affects the body's ability to control blood sugar levels. In dogs and cats, their body either doesn't produce enough insulin or doesn't utilize the insulin the way it should, and then blood sugar levels rise. Elevated blood sugar levels can lead to cataracts, liver disease, kidney disease, heart disease, and even death. Symptoms can begin quite gradually and can include weight loss or weight gain, excessive thirst and urination, urinary tract infections, weakness, and cataracts.

Consult your veterinarian if you see these symptoms in your dog or cat. A blood sugar test confirms the diagnosis.

Causes

Diabetes may be inheritable. Several dog breeds are more prone to it than others—including Golden Retrievers, German Shepherds, Miniature Schnauzers, and Poodles—but any dog or cat can develop diabetes.

Obesity is one of the leading known causes of diabetes. A diet high in unhealthy cereal grains, especially in cats, is also a factor. Certain medications, especially corticosteroids, can affect pancreatic function and cause diabetes. Unfortunately, we don't yet know all the causes of diabetes.

Dr. Martinez says, "High-carbohydrate diets in both humans and other animals are implicated in the obesity and diabetes epidemic." Cats in particular are very sensitive to high-carbohydrate diets.

Prevention

Because so many factors can contribute to diabetes, including inherited traits, there are limited ways to prevent it. However, you can help your pet by keeping him or her on a high-quality diet, avoiding excessive sugars and cereal-grain carbohydrates. Maintain your pet's weight at a healthy level, and keep your pet active.

Exercise is particularly important. Activity—whether it's walking, playing, or aerobic exercise—builds muscle, which in turn raises the body's metabolic rate. All of these things burn calories, help keep weight stable, and can potentially ward off diabetes.

When your pet needs medications that may potentially affect the pancreas, talk to your veterinarian. These can include thyroid drugs, corticosteroids, and tetracycline (an antibiotic). Ask if you can give your pet another medication instead. If you must give your pet that particular medication, can you start with the minimum dosage and the shortest amount of time the medication requires to be effective? Talk about your concerns.

Remedies

The first recommendation for dogs and cats is to feed a high-quality diet. Dr. Messonnier recommends a homemade diet: "The diet should be comprised of 50 percent high-quality complex carbohydrates (vegetables and oats), with no simple sugars. Fat should be restricted with no more than 20 percent. Protein can be from 15 to 30 percent."

CAT CHAT

Cats normally require a diet higher in meat proteins than is recommended for pets with diabetes. Talk to your veterinarian about this and find out what he or she recommends for your cat.

Increasing the fiber in your pet's diet is very important because the fiber will slow digestion; doing so helps maintain blood sugar levels. Cooked pumpkin and squash are very good for adding fiber to the diet. Dark green vegetables, finely diced and lightly steamed, are, too. Sugar-free Metamucil is also a good source of fiber. A pinch is great for a cat or small dog, while a medium-sized dog could have ½ teaspoon and a large dog 1 teaspoon. Mix it in with the pet's food.

Keeping active is important for all diabetic patients, canine, feline, or human. Keep up on walks and play sessions.

Bilberries stimulate insulin production and reduce blood sugar levels. They also effectively stimulate blood circulation, which is always an issue with diabetic patients. Other herbs beneficial to those with diabetes include burdock root, dandelion, ginseng, marshmallow, and yucca.

Perfect Form, by The Honest Kitchen, is a supplement that supports the digestive system. It contains fennel, papain, papaya, pumpkin seed, plantain, pectin, and slippery elm. This supplement adds natural digestive enzymes to the system and calms it at the same time.

Talk to Your Veterinarian

Your veterinarian can teach you how to monitor your pet's blood sugar. Doing so allows you to more effectively manage the diabetes through diet, exercise, and supplements. Your veterinarian may also recommend medication for the disease; if that's needed, monitoring your pet's blood sugar is a necessity.

Diarrhea

When the food your dog or cat eats moves too quickly through the intestinal tract, the body expels the feces in a softened or liquid form called diarrhea. The bowel contractions or spasms can occur rapidly, requiring multiple trips to the litter box or outside.

Diarrhea may be short-lived, occurring several times over an hour or so, or it may be long-lasting. A short bout of diarrhea isn't usually a problem for your pet, but diarrhea that continues for more than several hours can result in dehydration and prolonged discomfort.

 CAT CHAT

Kittens can become dehydrated very quickly from diarrhea. Call your veterinarian immediately if your kitten has diarrhea.

Causes

Many things can cause digestive upset and diarrhea: a change in diet (especially abrupt or rapid food changes), food ingredients, supplements, or treats. Exposure to bacteria such as salmonella or E. coli can also cause diarrhea, as can giardia and coccidian.

A puppy or kitten who eats inappropriate things, especially things that aren't foods, may have loose stools. Internal parasites and several diseases, including lactose intolerance, can also cause diarrhea.

Prevention

It's tough to prevent diarrhea because so many things can cause it. Using quality ingredients and making diet changes slowly and gradually are important to preventing diarrhea. For example, if you're changing your pet from a commercial food high in cereal grains to a homemade meat-based diet, do so gradually over several weeks. It can take time for a cat or dog to adjust to the new diet; changing too quickly may cause gastrointestinal upset.

Have your vet check your pet for internal parasites on a regular basis, especially if you live in an area where they're common, such in warmer climates. Your vet should check all puppies and kittens as well.

> **DOG TALK**
>
> Many dogs have diarrhea if they become overly excited or stressed, such as when they arrive at a dog show or performance event. Bach Flowers Rescue Remedy or a similar homeopathic remedy can work wonders in calming these dogs. Rescue Remedy was designed specifically to help calm anxiety and fear. See Chapter 4 for more information.

Remedies

Dehydration can result from diarrhea, especially in very small dogs and cats, puppies and kittens, and elderly animals. However, a bad case of diarrhea can cause dehydration in even the healthiest adult animals, so it's important you remain attentive. Make sure your pet has access to water at all times. If your pet doesn't want to drink, offer him or her ice or broth.

It's a good idea to fast healthy adult animals for several hours after a bout of diarrhea to help calm the intestinal tract. Put the pet on a bland diet, like chicken and rice, or chicken and pumpkin. As the diarrhea clears up, gradually return the pet back to his or her normal diet.

Many pet owners use a homeopathic remedy called arsenicum album to treat their pet's diarrhea. You can also use it to treat digestive disorders, allergies, anxiety, and a variety of other pet health issues. Other homeopathic remedies for diarrhea include nux vomica and podophyllum.

Slippery elm provides soothing protection for the intestinal tract, while boswellia is an anti-inflammatory. Other herbs that provide gastrointestinal comfort include aloe vera (don't use it with cats, as it can be toxic when ingested), boswellia, calendula, and raspberry leaf.

PetAlive has a remedy called Natural Moves that contains several herbal remedies, dietary fiber, and homeopathic ingredients.

After your pet's diarrhea has slowed, add small amounts of probiotics and digestive enzymes to the bland diet to get the intestinal tract functioning well again. Yogurt, kefir, and papaya are all good. Only Natural Pet's Probiotic Blend is good for this ailment, as is PetAlive's Digestive Support.

Talk to Your Veterinarian

Many veterinarians recommend using an over-the-counter product such as Pepto Bismal or Immodium for diarrhea with no other known problems, but discuss this with your veterinarian before using it. He or she may have other recommendations, or can provide instructions as to the appropriate dose.

Talk to your veterinarian if you have a very small, very young, or elderly pet as soon as the diarrhea begins. These pets are at the highest risk for dehydration. Parvovirus is deadly for puppies, and it's characterized by foul-smelling, bloody diarrhea. Take your puppy to your vet immediately if you see this.

For healthy adult pets, call your veterinarian if there is blood in the feces, or if the diarrhea is accompanied by vomiting. You need some help, too, if your pet is weak or depressed, or if it's running a fever.

Ear Infections

Ear infections can be painful, annoying, and messy. Unfortunately, they can also become chronic. An infected ear is red and contains dirty-looking matter, and the dog or cat may paw or scratch at it. Some pets rub up against furniture or the carpet to try and get some relief from itching.

Causes

Many different things can cause ear infections, including ear mites, foreign objects in the ears, bacteria, and even yeast infections. Food allergies can cause ear problems, as can frequent swimming. Several diseases can cause ear problems, including hyperthyroidism.

Although some dog breeds more commonly have ear problems than others—including Golden Retrievers, Cocker Spaniels, and Basset Hounds—we don't yet know whether the tendency toward ear infections is an inherited trait.

Prevention

You can prevent most ear problems by feeding your pet a high-quality diet. Cereal grain allergies cause many allergy symptoms, including an allergic response in a pet's ears.

It's important that you keep your pet's ears clean. Removing dirt, excess wax, and other debris from the outer ear and inside the ear flap can help prevent bacterial growth. To clean your pet's ears, slightly dampen a cotton ball or cotton pad with mineral oil, tea tree oil (on dogs only), or aloe vera, and use it to gently wipe the outside of the ear and inside of the ear flap. Weekly cleaning is usually sufficient. Many essential oils, including tea tree oil, can be toxic to cats, so don't use this on your cat's ears. See Chapter 4 for more on essential oils.

GO NATURAL

The best tea tree oil is made from the Malaleuca tree, a native of Australia. Although oil can come from other trees and plants, the Malaleuca tree oil is a topical antiseptic, a naturally mild antibiotic, and an effective pest repellant. Don't use it on cats, though.

Remedies

Usually, keeping your pet's ears clean is sufficient for good ear health.

Herbs known for boosting the immune system, including alfalfa, chamomile, dandelion leaf and root, echinacea, goldenseal, hawthorne, licorice root, milk thistle, sage, slippery elm, and white willow, are all good for ear infections.

The Honest Kitchen's Invigor tea supports the immune system of dogs and cats. It contains kelp, astragalus, hawthorne berries, olive leaf, spirulina, and watercress.

Talk to Your Veterinarian

If your pet's ear is red and swollen, or if he or she is scratching it, or if your pet appears to be in pain, call your veterinarian. Your pet may need conventional veterinary medicine to alleviate the mites, allergy, or infection. After that, you can use natural remedies to maintain good ear health.

Epilepsy

Epilepsy is a seizure disorder caused by abnormal electrical activity in the brain. In a grand mal seizure, the dog or cat is unconscious, the legs are rigid, and there may be jerking movements. You may also see jaw chomping, drooling, and uncontrolled urinating or defecating. A petite mal seizure is less intense; the dog or cat isn't unconscious, and uncontrolled urinating or defecating doesn't usually occur.

Causes

Some dog breeds are more prone to epilepsy, and this is an inherited trait in these breeds. Such breeds include Beagles, Dachshunds, German Shepherds, and Keeshonden. Other breeds have demonstrated a tendency toward epilepsy, but we don't yet know whether this is an inherited condition; these breeds include Fox Terriers, Golden Retrievers, Labrador Retrievers, Poodles, Miniature Schnauzers, St. Bernards, and Siberian Huskies.

Brain trauma and diseases can also cause epilepsy. Heat stroke, brain abscesses, tumors, poisoning, and many other issues that affect the brain can cause seizures.

Prevention

The first seizure is always frightening, both to the pet and the owner, because it's unexpected and often traumatic. Preventing the first seizure is impossible because no one can predict that a seizure is going to happen.

If you can identify the cause of your pet's seizure, then you can prevent future seizures by addressing the problem. A veterinarian should see a pet who's had a seizure within a day of the first seizure so the cause can be identified, if possible.

There are several natural remedies and veterinary medications that may prevent future seizures. When you can't totally prevent your pet's seizures, you may be able to use these treatments to reduce the frequency and strength of the seizures.

Remedies

There's no cure for epilepsy, unless your pet has a curable underlying medical condition. Natural remedies can sometimes calm the nervous system, thereby reducing the frequency and duration of seizures.

L-Carnitine, an amino acid, is effective at controlling or at least reducing the frequency of seizures. Side effects are rare and it's considered safe for dogs and cats.

Several herbal remedies have calming effects on the nervous system, including passion flower, skullcap, gingko biloba, and valerian. The Bach Flower essence Scleranthus, a homeopathic remedy, treats neurological problems, including seizures. See Chapter 4 for more on flower essences, including Bach Flower Remedies.

> **GO NATURAL**
>
> Eliminating any known allergens, preservatives, and artificial colorings and flavorings from the pet's diet is beneficial for pets with seizures. Usually, these changes won't stop seizures unless one of the removed items is causing the underlying problem; nonetheless, removing them from the pet's environment will safeguard the body's overall health.

Talk to Your Veterinarian

Any seizure must be taken seriously. Not only may there be an underlying health problem initiating seizures, but also a seizure itself is heartbreaking to you and distressing to the animal. Continued seizures significantly affect your pet's quality of life.

After your pet's first seizure occurs, make an appointment right away for your veterinarian to examine your pet. If you wish to use natural remedies, share that information with your vet. Many times, you can work with your vet to reach a balance between natural care and veterinary medicine.

Feline Immunodeficiency Virus

Feline immunodeficiency virus (FIV) is a dangerous and contagious disease found in cats. FIV is a *retrovirus*, and is similar to AIDS. Like AIDS, this is an autoimmune disease. Some cats exposed to the disease never become sick and others will take years to develop symptoms of the disease. A cat with an already compromised or weak immune system is more prone than a healthy cat to developing the disease.

Secondary infections are more dangerous to a cat with FIV because his immune system is already stressed by the disease. The most common secondary infections connected with FIV include dental disease, diarrhea, skin infections, ear infections, and seizures.

DEFINITION

A **retrovirus** is an RNA (not DNA) virus. These often produce tumors. A **secondary infection** is one that occurs as a direct or an indirect result of the primary disease, or because the animal's immune system is overworked from attacking the primary disease.

Causes

An infected cat transmits FIV to another cat through a bite. Because male cats are more prone to fighting, especially unneutered male cats, experts say the best prevention for FIV is keeping the cat inside. Although many believe that cats who live in the same home and groom each other can't transmit the disease, that thinking is now being called into question by many researchers. An infected mother cat can give FIV to her kittens as they pass through the birth canal or the kittens may contract it through her milk.

Prevention

The ideal prevention is to make sure your cat isn't exposed to FIV in the first place. Get a kitten or adult cat tested for the disease prior to adopting the animal. Have your vet test cats already living at home with you, too, to make sure the disease isn't already there and lying dormant. Keep your cats inside to prevent them from acquiring the disease from other outdoor cats.

CAT CHAT

All cats diagnosed with FIV should be kept inside. An infected cat allowed outside can potentially infect every other cat in the neighborhood.

Remedies

The most important thing to do for FIV-positive cats is to manage their stress and keep their immune system as healthy as possible. Healthy cats can fight off the disease for a long time; in fact, some cats with this disease live a long, normal life.

A good diet is imperative, and most experts recommend a home-cooked diet over a raw one. The possibility of a bacterial contamination in raw meat is too dangerous for a cat with a weakened immune system. Supplement the animal's diet with antioxidants and digestive enzymes.

Any herbs known for boosting the immune system, including alfalfa, chamomile, dandelion leaf and root, echinacea, goldenseal, hawthorne, licorice root, milk thistle, sage, slippery elm, and white willow, are helpful to FIV-positive cats.

Talk to Your Veterinarian

If your cat has been diagnosed with FIV, call your veterinarian at any sign of illness—no matter how small or insignificant. Unfortunately, many FIV-positive cats die not of the disease, but of a secondary infection. Make sure your veterinarian knows about any natural immune system boosters you're giving your cat because some herbs and medications don't work well together.

Feline Infectious Peritonitis

Feline infectious peritonitis (FIP) is a systemic infection caused by the feline corona virus. There are two forms of the disease, characterized by the terms *wet* and *dry*. Wet FIP is characterized by fluids leaking from the blood vessels and accumulating in the animal's chest or abdomen. These cats have a poor prognosis.

Dry FIP causes abscesses to form throughout the body. The animal's prognosis depends entirely upon where the abscesses form. Blindness can result if they occur in the eyes, paralysis if they form in the spinal cord, and kidney failure if they form in the kidneys.

Causes

FIP is caused by a virus transmitted from one cat to another via saliva or feces. The virus remains viable for a few hours on surfaces, so it can also be passed to a cat by contaminated food and water bowls, bedding, and even an owner's clothing. Persian cats have a potentially inherited tendency toward the disease.

Prevention

The only way to prevent this disease is to test all cats in the household to make sure no one is harboring the disease. Any cats you consider adopting into the household need to be tested, too.

Unfortunately, FIP tests aren't 100 percent accurate. The test may not reveal cats who are carrying the virus and aren't actively sick. Dr. Martinez says, "There are many false positive and false negative scenarios. Kittens originating in feral cat colonies are at a much greater risk of developing the disease as they are often infected at a very young age."

> **PET ALERT**
>
> To prevent the spread of infectious feline diseases, anyone in the household who works at a veterinary clinic or who volunteers at an animal shelter should change clothes prior to entering the home. He or she should also wash his or her hands and any other skin that may have touched other cats.

Remedies

Natural remedies can't cure FIP; for these cats, the goal is to maintain a healthy immune system. A quality home-cooked diet (no raw meat) is beneficial, as well as antioxidant and digestive enzyme supplements.

Any herbs known for boosting the immune system, including alfalfa, chamomile, dandelion leaf and root, echinacea, goldenseal, hawthorne, licorice root, milk thistle, sage, slippery elm, and white willow, are potentially beneficial. You may also give cats with FIP the Bach Flower essences crab apple, larch, and olive.

Talk to Your Veterinarian

Once your pet has been diagnosed, discuss with your veterinarian your desire to use natural remedies to support your cat's immune system. Let your vet know anything you're giving your cat so if he or she prescribes any medications, you can avoid negative interactions.

There is no cure for FIP. If any changes occur in your pet, or if you see any signs of infection or other disease, call your vet right away.

Feline Leukemia Virus

Feline leukemia virus (FeLV) is another dangerous and contagious disease found in cats. Like FIV, FeLV is a retrovirus similar to AIDS.

Cats with FeLV may show signs of respiratory infections, loss of appetite, dental disease, diarrhea, and chronic skin infections. Cats may also develop seizures, cancerous tumors, or cancer of the blood cells called lymphocytes.

Causes

This disease can be transmitted to another cat through the infected cat's saliva and nasal excretions. Cats in close contact with each other who share food and water bowls, litter boxes, and beds can easily transmit it from one cat to another.

Outside cats who fight can pass it to one another via bite wounds. One feisty cat could spread it to an entire neighborhood's cat population.

Prevention

The only way to prevent this disease is to test all cats in the household to make sure no one is harboring the disease. Any cats that might be adopted need to be tested, too.

 CAT CHAT

As with so many serious feline diseases, there's no cure for FeLV, but FeLV isn't a death sentence. Cats with good natural and veterinary support can potentially live many years.

Remedies

Natural remedies can't cure FeLV; for these cats, the goal is to maintain a healthy immune system. A quality home-cooked diet (no raw meat) is beneficial, as well as antioxidant and digestive enzyme supplements.

Any herbs known for boosting the immune system, including alfalfa, chamomile, dandelion leaf and root, echinacea, goldenseal, hawthorne, licorice root, milk thistle, sage, slippery elm, and white willow, are helpful.

Talk to Your Veterinarian

Once your pet has been diagnosed, discuss with your veterinarian your desire to use natural remedies to support your cat's immune system. Let your vet know anything you're giving your cat so if he or she prescribes any medications, you can avoid negative interactions.

There is no cure for FeLV. If any changes occur in your pet, any signs of infection or other disease, call your vet right away.

Feline Lower Urinary Tract Disease

Feline lower urinary tract disease (FLUTD) covers several problems that can occur in the urinary tract and bladder of cats, including the formation of crystals (stones) in the bladder and obstructions of the urethra.

Symptoms in your cat include straining when trying to urinate, spending a great deal of time in the litter box, increased thirst, and urinary incontinence. The cat may lick the genitals more than normal and there may be blood in the urine or in the litter box.

Causes

The most common cause of FLUTD is the formation of crystals called uroliths in the bladder. These can also form in the kidneys.

The pH of the urine is most likely responsible for the formation of these crystals. Cats with high pH levels in their urine are more apt to form crystals than cats with lower pH levels.

Some cats have a malformed bladder, which can also cause FLUTD. These cats have a pouch or sagging portion of the bladder that prevents them from completely emptying it.

A blockage occurs when a crystal moves into the urethra, blocking the flow of urine. Without veterinary care, a blockage will cause renal failure and death in as little as two to three days. Although blockages can occur in both male and female cats, it is more common in males.

> **CAT CHAT**
>
> FLUTD is more common in cats eating a dry kibble diet than those eating canned or homemade diets. Dry kibble tends to cause dehydration, which can increase a cat's risk of developing this disease.

Prevention

It's very difficult to predict which cats will develop this disease. For example, many cats can eat dry kibble with no health issues at all, while others develop problems. Most veterinarians recommend either a canned food diet or a homemade diet for cats who appear to be at risk through examination, blood work, or urinalysis.

"Raw or cooked meats," says Dr. Martinez, "acidifies the urine, dissolves urinary crystals, and inhibits bacterial growth. Moist food and meat treats help keep your cat's urinary tract flushed and clean."

Remedies

The single most important thing to preventing and treating this disease is managing the cat's urinary pH. A high pH (alkaline) level in the bladder tends to lead to the development of crystals; a lower pH (acidic) level tends to dissolve any crystals that form.

Adding vitamin C to your cat's diet can create a more acidic balance in the bladder. Too much vitamin C can cause diarrhea, however, making your cat even more uncomfortable. Add vitamin C to your cat's food a tiny bit at a time, and watch your cat for any side effects.

Cranberry is the tried-and-true supplement for anything to do with bladder or urinary tract health. Add a little juice to your cat's meals—straight from the berries—or add a cranberry capsule.

Any herbs known for boosting the immune system, including alfalfa, chamomile, dandelion leaf and root, echinacea, goldenseal, hawthorne, licorice root, milk thistle, sage, slippery elm, and white willow, are potentially beneficial.

Talk to Your Veterinarian

Get your cat to the veterinarian right away if you see any symptoms of FLUTD, because it's potentially life-threatening, especially if there is a blockage. If there's no blockage, talk to your veterinarian about potential natural remedies you can use to help your cat.

The Least You Need to Know

- Not all health issues are inheritable, although many dogs and cats may inherit the tendency to develop some diseases.
- Natural remedies can have a place in the pet owner's cupboard, but some health issues also need conventional veterinary care.
- Diabetes is a growing health concern affecting dogs and cats, and there's a clear correlation with the obesity epidemic.
- Several feline diseases—including FIV, FIP, and FeLV—are contagious and potentially deadly.

Fleas to Intestinal Parasites

In This Chapter

- The scourge of pet-dom—the tiny flea
- Understanding gastrointestinal diseases in dogs and cats
- Other pet ailments
- Understanding causes and prevention
- Using natural remedies
- Knowing when to call the veterinarian

The health problems in this chapter include a wide variety of disease and health issues. Gastrointestinal disease, for example, can be merely irritating for your pet or it can cause serious health issues, including malnutrition. Then, intestinal parasites are not only health risks, but also just plain gross.

For each health problem, I offer a number of remedies. These range from a change in your pet's diet, exercise, or supplements, to herbal and homeopathic remedies. Acupuncture and chiropractic therapies may also be appropriate.

Even if you're raising your dog or cat using natural techniques, working with your veterinarian is also important. Your veterinarian, conventional or holistic, is also concerned about your pet's well-being.

Fleas

Despite being so tiny, fleas can cause so much misery—clearly size doesn't matter when there are hundreds and thousands of them.

Fleas are tiny insects that live by biting and feeding off their host—in this case, dogs and cats. Each time a flea bites, it takes one drop of blood. One flea isn't going to do a great deal of harm, but where there's one flea there are likely hundreds more.

These tiny flea bites can be a huge problem for young puppies, kittens, small dogs, and elderly dogs and cats because each time a flea bites, a drop of blood is lost. That may not sound like much, but it adds up. Small dogs, puppies, kittens, and elderly dogs and cats can quickly suffer from this blood loss. Flea bites are also a serious problem for a pet who's allergic to flea saliva. For many pets, bites cause severe itching; infested pets will scratch, chew, and even lose hair in the area of the bites.

CAT CHAT

The flea that torments both cats and dogs is a type of flea called the cat flea. If you see salt and pepper material on your cat's bed, the dark bits are excreted blood and the white specks are flea eggs.

Causes

Unfortunately, fleas can be found throughout the world. In the United States, fleas are active year round in the southern, southeastern, and Gulf coast states, and along the Pacific coast. Fleas are active from March through December from Chicago and south of there, and are active in the summer months in the rest of the country.

Prevention

To protect your pet from a flea infestation, consider controlling the fleas in your home and yard. In years past, doing so meant using pesticides and insecticides everywhere. That is much too toxic, however, and has fallen out of favor with most pet owners.

One of the best tools for prevention in the house is a good vacuum cleaner. Vacuum the house daily during flea season. That means vacuuming the floor, carpet, pet's bedding, and furniture. Don't forget to vacuum the car, too. In addition, wash the pet's bedding regularly—and that includes your linens if your pet sleeps on your bed.

Remedies

In the past, pet owners often used garlic and brewer's yeast to discourage fleas from biting, but this remedy has fallen out of favor with many pet experts. Garlic isn't as healthy for dogs and cats as we once thought, and brewer's yeast alone isn't very effective.

> **PET ALERT**
>
> Pet owners sometimes use pennyroyal oil as a natural means of flea control. Recently, though, there have been more cases of toxicity. Use this only sparingly—if at all—and don't use it on cats, kittens, puppies, or elderly animals.

There's a wide variety of commercial herbal shampoos, however, that are effective at removing the fleas from your pet. Dr. Shawn's Flea and Tick Shampoo uses lemongrass and neem oils to combat fleas. Only Natural Pet offers a shampoo that combines natural herbal extracts with lavender and jojoba oil. (See Appendix B for more information on this and other products mentioned in this chapter.)

To keep fleas off your pet after bathing and between baths, use Dr. Shawn's Herbal Flea & Tick Spray, which contains peppermint, spearmint, lemongrass, clove, cedar, and lemon eucalyptus. Only Natural Pet offers a complete line of natural oils, drops, and sprays to combat fleas and ticks.

You need to control the fleas in the house. Although vacuuming is the first step, it's often not enough. Sentry makes a spray called Natural Defense Household Spray. You can use it in the house, in crates, on bedding, in cabinets, and more. It contains peppermint, cinnamon, lemongrass, and thyme oils.

Diatomaceous earth and boric acid can also be used in the house to combat fleas. Sprinkle it liberally throughout the house, let it set for a little while (according to the package directions), and then vacuum.

Talk to Your Veterinarian

If your pet is having a reaction to flea bites and is scratching, chewing, and acting miserable, call your vet. Your pet may need veterinary care to overcome the flea bite reaction or dermatitis.

Gastrointestinal Disease

Gastrointestinal disease is an umbrella term encompassing a wide variety of disorders of the gastrointestinal tract, including inflammatory bowel disease (IBD), digestive disorders, appetite loss, malabsorption, and malnutrition, as well as several other health problems.

Symptoms of gastrointestinal disease usually include vomiting, diarrhea, flatulence, a rumbling stomach or abdomen, soft and smelly stools, overly large stools, and bad breath. It's not uncommon for your pet to lose his or her appetite.

You need your veterinarian's help to accurately pinpoint what's going on in your dog or cat's gastrointestinal system. A vet should not only treat these various health problems individually, but he or she should also work to prevent several potential problems. One such problem is a bloated stomach that turns, called *torsion*, which can become life-threatening in a very short period of time. Don't try to treat gastrointestinal disease without expert help.

Causes

The cause of any particular gastrointestinal problem can be hard to figure out, simply because so much is involved in that body system. Some of the most common problems are caused by or are related to the pet's diet, the pet ingesting foreign objects, or inheritable traits. German Shepherds, for example, have a very sensitive gastrointestinal system.

GO NATURAL

The diet for a dog or cat with a gastrointestinal disease needs to be bland and calming so the intestinal tract can heal. Cottage cheese, yogurt, cooked eggs, and pumpkin are all gentle on the digestive system.

Prevention

It's often difficult to prevent gastrointestinal health issues simply because, until the problem occurs, an owner has no idea the pet is prone to the disease, or is sensitive to a particular food. Feeding your pet a high-quality diet and avoiding spicy foods, too much fat, and cereal-grain glutens will help prevent many digestive upsets.

Puppies and kittens shouldn't be allowed to play with items they are able to swallow, such as pieces of string or yarn for kittens or dirty socks and the kitchen trash for puppies. Although it can be almost impossible to determine what a puppy or kitten might find attractive, making the home as safe as possible is the best prevention.

Remedies

Your veterinarian will have to determine the treatment for any specific gastrointestinal diseases, but there are some remedies you can use to create and then maintain a healthy intestinal tract. Always check with your vet before beginning any of these remedies to make sure they won't react badly with treatments he or she is prescribing.

Adding natural fiber to your pet's diet is the first step in treating a gastrointestinal disease. Cooked pumpkin, cooked squash, lightly steamed dark green vegetables, and flaxseed meal are all good sources of fiber. (See Chapter 13 for more about supplementing your pet's diet.)

Increasing your pet's digestive enzymes is very important. Yogurt and kefir, both containing live active cultures, are great for achieving this, as are papaya and pineapple.

Some herbal remedies include slippery elm, ginger, alfalfa, peppermint, chamomile, marshmallow, and fennel. Consider using the homeopathic remedy nux vomica for vomiting and nausea.

The Honest Kitchen has designed a supplement called Perfect Form to aid the digestive health of dogs and cats. It contains fennel, papaya, papaya, pumpkin seed, plantain, pectin, and slippery elm.

> **CAT CHAT**
>
> If your cat is a reluctant eater, try mixing new foods or remedies with chicken broth or cottage cheese. Remember to add new foods very gradually.

Talk to Your Veterinarian

Take gastrointestinal upsets very seriously; they may signal something more serious than a tummy ache. Pay attention to what's normal and what's not normal for your pet's digestive system. Call your veterinarian if your dog or cat is panting, pacing, or whining, or if he or she appears to be in distress. Call if your pet has vomited and/or has had diarrhea for more than a few hours, can't keep water down, or has had blood in the diarrhea or vomit (a serious danger sign).

Diarrhea in puppies and kittens needs immediate veterinary treatment, as these baby animals can dehydrate quickly. Elderly animals may need help right away, too, especially if they are suffering from a chronic disease.

Hairballs

Cats make a particular sound when they're trying to cough up a hairball. Every cat owner knows to come running when they hear that sound. Not only does the cat sound like he or she's in distress, but you know there's going to be something to clean up.

Causes

When cats groom themselves, they swallow some hair. Most of the time, that hair simply moves through the stomach and into the intestinal tract with no problem, and it's then expelled in the feces. Sometimes, a ball of hair will form in the stomach and become too large to pass into the small intestine. In this case, the cat hacks the hairball back up.

Prevention

The best hairball prevention for your cat is grooming on a regular basis. Every hair on the grooming comb or brush is one less your cat would have otherwise swallowed. In addition, add a teaspoon of cod liver oil or fish oil to your cat's food every day. Not only is it good nutrition, but it will also lubricate those hairballs while they're small and allow the cat to eliminate them naturally.

Some commercial foods contain extra ingredients—usually oils— that help the hairballs pass through the intestinal tract. Don't choose the food just for this, however. As I discussed in Part 2, read the labels and choose the best food for your cat. If you find one that also helps with hairballs, that's wonderful.

 DOG TALK

Dogs rarely have problems with hairballs, and we really don't know why. Perhaps they don't groom themselves as much or their stomach is better able to move the hair along.

Remedies

If your cat has been coughing up hairballs, begin adding fish oil to his or her food to help prevent future hairballs. Try putting a fingertip's worth of slightly softened butter on your cat's paw. If your cat's unable to just flick it off, she will slowly lick the butter and swallow it, allowing it to lubricate the system.

Make sure your cat is getting enough fiber in her diet. Some cooked pumpkin or steamed greens will also keep the hairball moving through her system.

Talk to Your Veterinarian

Call your veterinarian if your cat continues to cough and retch without bringing up a hairball. The hairball may be too large or there may be another unrelated problem.

Heart Disease and Failure

The heart is the foundation of the circulatory system; without the heart's pumping action, blood can't move through your pet's body. There are several types of heart disease, all of which can progress to heart failure.

In cats, there are three types of *cardiomyopathy*:

- Dilative cardiomyopathy is when the heart is enlarged and has thin and weakened walls.

- Hypertropic cardiomyopathy is when the heart walls become thick and still.

- Restrictive cardiomyopathy isn't as well understood by pet health experts, but we do know the heart walls are less efficient at pumping blood with this diagnosis, perhaps due to stiffness.

DEFINITION

Cardiomyopathy is an umbrella term for a variety of diseases or disorders that involve the muscles of the heart. When the muscles of the heart are malformed, diseased, or injured, the heart cannot function correctly and eventually will fail.

Dogs can also suffer from dilated cardiomyopathy, but they can also have congenital heart disease, which means the animal was born with this defect. Acquired heart disease is caused by something else, such as a bacterial infection, Lyme disease, thyroid disease, or another illness that has affected the heart's health and function.

Heart failure occurs when heart disease has progressed to the point at which the animal is unable to function and is in the process of dying. Heart failure, often called congestive heart failure, isn't a disease in and of itself; rather, it's the end result of heart disease.

Symptoms of heart disease may present gradually, and often go undetected. The pet may not play as much as he or she used to, and the owner may simply attribute the change to the fact that the pet is growing older. Other symptoms may be coughing (especially during activity or at night), fainting, and collapse. Many pets will develop a swollen abdomen as the heart becomes less able to pump fluids through the body.

DOG TALK

The canine parvovirus can affect the heart muscle. Puppies that survive the parvo illness may have lasting repercussions, like a damaged heart and even heart failure.

Causes

There are many causes of heart disease. Some can be inherited. American Short Hair and Maine Coon cats are known to have an inherited tendency toward hypertropic cardiomyopathy. Boxers, Doberman Pinschers, English Springer Spaniels, Cocker Spaniels, German Shepherds, Great Danes, Old English Sheepdogs, St. Bernards, and Schnauzers have an inherited tendency to develop dilated cardiomyopathy. Some diseases can cause problems with the heart, too, as can injuries and infections.

In years past, thousands of cats developed cardiomyopathy, until we discovered cats needed taurine in their diets. Today, some experts believe some dogs—including Cocker Spaniels, Golden Retrievers, and Newfoundlands—may need more taurine in their diets.

Prevention

One of the best ways to prevent heart disease is for cat and dog breeders to be aware of the disease in their own breed. It's crucial to support research that will allow breeders to identify affected animals and avoid breeding them.

Remedies

Natural remedies can't cure heart disease—even modern veterinary medicine can't do that. Several natural remedies can help your pet live more comfortably. Thorne Research has Bio-Cardio, which contains CoQ10 and other nutrients and botanicals, while PetAlive has Heart & Circulation Tonic.

Several herbs help the heart and circulatory system, including hawthorne, goldenseal, red clover, gingko, dandelion, parsley, and ginseng. Some healthful nutritional supplements include CoQ10 and vitamins A, B complex, C, and E.

Working with your veterinarian is vital, even if you wish to use natural remedies. Make sure your veterinarian knows what remedies you wish to use so the two of you can make sure the remedies and medications don't cause a bad reaction.

Talk to Your Veterinarian

Maintain a working relationship with your conventional or holistic veterinarian. He or she may wish to see your pet on a regular basis, perhaps every four to six months depending on your pet's condition. If you see a change in your pet, call your vet immediately. It's a potential emergency if your pet can no longer go for walks, play, or move easily around the house; becomes faint or collapses; or has bluish gums.

Heartworms

Heartworms are worms that live in the heart of the host animal. Infected animals may suffer from heart inflammation, vomiting, loss of appetite, weight loss, coughing, and even heart failure. Dogs and cats with heartworm, if untreated, will die.

Although originally found in the southeastern United States, heartworms are now found in animals all over the United States and in Canada. In the United States, only the upper Midwest still has low numbers of infected animals.

The signs of a heartworm infestation and heart disease are very similar, and your veterinarian must make a diagnosis. A heartworm test is easy to do in the vet's office.

Causes

When a dog or a cat is bitten by a mosquito, the larvae of the heartworm are carried by the insect in the mosquito's bloodstream, and are injected into the dog or cat. These larvae grow and move through the bloodstream. When the larvae mature, they migrate to the heart. Though once thought only to be a danger to dogs, cats are now suffering from heartworms in growing numbers.

Prevention

Keeping mosquitoes off your pet is the best prevention. Because mosquitoes are the intermediary host that provides a step in the middle for the transmission of heartworms, an infected insect must bite your pet for your pet to get these parasites.

Remedies

You can choose from several natural remedies for keeping mosquitoes off of or away from dogs. You can work rosemary tea or lavender oil diluted with water into the dog's coat, and you can apply an apple cider vinegar rinse. Any of these could potentially work. Don't use any of these remedies on cats, however. Most concentrated oils are toxic to cats, especially citrus oils, lavender, and pennyroyal. Keeping your cat inside the house is the best heartworm prevention.

> **CAT CHAT**
>
> Because cats are smaller than dogs, are more sensitive to their environment, and groom themselves extensively, be cautious using anything on your cat's coat. Never think of your cat as a small dog.

Talk to Your Veterinarian

Conventional medicine has several heartworm preventives available. Although many pet owners who live in heartworm-infested regions prefer not to use these medications because they are systemic medications that carry some risk with use, there is no known natural remedy for preventing an infestation.

Hip Dysplasia

This is a debilitating deformity of the hip and thighbone joint. In most instances, the animal's hip socket is deformed to some extent. Instead of being cup-shaped, the socket may be shallow or—in severe cases—almost nonexistent. The ligaments, muscles, and connective tissues may also be too lax to hold the thighbone in place.

In severe cases, a dog can begin limping and demonstrate a reluctance to jump at as early as 8 to 12 months of age. In other pets, the lameness will show up later, as arthritis sets in on the damaged bones and joints. A veterinarian can diagnose hip dysplasia through joint palpation and x-rays.

Causes

Experts once thought hip dysplasia didn't occur in cats, but we now know this isn't true. This disorder has both an inherited and an environmental factor. Many breeds have a tendency toward this disorder, including German Shepherds, Labrador Retrievers, Golden Retrievers, St. Bernards, Newfoundlands, Bernese Mountain Dogs, and many others. Although it's inheritable in cats, we don't yet know if any breeds are more prone to it than others.

Diet is also linked to animals developing hip dysplasia. Too many calories in early puppyhood, which can lead to rapid growth, may be a contributing factor. Diets low in calcium and other essential minerals are also connected to the disorder's development in pets.

Obesity in young dogs, puppies who over-exercise, or puppies and young dogs who run repeatedly on a hard surface day after day can injure the hip joints and possibly cause dysplasia.

Prevention

The first step to preventing hip dysplasia is for cat and dog breeders to make sure their breeding animals aren't dysplastic. They should x-ray an animal's hips before including him or her in a breeding program.

A high-quality diet that isn't too high in fat or calories, with good sources of proteins, vitamins, and minerals, is very important for growing puppies. Their growth should be steady and even, without huge growth surges.

Exercise needs to be slow and steady in puppyhood, without too much exercise or stressful, repetitive-motion exercises. For example, jogging with your dog on varied surfaces is fine; but long, hard runs on concrete sidewalks are not.

CAT CHAT

It's hard to gain a cat's cooperation in exercise, especially if his or her joints are stiff and sore. Movement is important, though, so use your imagination to keep your cat moving.

Remedies

Keeping your pet lean and fit can go a long way toward keeping him or her strong, even if the animal develops hip dysplasia. When their muscles, ligaments, and tendons are strong and tight, they can help maintain joint integrity, even when the socket is deformed.

The exercises meant to keep your pet fit can potentially damage the joint, though, so choose these wisely to limit any damage. Swimming is a great exercise for dogs who like water, and for the few cats who do, too. Long walks, easy jogs, low-level agility, and carting are all great for dogs. Avoid dog sports that are fast-paced and that require athletic turns, spins, and high jumps.

The first remedies experts recommend include vitamin C, glucosamine, and chondroitin. Fatty acids are good for reducing inflammation, as are licorice root and yucca. Dandelion and nettle are effective in helping joints heal, and alfalfa is a good pain reliever.

The Honest Kitchen's Lithe Tea is effective for dogs with hip dysplasia (but it is not recommended for cats). It contains alfalfa, white willow bark, yucca, ginger, red clover, and boswellia.

Warmth is also important for these pets; cold can cause their joints and muscles to stiffen. For the same reason, massage is also good therapy for these animals.

Acupuncture and chiropractic therapies are great treatments as well. Dr. Narda Robinson says, "We're starting to look at the value of laser therapy for dogs with hip dysplasia." Although the technique has value for pain relief in people, we don't yet know if the same applies to dogs and cats.

Talk to Your Veterinarian

Talk to your veterinarian if your pet has trouble getting up and down, refuses to jump, is limping and favoring one leg, appears sore to the touch, or stops doing favorite activities. If you wish to use natural remedies to help your pet feel better, tell your vet. He or she may recommend some medications to help the pain and inflammation; confirm with the vet that the natural remedies won't interact with those.

Your veterinarian may also recommend surgery. Your vet can tell you about a variety of available options, depending on the damage to the joint.

Hyperactivity

Behavioral hyperactivity can be either a medical condition or a behavioral one. To make things even more confusing, symptoms may vary among individual animals. An owner may complain that the dog or cat is too active, fidgets, or can't relax. Dog trainers often notice a puppy or young dog in class is more active than is normal for a dog of that breed or age.

The hyperactive cat may be more active at night than an owner prefers. The cat may roam the house yowling, clawing at the furniture, and chasing imaginary mice. The cat may incessantly disturb the owner at night.

Many times, owners simply accept the pet for who he or she is and try to learn to live with the pets' behaviors. Other owners will give up and find a new home for the pet or surrender the animal to the local shelter. Others will ask for help because the pet is difficult to live with.

DOG TALK

Hyperactive puppies and young dogs often have difficulty learning, retaining what they've learned, and concentrating. Obedience and even housetraining can be a challenge.

Causes

Hyperactivity can have several causes, one of which is delayed social maturity. Some breeds—Labrador and Golden Retrievers, for example—have very long puppyhoods and adolescence. By 2 and 3 years old, when many dogs are mentally mature, these dogs are not. They haven't yet learned the social manners other dogs have already learned, nor have they learned self-control; instead of controlling themselves around distractions, these dogs simply react.

Diet can also be a part of this disorder. Many dogs and cats eating foods high in simple sugars (cereal grains) can't handle the blood sugar highs and lows these foods provide.

Hyperthyroidism (overactive thyroid) and adrenal gland disorders can cause hyperactivity; these disorders must be diagnosed by your veterinarian.

Prevention

Breeders of dogs or cats who have the tendency to have higher activity levels should make sure new puppy or kitten owners are aware of this. It's much better to educate new owners before the fact than it is to deal with unhappy owners later.

Remedies

Exercise is important for hyperactive dogs and cats. Vigorous exercise every single day can help use up some of that excess energy.

CAT CHAT

Cats who tend to be active at night need exercise early in the evening, but don't exercise with the animal late at night or the cat will still be excited when you try to go to bed.

A good diet is the first step toward alleviating hyperactivity. A diet with moderate to high animal protein and very low levels of simple sugars is very important for both cats and dogs. Carbohydrates should be from foods that help keep the blood sugar in balance, such as sweet potatoes, pumpkin, squash, and dark green vegetables.

For dogs, training is also very important because it teaches dogs self-control and the rules for living with people. Contact a dog trainer or a behavioral consultant for help if you feel overwhelmed.

Spaying and neutering can often help these pets. In puberty and afterward, many pets get anxious and have a strong desire to breed. Although the surgeries themselves don't calm the pets, spaying and neutering can significantly decrease the sexual hormones that generate hyperactivity.

With cats, training is a little more difficult for many pet owners, but using rewards the cats like is very effective. Teach the cat to claw on his or her cat tree and not the furniture. Teach your cat to settle down, and don't allow the animal to run madly around the house. A behavioral consultant can help you if you're not sure how to approach cat training.

St. John's wort is one of the best herbal remedies for these pets. You can give it to your pet in capsule form or you can sprinkle it in his or her food.

Talk to Your Veterinarian

If natural remedies are not helping calm your pet, talk to your veterinarian. A thorough exam and bloodwork might be warranted to see if there is a physical cause for your pet's hyperactivity. Thyroid disease can be one cause, but this is quite rare.

Intervertebral Disc Disease

Although intervertebral disc disease is more common in small dogs than in large ones, and less common in cats, this painful and debilitating disease can happen to any cat or dog. There are two types of disc disease. In the first type, the capsule surrounding the disc ruptures, allowing the disc to poke through and push against the spinal cord. This type is most common in small dogs with long backs, including Dachshunds, Shih Tzus, Lhasa Apsos, Beagles, Cocker Spaniels, and Pekingese. In the second type, the entire disc, with capsule surrounding it, bulges outward. This type is more common in large dogs, including German Shepherds and Labrador Retrievers.

In both instances, the pain can be quite severe, causing the dog to cry out in pain. The dog may refuse to lower his head to eat or drink, and may refuse to jump in the car or up on a seat. He or she may turn down play or exercise. Some dogs will experience paralysis in one or more legs.

Causes

Intervertebral disc disease is an inherited disease for several breeds, especially in Dachshunds. We need to continue research to confirm heredity in other breeds.

Injuries can also cause damage to the discs. Jumping high for a toy, running hard, making quick turns, and being hit traumatically can all cause injuries to the discs.

Prevention

The only realistic prevention is for breeders to make sure all of their breeding animals have strong backs and no disc disease. Supporters should also champion research for breeds they know to have back problems.

Remedies

Your vet may recommend acupuncture if your dog has disc disease. Chiropractic therapy is becoming more popular for pets, though we don't yet know how effective it is as a treatment for disc disease.

Reducing pain and inflammation are important, as well as keeping the pet lean and fit. Ensuring these things can go a long way toward keeping your pet strong and decreasing the likelihood he or she will develop disc disease.

It's important to keep your pet moving with low-impact activities. This keeps the body strong and agile. Swimming is a good exercise for dogs who like water and for the few cats who do, too. Make sure your cat walks and plays every day. Dogs need long walks and easy play sessions.

Your pet will appreciate warmth, too, to ease the pain of a sore back. An extra blanket, a hot water bottle, or a heated bed can all provide extra warmth.

Recommended food and herbal remedies include vitamin C, glucosamine, and chondroitin. Fatty acids are good for reducing inflammation, as are licorice root and yucca. Dandelion and nettle are effective in helping joints heal, and alfalfa is a good pain reliever. The Honest Kitchen's Lithe Tea is effective for dogs with any skeletal or joint disease (but it is not recommended for cats). It contains alfalfa, white willow bark, yucca, ginger, red clover, and boswellia.

Talk to Your Veterinarian

If paralysis is a result of the disc disease, your veterinarian may recommend surgery. You can treat milder forms of disc disease with rest and anti-inflammatory medications. If you wish to explore natural remedies, discuss this with your veterinarian.

Intestinal Parasites

Intestinal parasites live in and feed off of a host animal. They most commonly infest puppies and kittens, although older pets can also be infested.

Tapeworms have an intermediary host—fleas that transmit larvae to the dog or cat when they bite the animal (see the earlier section on fleas). Other intestinal parasites, such as roundworms, hookworms, and whipworms, live and reproduce in the host animal and can be contagious to others via the feces. Intestinal parasites can also infect people.

As intestinal parasites live primarily in the intestinal tract, most symptoms mimic those of gastrointestinal disease and can range from flatulence to bloody diarrhea. The most common symptoms include weight loss, often accompanied by a bloated abdomen, as well as an unkempt and disheveled appearance.

Causes

Intestinal parasites can be transmitted through contact with another animal's feces, which means cleanliness is very important. Be sure to keep puppies and kittens away from other animals' feces when they are outside.

Prevention

Strong, healthy pets are less likely to become infested with parasites even when exposed to them. Therefore, all of the things that help keep our pets healthy—excellent diet; supplements that include vitamins, minerals, and antioxidants; exercise; and quality health care—contribute to preventing parasites.

Keep your yard and litter boxes clean to prevent the spread of parasites. After all, you don't want your pet to infect others or continue to re-infest himself.

Remedies

Garlic has long been the first defense for de-worming animals, pets and livestock. In recent years, however, it has fallen out of favor among animal caregivers. A member of the Allium family, the same family as onions, garlic can be toxic to some pets, especially cats.

There are some commercial remedies for parasite elimination. Only Natural offers a remedy called Para-Gone Worm Elimination, PetAlive offers Parasite Dr., and Nature's Herbs offers a Chinese herbal formula called Parasite Relief for Dogs and Parasite Relief for Cats. These are both natural remedies that contain herbs but no medications.

Natural remedies include licorice root, chamomile, dandelion leaf, licorice root, yarrow, yucca, and goldenseal. Reishi and maitake mushrooms may also be effective.

Talk to Your Veterinarian

Identifying intestinal parasites can be difficult because many can only be identified when one observes diluted stool under a microscope. If your pet is having health issues or just looks unhealthy, talk to your veterinarian—your pet may be suffering from intestinal parasites or another illness you must address.

The Least You Need to Know

- Fleas and intestinal parasites can make your pet miserable. Natural remedies may help, but your pet may need veterinary care.

- You can often eliminate gastrointestinal disease with good food, supplements, and natural remedies.

- Hip dysplasia and disc disease can't be cured by natural remedies, though they may help alleviate discomfort.

- Natural remedies may help with many health problems, but always keep open the lines of communication between you and your veterinarian.

Kidney Disease to Urinary Issues

In This Chapter

- Understanding kidney and liver diseases
- Obesity—a growing problem
- Other pet ailments
- Understanding causes and prevention
- How natural remedies can help
- Knowing when to call your veterinarian

Unfortunately, kidney disease is far too common in older pets, and it often doesn't reveal many obvious symptoms for pet owners to recognize. Liver disease is a frightening disease, too. This chapter addresses a number of serious illnesses, as well as a few just plain annoying ones.

In this chapter, I discuss the causes of these diseases, as well as ways to prevent them that include natural remedies. For some diseases, there are realistic ways to avoid them altogether. As always, if you have questions or concerns about your pet's health, talk to your veterinarian. Whether he or she practices conventional veterinary medicine, holistic medicine, or a combination of both, your vet's help is vital to caring for an injured or ill pet.

Kidney Disease

There are several kidney ailments that fall under the umbrella description of kidney disease. Some, like polycystic kidney disease, are congenital, meaning the pet is born with them. Some are inherited, such as renal dysplasia. Kidney disease is also a disease that affects elderly pets; as they age, many older pets develop renal failure.

Symptoms of kidney disease may include increased thirst, frequent or significantly decreased urination, blood in the urine, vomiting, diarrhea, weight loss, unhealthy skin and coat, and pain around the kidneys. Your veterinarian will have to make the final diagnosis regarding this disease as many of these symptoms can also apply to other diseases.

> **PET ALERT**
>
> Antifreeze poisoning is one of the most common forms of pet poisoning. Pets are often attracted by the product's sweet taste. As little as 1 teaspoon of antifreeze can be lethal to a cat, and not much more can kill a dog. The poison, ethylene glycol, causes sudden kidney failure. You can help prevent antifreeze poisoning by purchasing the available non-lethal antifreezes.

Causes

Just as there are many different types of kidney disease, there are many causes of kidney disease. Pets with polycystic kidney disease develop cysts on the kidneys. The damage done to the kidneys depends on how many cysts develop. Renal dysplasia occurs when tissue in the kidneys are malformed. Age, infections, parasites, trauma, and toxins can all lead to kidney disease.

Kidney disease can happen in any dog breed or any mixture of breeds, but inherited tendencies have been seen in many breeds, including Alaskan Malamutes, Basenjis, Beagles, Bernese Mountain Dogs, Bull Terriers, Cairn Terriers, Cocker Spaniels, Doberman Pinschers, Golden Retrievers, Labrador Retrievers, Lhasa Apsos, Miniature Schnauzers, Soft-Coated Wheaten Terriers, Shih Tzus, and Standard Poodles.

Cats can develop kidney disease, just as dogs can. Breeds that appear to have an inherited tendency to develop certain forms of the disease include Abyssinians, Siamese, Russian Blues, Burmese, and Balinese. Mixed-breed cats aren't immune, and can certainly develop it.

Prevention

Keeping your pet as healthy as possible is the best prevention. Feed your cat or dog a high-quality diet, prevent exposure to poisons and other toxins, and limit medications that can cause kidney damage (if possible).

Breeders should use only those cats and dogs who don't have kidney disease, and whose ancestors haven't had it, for breeding stock. Even though there are many causes of certain forms of this disease, eliminating the inherited diseases would be wonderful.

Remedies

Feed your pet a high-quality, preferably home-cooked diet (see Chapter 12) because many questions have surfaced concerning the relationship between processed commercial diets and kidney disease. Many people are investigating whether there's an actual, concrete connection. Cooked food is better than raw for pets with kidney disease because they often have compromised immune systems.

GO NATURAL

Consider providing a diet high in fatty acids as a means of helping pets with kidney disease, though research has thus far shown the amounts normally given to pets—especially those found naturally in foods— are ineffective. Talk to your veterinarian to see if he recommends an increase in fatty acid supplements.

For many years, experts have recommended that pets with kidney disease be fed diets lower in proteins to ease the kidneys' work. Many experts are revisiting this approach because lowered protein levels can also lead to health issues. Most experts are currently recommending that pet owners maintain protein levels, though owners should take a close look at the actual sources of proteins.

Eggs are an excellent source of protein, and they contain all of the amino acids pets need for good health. Cooked eggs, combined with easily digested meat such as chicken and turkey, are better than red meat. Although plant proteins aren't complete, they promote alkaline urine and thus are good for damaged kidneys.

Water is important, and pet owners should encourage pets to drink as much as they want. Adding low-sodium vegetable or chicken broth to the pet's water may help encourage consumption.

Water-soluble vitamins tend to pass quickly through pets with kidney disease. It's therefore important to supplement the diet with vitamins B complex and C.

Phosphorus is a damaging mineral for pets with kidney disease. Many veterinarians may recommend medications to lower phosphorus levels. Supplementing the diet with calcium can also help because calcium binds to phosphorus, but discuss this supplement with your veterinarian prior to adding it to the diet.

You can also use several herbal remedies to treat kidney disease, including astragalus, burdock, dandelion leaf, echinacea, hawthorne, marshmallow (the plant, not the candy), and ginkgo biloba. Two homeopathic remedies that are recommended for pets with kidney disease are natrum muriaticum and arsenicum album.

Talk to Your Veterinarian

Your veterinarian must diagnose kidney disease. Following a definitive diagnosis, talk to your veterinarian about any natural remedies you may like to try. It's important that those don't interfere with or react to any medications he or she may wish you to use. Always call your veterinarian if your pet's symptoms reappear or get worse.

Liver Disease

The liver is a complex organ that's vital to good health. The liver is one of the few organs that can heal itself after damage, but it can only do so if the disease is caught early. When a pet's liver is severely damaged—either from an inherited, congenital disease or from another disease—the prognosis can be poor.

The first symptom of liver disease may be some tenderness in the abdomen, usually near the rib cage. The abdomen may be slightly enlarged. Your pet may become jaundiced, which you can see when the whites of the eyes turn yellow. The gums, tongue, and inner ears will appear yellow, too.

DOG TALK

Many purebred dog clubs are now helping to establish and support research into genetic screening for health problems found in their breed, including liver disease. To help support these efforts, contact the national breed club of your choice and ask how you can donate.

Causes

There are several inherited forms of liver disease, but liver problems can also be caused by toxins, medications given over long periods of time, and other diseases.

Dogs and cats can both suffer from liver disease. Although there don't seem to be any particular cat breeds affected more than others, several dog breeds are. Bedlington Terriers, Doberman Pinschers, Skye Terriers, and West Highland White Terriers are more prone to copper toxicosis than other breeds. Miniature Schnauzers, Maltese, West Highland White Terriers, and Irish Wolfhounds are more prone to liver shunts.

Copper toxicosis, also called copper-associated hepatitis, is the body's inability to metabolize copper. This allows toxic levels of copper to build up in the liver, causing liver failure and eventually death.

Liver shunts are abnormal veins that allow blood to bypass the liver. The liver cannot do its job of removing toxins from the bloodstream. Ammonia and other toxins can build up and can result in hepatitis encephalopathy, a brain dysfunction caused by high levels of ammonia in the bloodstream. The pet will stagger as if drunk, be mentally dull and disoriented, drool, and may even have seizures.

Prevention

As with all potentially inherited diseases, breeders should screen their breeding animals and use only those without liver disease to eliminate or decrease the number of inherited cases.

Eliminating the use of many household and yard chemicals and toxins can put less stress on the animal's liver. Because one of the functions of the liver is to remove toxins from the body, too many toxins in the animal's environment—such as from pesticides, insecticides, fertilizers, cleaning chemicals, and herbicides—place stress on or potentially damage the liver.

Remedies

Milk thistle is the number one treatment for any liver disorder. Long known by natural remedy experts for its ability to help the liver heal itself, even conventional medical practitioners often recommend it.

Milk thistle works by increasing bile production and flow, and by acting as an antioxidant that slows liver inflammation. It also strengthens and repairs damaged cells.

GO NATURAL

Milk thistle is a flowering plant from the daisy family. It's native to Mediterranean Europe, North Africa, and the Middle East. For more than 2,000 years, people have used it as a tonic for treating liver disease. There's no way we can know how long people have used it for domesticated animals.

Other herbal and food remedies include turmeric, artichoke, boswellia, burdock, licorice, dandelion, goldenseal, red clover, yellow dock, and yarrow. The combination of milk thistle, red clover, and licorice root seem to be the most effective. Yogurt with digestive enzymes is great because it adds nutrition and assists the body with food digestion, thereby allowing the liver to heal better because it doesn't have to work as hard.

CoQ10, B complex, and vitamin C are also good for dogs and cats with liver disease. Pet owners often use the homeopathic remedies carduus marianus and chelidonium majus as well. These remedies serve a variety of functions but primarily assist the liver by keeping the immune system strong, helping the digestive system function better, and aiding the circulatory system.

Although veterinarians sometimes recommend a low-protein diet, this shouldn't be a blanket recommendation for all pets with liver disease because the liver needs protein for healing. Digestive enzymes—such as yogurt, kefir, papaya, and pineapple—help the body more easily process proteins. Proteins such as those present in eggs, cottage cheese, and yogurt may be more easily digested than red meat.

CAT CHAT

Overweight cats who stop eating for any reason—whether because of a change in food or because of another health-related issue—can develop fatty liver disease. This occurs when the body begins using fat reserves for body processes because the liver can become overwhelmed with fat and fail.

Talk to Your Veterinarian

The liver has amazing powers to heal itself—more than any other organ in the body—but it often needs help to do so. Pay attention to symptoms that may indicate liver disease, and talk to your veterinarian right away if you see any of them appear.

If you're currently treating your pet for liver disease and you see an increase in symptoms or any decline in your pet's health, call your veterinarian immediately. If the condition progresses too far, the liver can reach a point when it can no longer heal itself.

Mange

Mange is caused by mites, tiny insects that live on and in the skin. Mites are usually not a problem and can often live symbiotically with their host, not causing any health issues. However, at certain times of life—puberty, for example—or if the animal is stressed or ill, the mites can get out of control. Following are some common types of mange:

- **Demodectic mange** is common in puppies, kittens, and adolescent dogs, and adolescent males seem to get it more often than females. This mite is too small to be seen without magnification, so it is usually diagnosed by a skin scraping, which is then examined under a microscope. This type of mange is not contagious.

- **Sarcoptic mange** (often called scabies) is more prevalent in puppies and dogs than in cats. This is caused by a tiny mite that again must be diagnosed through a skin scraping examined under a microscope. This mange is highly contagious to other pets and people. It causes extreme itching; the pet might scratch or chew himself raw and bloody.

- **Notoedric mange** most often appears in kittens and cats. This mite is diagnosed by skin scrapings examined under a microscope. It is highly contagious to other animals and people. It causes hair loss and crusty spots on the skin that can develop secondary infections.

- **Chyletiella mange** (often called walking dandruff) is caused by a large red-colored mite that can often be seen on dogs and cats, but most often on puppies, without magnification. It tends to be found in kennels and pet stores where there are large numbers of animals. It causes crusty, flaking skin that may or may not be itchy. This is contagious to other animals and people.

- **Otodectic mange** (usually known as ear mites) occurs in puppies, kittens, dogs, and cats. These tiny mites cause severe itching, so much so that it is often diagnosed simply by the amount of scratching at the ears the pet does. These mites are highly contagious to other animals but not to people.

Although each type of mange has individual characteristics, most cause itching, rubbing, scratching, and skin irritation. Scabies can cause animals to scratch and chew at themselves in a torment of itching. Many animals will cause open sores with their scratching.

Causes

Demodectic mange likely has an inherited tendency, and isn't contagious. Generally, it flares up when the animal's immune system is out of kilter, such as during adolescence. Other forms of mange are contagious to other pets in the household and even to people.

Prevention

A healthy pet with a strong immune system is the best prevention for any type of mange. Then, even if the pet is exposed, the body can either resist succumbing to the mites' adverse effects or it can succumb to a lesser degree than if the pet were sickly.

Do not breed animals who have suffered an outbreak of demodectic mange. Because reaction to these mites has a potentially genetic link, the easiest way to prevent it is to not breed animals who have a history of demodectic mange.

Remedies

A high-quality diet high in antioxidants is good mange prevention. Many experts recommend fatty acid supplements, including fish oils (such as cod liver oil).

Once an outbreak has occurred, there aren't any known natural remedies that cure or control it. Some caregivers have used natural remedies in conjunction with veterinary care, including an apple cider vinegar rinse (safe for cats and dogs), a tea tree oil rinse (for dogs only), and a lavender oil rinse (for dogs only). See Chapter 4 for more information on essential oils.

Boosting your pet's immune system is important during and after a mange outbreak. Herbs such as burdock, dandelion, echinacea, licorice root, sarsaparilla, and yellow dock are immune boosters.

Talk to Your Veterinarian

Your veterinarian must diagnose a mange outbreak. He or she must first determine whether mites or something else is to blame. Next, your vet must figure out what type of mite is involved in the outbreak. Because natural remedies can't cure mites, talk to your vet about any remedies you would like to use in conjunction with his or her recommended treatments.

Obesity

Some veterinarians and nutrition experts believe that as many as 40 percent of all dogs and cats in the United States are overweight and potentially obese. Wild canines and felines aren't obese; this isn't a natural condition. Wild canines and felines work for their food by hunting and scavenging. They move around a lot, and they put forth a great deal of energy to hunt and to protect themselves and their offspring.

Domestic dogs and cats who have food placed in front of them by their owners often eat too much. Because they aren't nearly as active as their wild counterparts, they often put on too many pounds. Unfortunately, obesity can be as bad for our pets as it is for us. It can lead to many other serious illnesses, including diabetes, joint pain, and arthritis.

Causes

The causes of obesity in dogs and cats are usually overeating, eating the wrong foods, and a lack of exercise. One, two, or all three factors may contribute to an animal's obesity.

Some breeds are more prone to obesity than others, so a genetic predisposition may be a part of the equation. Basset Hounds, Beagles, Labrador Retrievers, Mastiffs, and Pugs gain weight easily. Indoor cats tend to be heavier than cats who go outside.

Some health problems, including thyroid disease, can lead to weight gain. Some medications can, too, including steroids.

Prevention

The best way to prevent obesity is to be attentive to your pet's weight. All dogs and cats, no matter what breed or mixture of breeds, should have a waist. The body should be slightly slimmer between the ribs and hips, cinching at the waist. Certainly, the animal should have some meat on the ribs, but you should be able to feel individual ribs. Dogs and cats don't become obese suddenly; it happens over time. If you pay attention, you can make changes before the pet is obese.

Obviously, it is important to feed your pet a high-quality diet. Limit treats to good foods, such as bits of meat or fish, or slices of apple, banana, or carrot.

Keep your pet moving. Daily exercise and regular playtimes are very important and can help burn calories.

GO NATURAL

Zookeepers use environmental enrichment to keep their animals' minds and body busy. Do this for your pets by hiding toys and treats in different places so your dog or cat must hunt them down.

Remedies

If your pet is already obese and you want to make some changes, begin with a visit to your veterinarian. Make sure your pet is otherwise healthy before you change anything. If your cat is obese, Implement any changes under your veterinarian's supervision so you can prevent fatty liver disease, which can occur in cats who stop eating, either because of a diet, a change in food, or another health-related issue.

Feed your pet a high-quality diet. If your pet is eating a commercial food, consider changing to a raw food or home-cooked diet (see Chapters 11 and 12). Feed your cat or dog a diet high in animal proteins, a moderate amount of complex carbohydrates, and no cereal grains.

Measure the amount you feed your pet, so you can cut back accurately on the amount you feed him or her if you see weight gain. If your pet acts hungry, increase the fiber in the food to help him or her feel fuller. Adding some cooked or canned pumpkin to the food is a tasty, low-calorie way to increase fiber.

Increase your pet's exercise and play routines. Do so gradually because sore muscles are no fun, and because forcing your pet to do too much may cause injury.

Acupuncture can help the pet feel more balanced as changes occur in his or her body. We don't know if chiropractic therapies aid weight loss, though many chiropractors feel it can help treat soreness or strains that may occur during exercise.

Talk to Your Veterinarian

If you aren't sure whether your dog or cat is at a healthy weight, or if your pet is obviously overweight, talk to your veterinarian. He or she can help you with your pet's weight-loss program. Discuss guidelines as to how much weight your pet should lose each month and what your pet's ideal weight might be. If your pet doesn't seem to lose any weight, even with your help, take your pet in for a thorough examination and bloodwork. Several diseases, including thyroid disease, can make weight loss difficult.

Pain

Pain can be extremely debilitating. A dog or cat in pain may become depressed, lethargic, or aggressive, and he or she may stop participating in normal activities.

> **CAT CHAT**
>
> Many cats are stoic. They may hide illnesses, injuries, and even pain. It's important to pay attention to your cat's normal behavior and routine. When these change for no apparent reason, take a close look at why.

Causes

Pain has a cause; it doesn't appear without a reason. It can be caused by an illness, an injury, overexertion, or playing too rough. It's important that you address the original cause of the pain to prevent further and future occurrences. If you know your pet played too hard the day before, then you know the cause of the soreness and pain.

If you don't know what caused your pet's pain, consult with your veterinarian to find the source. After your vet has diagnosed the problem, you can begin treating it, whether you take a natural or conventional approach, or a combination of both. Of course, you must also address the pain as your pet is healing.

Prevention

It's impossible to protect your pet completely so he or she will never feel pain—he or she would never be able to play, perform dog sports, chase a mechanical mouse, or do anything else that's fun and exciting. Illnesses can cause pain, too. Although you can prevent many of those illnesses with good health care, you can't prevent all of them. Still, you can keep your pet somewhat safe by being careful and protecting him or her when you can.

Remedies

Natural pain remedies don't have the quick reaction time of conventional medications. It may take a day or two for them to calm the pain.

Feverfew is the herbal pain reliever people most commonly use. People often use it for migraines, so it has some pain relieving strength. Skullcap, licorice root, St. John's wort, turmeric, and yucca are also good for soreness and pain.

For pain, experts often recommend the homeopathic remedies arnica montana, bellis perennis, hypericum perforatum, and calendula officinalis. Some people like essential oils for their calming effect on dogs stressed out by discomfort. Lavender and peppermint oil are especially calming to dogs. Again, though, don't use essential oil remedies on cats.

Acupuncture is often valuable to dogs and cats suffering from pain, depending on the cause. Chiropractic therapy may also be worthwhile. See Chapter 2 for more information on these therapies.

Talk to Your Veterinarian

If you know your pet is sore from overexertion, what he or she did to cause pain, and that he or she isn't hurt seriously, then you can probably treat the pain at home. If you don't know the cause of the pain or if it gets worse, talk to your veterinarian. Remember, pain is a signal something's wrong.

Skin and Coat Problems

Dogs' and cats' skin and coats reflect their overall health. A healthy dog or cat has a nice shiny coat and clear, supple skin. An ill dog or cat is apt to reflect his or her unhealthiness in the skin and coat. The animal may have dry or flaky skin, and a dull, dry-looking coat. He or she may shed more or even have patches of thin coat.

If your pet has skin and coat problems, see your veterinarian before doing anything else. Make sure there aren't underlying health issues causing the skin and coat problems.

Causes

Several health problems—thyroid, liver disease, kidney disease, and others—can cause an unhealthy coat. After your veterinarian has ruled those out, you can consider other issues that may be causing the lackluster coat.

Other things can cause a coat to become unhealthy. A less than optimal diet or a diet lacking certain ingredients, dirty living conditions, and a lack of grooming can all affect the coat. Internal and external parasites such as intestinal worms, mites, and fleas can affect nutrition, cause allergic responses, and make your pet chew and itch.

 DOG TALK

The type of coat a dog has—short, long, thick, thin, flowing, curly, or straight—has no bearing on the quality of the coat. That instead is based on heredity and the health of the dog.

Heredity also plays a part in the health of an animal's coat. If your dog's or cat's ancestors had a tendency to have skin and coat problems, your pet may face the same issues, too. Allergies can be inherited, too, as can the tendency to have demodectic mange (see the discussion earlier in the chapter).

Prevention

Keeping your pet healthy, with a strong immune system, is one of the best ways to prevent skin and coat problems. If your pet is healthy on the inside, he or she is more likely to be healthy on the outside. Being healthy on the inside means a high-quality diet that's high in all of the essential nutrients, including the fatty acids, which are important for healthy skin and a shiny, full coat.

Grooming your pet on a regular basis—which means brushing or combing, and hair trimming—will help with skin and coat health. How often you must groom your pet and how involved the grooming process must be is dependent on the breed. Bathe your pet only when necessary. Bathing removes the natural oils from the skin and coat. Certainly, if your pet is dirty, go ahead and bathe him or her.

Controlling the parasites, inside and out, is also important. Work with your veterinarian to control internal parasites. Use good grooming techniques to control the external ones.

Remedies

The first step to a healthy coat is to feed your pet a good diet with whole foods that supply the essential fatty acids. You may want to supplement the diet with fish oil, cod liver oil, or flaxseed meal. Just add one of these supplements; all three may be too much.

Give your pet some yogurt, kefir, papaya, or pineapple for additional digestive enzymes. A high-quality diet won't do any good if your dog can't digest it properly.

The Honest Kitchen's remedy Sparkle is designed to help the skin and coat. It contains dandelion leaf, rosehips, burdock root, nettle leaf, and nutritional yeast. (See Appendix B for information on this and other products mentioned in this chapter.)

Only Natural Pet offers several skin and coat supplements and remedies for dogs and cats. Super Daily Vitamins & Enzymes for Skin and Coat contains vitamins and fatty acids, including omega-3 and -6. It also contains digestive enzymes.

Talk to Your Veterinarian

If your pet is scratching badly or if bald patches appear, talk to your veterinarian about any potential allergies, mange, or other health issues. If you're using natural remedies for the skin and coat and there's no improvement, call your vet for help identifying the problem.

Urinary Incontinence

Urinary incontinence isn't a house-training problem. If your dog is leaving surprises for you in another room, behind the sofa, or at a closed door that leads outside, you've got a house-training issue. When a dog relaxes in sleep and urinates, or dribbles a little all the time, that's urinary incontinence.

The first signs of urinary incontinence are dribbles of urine on the floor or wet spots where the dog has been sleeping. The coat around the genitalia may be damp all the time.

Causes

Hormone-related incontinence is the most common form of incontinence, and occurs most frequently in older spayed female dogs. It's less common in males. Although it can develop in older spayed female cats, it's not nearly as common as in dogs. Incontinence can also be caused by neurological problems, tumors, spinal cord injuries, bladder problems, kidney disease, and birth defects. Your veterinarian will need to examine your pet to determine the cause of the problem.

CAT CHAT

Obesity can cause urinary incontinence in cats. When obese cats who are otherwise healthy lose weight, the incontinence usually stops.

Prevention

Occasionally, vets have recommended that female animals not be spayed because most pets with incontinence issues are spayed females. That's not necessarily a good recommendation, even if many spayed female dogs never develop incontinence, considering intact female pets can develop other health issues such as pyometra, an infection that develops in the uterus and can be life threatening. In addition, dealing with the every-six-month season can be messy and will attract any intact male dogs in the neighborhood.

At this point, the best recommendations seem to be to keep your dog at a healthy weight and to help them maintain a good fitness level as they age.

Remedies

Experts most commonly recommend the traditional Chinese medicine (TCM) remedies Rehmannia Six and Rehmannia Eight as natural remedies for urinary incontinence. These remedies contain a variety of herbs that have therapeutic value for the kidneys, bladder, and urinary tract. Because the herbs needed vary from one pet to another, a TCM practitioner needs to provide some guidance.

There are a number of commercial remedies for this problem. Nature's Herbs offers a Chinese herbal remedy for cats and dogs. Only Natural has a product called Incontinence Homeopathic as well as an herbal formula called Tract-Ease for Kidney and Bladder Support. PetAlive has a homeopathic remedy called UTI-Free. Other herbal remedies include gingko biloba, mullein, and shiitake mushrooms.

Soy isoflavones are beneficial to animals with hormone-related incontinence, but you should only use this supplement with a veterinarian's supervision because soy can have such a strong effect on the body.

> **DEFINITION**
>
> **Soy isoflavones** are the organic compounds in soy that work in place of estrogen in the body. They can either block estrogen's effects or partially replace it.

Talk to Your Veterinarian

Since there can be many causes of urinary difficulties, it's a good idea to talk to your veterinarian when there are any changes in your pet's urinary habits. If your vet diagnoses old age–related incontinence, then you can discuss using natural remedies to assist your pet.

Call your vet, too, if the incontinence is occurring all the time and the urine is just running out of your pet. If the opposite occurs and your pet becomes unable to urinate, that needs immediate veterinary attention.

The Least You Need to Know

- Kidney and liver disease are serious pet illnesses; talk to your veterinarian about using natural remedies along with conventional medicine.
- More than 40 percent of pets in the United States are overweight or obese, which can lead to other serious health problems.
- Skin and coat problems have many causes, including diet and nutrition, parasites, and diseases.
- Urinary incontinence is not a housetraining issue and shouldn't be treated as one. It can be caused by many health issues, and the pet can't control the urine leakage.

The Aging Pet

Chapter 18

In This Chapter

- Understanding the aging process
- Helping your aging pet with natural remedies
- Making end-of-life decisions
- Allowing yourself to grieve

It's hard to watch a beloved pet grow older. As your pet's joints become stiff and the muzzle grays, it becomes obvious they simply don't live long enough. Twelve to 15 years go by so fast; it's unfair we can't have them in our lives longer.

Your dog's or cat's life span depends on the animal's state of health, genetics, breed or mixture of breeds, nutrition, and any stresses he or she has faced over a lifetime. Cats who go or live outside generally have shorter life spans than cats who live entirely inside.

Many people think that mixed-breed dogs or cats aren't as susceptible to as many health problems as purebred dogs and cats and thus have an advantage. Although this is sometimes true for individual dogs and cats, it is not true for all. Even mixed breeds are the result of their genetics—just as purebreds are—and being a mixed breed doesn't affect your dog's or cat's longevity.

The Aging Process

If your dog or cat isn't battling a terminal disease, the first signs of aging will probably appear gradually. Some dogs begin getting gray on the muzzle at 6 or 7 years of age, and that may be the only sign of aging for several more years. Every dog and cat ages differently, just as people do. Pet owners usually notice their pet is aging because of changes in behavior. You may notice your cat doesn't want to chase the fishing pole toy anymore or will only play for a minute or two before quitting. Your dog may not want to jump in the air for the tennis ball.

Older pets tend to sleep longer and more deeply. When my Australian Shepherd, Dax, was 13, she slept so soundly I would quietly approach her and watch to make sure she was still breathing. She scared me several times in her last few months.

Another sign of aging is hearing loss. Most pets retain some hearing at varying sound frequencies, but some go completely deaf. My oldest dog, Riker, is now 12 years old. When he began losing his hearing about a year ago, he was upset, fearful, reactive, and depressed. It took me a while to realize he was upset because he could no longer hear my voice. Here he was, my beloved pet, who I believe thought I wasn't talking to him anymore.

CAT CHAT

Generally, healthy indoor cats live for 15 to 18 years. It's not unusual, though, for cats to live for 18 to 20 years, with some living into their early 20s. Cats who live or go outside on a regular basis face a variety of threats, from exposure to disease, to dangers from other animals, to being hit by a car. Their lives are usually much shorter.

I handled this by changing my tone of voice until I found a pitch at which he could still hear my voice. He was overjoyed! I also made a habit of using hand signals to get his attention, smiling at him, and reaching out to him with my hands. When he walks into my hands, I pet him, rub him, and show him I still love him. His depression disappeared.

You may see your pet lose some vision or visual acuity, have dental problems, undergo changes in the intestinal tract, or experience changes in the thickness and texture of the coat. Your pet's joints may become stiff, and he or she may be slow to get up after sleeping. Most animals need to relieve themselves more often as they age. Some dogs and cats, like people, become grumpy as they get older.

Unfortunately, pets with terminal illnesses go through many of the same aging processes as healthy pets do—depending on age—but they also face the problems presented by their illnesses. The individual problems vary depending upon the illness involved.

It's important to work with your veterinarian—conventional or holistic—so you can deal with both your pet's illness and his or her aging.

DOG TALK

Small dogs often live from 14 to 16 years, medium-sized dogs from 12 to 14 years, large-sized dogs from 10 to 12 years, and giant-sized dogs from 8 to 10 years. These are just averages, though, and individual dogs may have different life spans.

Remedies That Can Help

Although it's impossible to prevent your pet from dying eventually, there are quite a few remedies available to help you make your pet more comfortable as he or she ages. The first is to keep your pet from extreme climates. Older pets can't handle extreme heat or cold; they get very uncomfortable and easily become overheated or chilled.

A high-quality diet is very important. In years past, vets recommended pet owners feed elderly cats and dogs a diet lower in protein to help their aging kidneys. There are several commercial diets that offer foods made with lowered protein levels. This has become a highly debated topic. Many nutrition experts are now saying elderly healthy pets should continue to eat a diet high in protein. There's no evidence that a lower-protein diet will prevent kidney failure later in life.

The elderly pet's diet should be high in antioxidants and fatty acids, but watch those calories. Don't allow older dogs or cats to become obese, which would only complicate the aging process. Digestive enzymes are often beneficial to older cats and dogs because the intestinal tract may not work as well as it did years ago.

It's important to keep older pets active. Continue walks and play sessions, but tailor them to your pet's changing abilities. Keep your pet's mind active, too. Interact with your pet, encourage games, and keep teaching him or her new things.

GO NATURAL

The muffin tin game is great fun. You need a 12-hole muffin tin and a dozen tennis balls. Place a treat, like cheese, in each hole, and then place a tennis ball on top. Encourage your dog to find the cheese. For cats and small dogs, play this with a miniature muffin tin and ping pong balls.

Some supplements and herbal remedies can help older pets, including vitamin B complex, vitamin C, CoQ10, and glucosamine chondroitin. Some commercial formulas include Only Natural Pet's Senior Formula Herbal Remedy and Super Daily Vitamins for Seniors. (See Chapter 13 for details on supplementing your pet's diet, and see Appendix B for details on ordering these supplements.)

You may also want to make some changes to your pet's environment:

- Make sure the litter box, cat food, and water dish are easily available, especially when your cat is unable to jump or climb.

- Your cat may need a litter box with lower sides so he or she can get in and out more easily.

- If your dog is stiff, place food and water on a stand that reaches about the height of his or her elbows. Doing so will make it easier for your dog to eat and drink.

- Provide your old dog or cat with a bed that provides support, while still being soft for old bones and joints. Eggshell foam provides this kind of comfort.

- In the winter, make sure your old pet has some warmth to prevent old joints from getting stiff. An extra blanket, a hot water bottle, or a heated pet bed would be appreciated.

- Give your old dog or cat a ramp so he or she can get into the car or up on the bed without injury.

Watch your pet, and help him or her when it is clear your pet needs some help. He or she may not appreciate it at the time, but help anyway. After all, some pets don't realize they are getting older and think they can still do the same things they did when they were younger. So help your pet, encourage him or her to use the ramp or new litter box, and praise your pet when he or she does.

Hospice

When your pet is approaching the end of life, care can become more difficult. Your cat or dog may need more veterinary care, especially if he or she has a terminal illness. At some point, you may need to decide whether veterinary care for that illness should continue.

Although hospice care for people is widely accepted, it's relatively new in veterinary medicine. Hospice care might consist of instructions on caring for your pet during this new stage of life, or you might need a veterinarian or veterinary technician to make periodic visits to your home. Sometimes pets need hospice care at the veterinarian's clinic. A new addition to this field are facilities that provide all care for pets during this end-of-life stage.

When you begin hospice care for your pet, you'll receive instructions from your vet for how to keep your pet comfortable for the rest of his or her life. Pain management is crucial, as well as nutrition and nutritional support. Ask your vet for advice on how to deal with urinary incontinence, vomiting, and diarrhea. Your vet or a pet hospice organization can help you with any issues so you and your dog or cat can go through this process together.

GO NATURAL

Your veterinarian may be able to provide hospice care for you and your aging pet. If your vet isn't able to do so, however, ask your vet for a referral to a pet hospice organization in your area.

The End of Life

Many aging pets astound their owners with their ability to cope with the aging process. After all, aging is completely natural. At some point, though, they'll need more help as they grow older. The natural remedies may not work as well anymore and your pet may need veterinary care to reach some level of comfort.

Some pets grow old and pass away at home, comfortable and well-loved. My husband and I lost our silver and black tabby cat, Tigger, that way. At the age of 17 years and 6 months, he fell asleep on our bed and died in his sleep. There was no sign of discomfort and he wasn't sick; he just died.

Although neither my husband nor I were with him in his last moments, and although we would have liked to have been there for him, one of our other cats was there. When I found them, our 3-year-old orange and white cat, Squash, was curled around him grooming him even though he was already gone.

Unfortunately, not all of our pets experience a pain-free and peaceful passing. Sometimes our pets may be in pain. They may be very sick and uncomfortable. Sometimes we need to let them go.

Deciding whether to euthanize a beloved pet is tough. Here are some questions to consider:

- Is your pet having more bad days than good days?
- Is your pet hiding and refusing to come out from hiding?
- Has your pet stopped playing?
- Is your pet no longer eager to eat? Is your pet drinking more water, drinking significantly less than normal, or has he or she stopped drinking altogether?
- Is your pet incontinent?
- Can your pet no longer stand or walk easily?

When your pet is obviously uncomfortable, and life is no longer joyful, talk to your veterinarian about euthanasia. Most veterinarians have their own guidelines for when it's best to euthanize pets, but they will listen to your concerns.

You can bring your pet to the veterinary clinic, or some veterinarians will come to the house. Neither approach is right or wrong; it needs to be what's best for you and your pet.

The process is simple. The vet usually gives your pet a mild tranquilizer first so he or she doesn't panic. Then the vet administers the euthanasia drug, and breathing and the heart stop fairly quickly. If your pet has been very ill, and the body is used to fighting for life, it can take a moment or two.

Honor the Grieving Process

Allow yourself to grieve after you lose your pet. After all, he or she was a treasured part of your family and life. Even though your cat or dog may have shared only a few years with you, he or she was important to you. It's normal to grieve.

The grieving process has five stages:

1. Denial may occur when you realize your pet is approaching the end of life.

2. Bargaining is when you may try to stave off death by trying new types of care, by using additional remedies, or by practicing your religion.

3. Anger may happen as death approaches, or it may occur after your pet dies.

4. Sadness may occur before or after your pet's death, or throughout the process.

5. Acceptance is when you are able to accept your pet's death and remember the happy memories you shared.

Not everyone goes through these stages in the same way; grieving is a very personal process. I find that I rarely get angry, but I do get very sad. And for me, sadness is usually the longest stage of grief. It begins before my pet dies, then lasts through the death and afterward. It takes a while for me to find acceptance. If you can recognize these stages of grief in yourself as you are going through it, it helps to understand what's happening emotionally. Just realize that grief is personal and what others feel is not necessarily right for you. You have to find your own peace.

> **GO NATURAL**
>
> Many veterinary colleges have hotlines for grieving pet owners. Ask your veterinarian for the one closest to you. Also search online for the "Rainbow Bridge." This has been a tremendous source of comfort for pet owners who have lost beloved pets.

Remember Your Companion

In your grief and hurt, don't erase the fact that your pet ever existed. Instead, remember him or her. Some pet owners go through old photos and create a scrapbook. Some pet owners like to save special toys, bowls, collars, or identification tags. It's important to find a way to remember your pet that's right for you.

As a writer, I write about my pets when they pass away. It's my way of honoring them and coping with the loss.

Here is part of what I wrote after we lost our Dax in 2008:

> My husband, Paul, and I lost our old dog today. This morning we helped her cross the Rainbow Bridge and she is finally free of the disease that has made her life uncomfortable for so long.
>
> Dax is an Australian Shepherd, and in her 13 years, earned obedience titles, herded sheep and geese, played in agility, and was an awesome therapy dog. She was honored by the AKC's ACE program for her therapy dog work.
>
> Dax's name comes from a *Star Trek* character, Jadzia Dax, who has a part of her who has lived many lives. When I first saw Dax at the age of 5 weeks, I said she had wise eyes. She was an old soul.

Dax worked hard and played hard. She always gave 110 percent, even when her liver disease caused her to feel bad. She was diagnosed with copper toxicosis at 6 years of age. Although she wasn't supposed to live for more than six months past diagnosis, with our help she lived another seven and a half years.

At 13, however, it was finally clear that our warrior woman was tired of fighting. Her liver had given up, her arthritis was painful, and she just plain didn't feel good. She fought so long to remain active and healthy and just couldn't do it anymore. It was time to say good-bye.

It's always hard to lose an old dog; they have been a treasured part of our lives. But every year we had with Dax was a bonus; with her liver disease we knew we could lose her at any time.

Dax leaves a legacy behind her. She gave hundreds of people love and affection during her therapy dog work, especially during the time when we visited hospice patients. She taught me a lot, too, especially how to live and train an intelligent, focused dog. Dax made a huge impact on our lives and we'll miss her.

I can't imagine living without my dogs and cats; life would be so sterile, quiet, and, well, boring. Our pets make us laugh when they play, roll over to invite a belly rub, and chase mysterious shadows on the wall. They provide warmth, affection, and comfort. They add so much to our lives, our families, and even our physical well-being.

By giving us so much, we also must give to them in return. Our pets need our love and affection. They need the best care we can provide for them, which includes good food, grooming, natural remedies and healing techniques, and veterinary care when that is appropriate.

The Least You Need to Know

- The aging process is normal; you need not fear it. You can help keep your older pets more comfortable during this process.

- Several remedies—including diet, supplements, and herbal remedies—can help individual aging complaints.

- When the end of your pet's life approaches, talk to your veterinarian about his or her policies and what your vet can offer to help you and your pet.

- Give yourself permission to grieve for your pet and treasure your memories.

Glossary

acupressure   An alternative therapy, similar to acupuncture, but performed with massage or pressure instead of using needles to penetrate the body. *See also* acupuncture.

acupuncture   An ancient alternative therapy from China that uses needles placed in specific spots on the body to treat disease or injuries.

alternative medicine   This denotes anything used for health care or illness prevention that falls outside the scope of conventional medicine.

amino acids   When proteins are consumed, they are broken down into amino acids, which are used for a variety of purposes within the body.

anaphylactic shock   A serious, life-threatening allergic response to a substance. Symptoms can include redness, swelling, seizures, and shock.

antibody   A protein-based substance, found in the body and produced by the immune system, that helps protect the body from disease.

aromatherapy   Using the fragrance of essential oils to create a change, either emotionally or physically.

Ayurveda   A system of alternative healing from India that includes the prevention of disease as well as healing it.

cardiomyopathy   An umbrella term for a variety of diseases or disorders that involve the muscles of the heart. When the muscles of the heart are malformed, diseased, or injured, the heart cannot function correctly and eventually will fail.

carnivore   An animal that eats meat almost exclusively.

chiropractic   An alternative therapy that uses manipulation of the spine to treat illnesses and injuries.

complete and balanced   Foods with this label contain adequate nutrition for the intended animal's health, according to the Association of American Feed Control Officials.

dinner   Foods with this label—as well as "banquet" and other similar descriptive terms—may contain a variety of ingredients (not just meat).

flower essences   A branch of homeopathy that uses flowers in the remedies.

food therapy   In traditional Chinese veterinary medicine (TCVM), this technique requires that the pet owner use specific foods, based on the energetic effect each food item has on the body. *See also* TCVM (traditional Chinese veterinary medicine).

for all life stages   Foods with this label provide adequate nutrition for all stages of life, from infant to old age.

free feeding   The practice of leaving food available to a pet all day.

free range   This means the animals involved are not caged all the time. This doesn't indicate they're never caged.

herb   A useful plant, often providing medicinal properties.

herbivore   An animal that eats plants exclusively.

holistic or **holism**   This is based on the idea that the whole pet—that is, all aspects of the pet's life—must be taken into account when providing for the animal's health.

home remedies   Natural health techniques, often passed on from one generation to the next.

homeopathy   An alternative remedy using small amounts of substances diluted in water or alcohol to affect a change in the mind or body.

human grade   Indicates that every ingredient and the processing method are equal to those used to meet human food standards.

integrated care   Combines conventional medicine and alternative, holistic, and natural health techniques in conjunction with conventional veterinary medicine.

law of similars   The primary principle of homeopathy, which says that if a disease causes a specific symptom, another substance that causes the same symptom can be used to treat that disease.

melamine   A chemical compound added illegally to foods to boost the foods' protein count in laboratory analysis.

mixed chiropractors   Practitioners who provide chiropractic services in conjunction with other therapies.

nosode   A homeopathic remedy made from a product of disease, such as a bit of infected tissue, used in place of a vaccination.

obligate carnivore   An animal that eats meat exclusively.

omnivore   An animal that eats both plants and animals.

organic   Indicates farmers or producers used environmentally sound techniques, with no synthetic pesticides or banned substances, to grow or produce a food or product.

passive immunities   Antibodies that provide immunity and come from mother's milk rather than from exposure to disease or vaccinations.

peptides   Groups or chains of amino acids that work together for a specific purpose, such as hormonal function.

periodontal disease   The inflammation of the gums and the deeper structures that support the teeth. *See also* plaque, tartar.

pheromones   Naturally produced chemicals that elicit a response from members of the same species.

phytonutrients   Organic compounds found only in plants.

plaque   A film of food particles, saliva, and proteins that form on the teeth. If not removed, plaque will convert to tartar.

Qi   Pronounced *chee*, the body's vital energy or life force.

Reiki   A healing technique originating in Japan that uses the warmth and energy from one being to affect a change in another.

retrovirus   A virus formed from RNA (rather than DNA) that often causes tumors.

secondary infection   An infection that occurs as a side effect of the original disease.

soy isoflavones   Organic compounds in soy that act like the hormone estrogen when absorbed into the body.

straight chiropractors   Practitioners who adhere to the original theories set forth by Daniel Palmer, the founder of chiropractic medicine.

tartar   A brown substance on a pet's teeth that is formed from proteins, saliva, and bacteria.

TCM (traditional Chinese medicine)   Medicine for people emphasizing that mind, body, spirit, and emotions must all be considered for good health.

TCVM (traditional Chinese veterinary medicine)   Veterinary medicine begun about 3,500 years ago that uses food, herbal remedies, massage, acupuncture, and acupressure to treat animals.

tincture   A liquid solution consisting of an herb mixed with alcohol, vinegar, or water.

titer   A concentration of a measured substance, such as disease antibodies, in blood serum.

vaccinosis   A chronic illness that results from vaccinations. It may include immune system problems, lupus, and cancer.

vital life force   *See* Qi.

Resources

Books

Bach, David. *Go Green, Live Rich.* Broadway Books, 2008.

Carlson, Delbert, DVM, Liisa Carlson, DVM, Debra Eldredge, DVM, and James Giffin, DVM. *Dog Owner's Home Veterinary Handbook* (4th ed.). Wiley Publishing, 2007.

Delaney, Kimberly. *Clean Home, Green Home (Knack: Make It Easy series).* Morris Book Publishing, 2009.

Holland, Debra, Ph.D. *The Complete Idiot's Guide to Grief and Grieving.* Alpha Books, 2011.

Martinez, Greg, DVM. *Dr. Greg's Dog Dish Diet.* Riparian Press, 2009.

Messonnier, Shawn, DVM. *8 Weeks to a Healthy Dog.* Rodale, 2003.

———. *Natural Health Bible for Dogs & Cats.* Prima Publishing, 2000.

O'Driscoll, Catherine. *Shock to the System.* Dogwise Publishing, 2006.

Plechner, Alfred J., DVM. *Pets at Risk.* New Sage Press, 2003.

Volhard, Wendy, and Kerry Brown, DVM. *Holistic Guide for a Healthy Dog.* Howell Book House, 2000.

Weiskopf, Joan. *Pet Food Nation.* Harper Collins Publishers, 2007.

York, Joan. *Alternative Health Remedies for Cats.* Booksurge Publishing, 2009.

Zucker, Martin. *Veterinary Guide to Natural Remedies for Cats.* Three Rivers Press, 2000.

Organizations

Veterinary Organizations

Academy of Veterinary Homeopathy
www.theavh.org
A professional organization for veterinarians practicing homeopathic techniques.

American Academy of Veterinary Acupuncture
www.aava.org
A professional organization for veterinarians who provide acupuncture services for pets.

American Holistic Veterinary Medical Association
www.ahvma.org
A professional organization for veterinarians interested in and practicing holistic veterinary care.

American Veterinary Chiropractic Association
www.animalchiropractic.org
A professional organization for veterinarians practicing chiropractic care.

American Veterinary Medical Association
www.avma.org
A professional veterinary organization that provides many informative files for pet owners.

Natural, Organic, and Holistic Products and Organizations

Aldaron Animal Essences
www.aldaronessences.com
An online store that provides flower essence formulas for dogs.

Canine Eye Registry Foundation (CERF)
www.vmdb.org/history.html
A registry founded to help identify and prevent inherited eye disorders and diseases.

Dr. Shawn's Pet Care Naturally
www.petcarenaturally.com
Dr. Shawn Messonnier's own line of natural pet care products.

National Center for Complementary and Alternative Medicine
www.nccam.nih.gov
Operated by the National Institutes for Health. Although for people, this is an excellent resource for basic information about alternative remedies.

National Organic Program
www.usda.gov
The U.S. Department of Agriculture's program for regulating what substances are and aren't allowed in organic foods.

Natural Dog Health Remedies
www.natural-dog-health-remedies.com
A website that provides suggestions for a wide variety of dog health issues.

Only Natural Pet Store
www.onlynaturalpet.com
An online store for natural, herbal, and homeopathic products.

Organic Trade Association
www.ota.com
An organization promoting organic businesses.

PetAlive
www.nativeremedies.com
An online store that offers a variety of natural remedies for dogs and cats.

Teddy's Pride
https://www.buyteddyspridesite.com
A dental product to help keep your pet's teeth and gums healthy.

The Honest Kitchen
www.thehonestkitchen.com
An online store that provides dehydrated pet foods and supplements for dogs and cats.

Thorne Research
www.thorne.com
A research organization that manufactures and sells alternative remedies and supplements for people and animals.

Tri-Animals
www.tri-animals.com
An online store for all-natural insect repellents and other essential oil products.

Hospice and Grieving

Angel's Gate
www.angelsgate.org
A hospice home for pets.

Argus Institute Pet Hospice
www.argusinstitute.colorado.edu/pethospice.htm
A hospice service for pets.

Beyond the Rainbow
www.texaspethospice.com
A hospice center for pets and their owners.

Brighthaven
www.brighthaven.org
A holistic retirement retreat for pets.

Pawspice
www.pawspice.com
An organization that promotes quality of life care for cancer treatments and provides hospice care for pets.

The International Association of Animal Hospice and Palliative Care
www.iaahpc.org
An association that promotes the philosophy that supports hospice for pets.

The Nikki Hospice Foundation for Pets
www.pethospice.org
A foundation that provides hospice care for pets.

Recipes

If you're interested in trying a home-cooked diet for your pet, the recipes in this appendix—all taste-tested by dogs and cats—are a good place to start. Once you try a few, you might decide you want to transition your pet to a home-cooked diet, where you control the ingredients.

For Dogs

Sesame Chicken

You can use leftover chicken in this recipe as long as it isn't heavily spiced. The sesame oil makes this an appealing dish, even for picky eaters. This recipe makes one day's worth of meals for a 50-pound dog of average activity, and provides about 1,300 calories.

> 2 cups chicken, cooked and shredded into small pieces
>
> 1 cup sweet potato, cooked and diced into small pieces
>
> 1 TB. sesame seed oil
>
> 2 large eggs, hardboiled and crumbled, with shells
>
> ¼ cup blueberries, frozen or fresh
>
> 1 cup fresh broccoli florets, finely chopped, lightly steamed

1. Gently mix chicken, sweet potato, sesame seed oil, eggs, blueberries, and broccoli.

2. Divide into two or three airtight containers (depending on your dog's feeding schedule) and store in the refrigerator.

Variations: If this recipe becomes your pet's favorite and you prepare it frequently, you can vary the ingredients so your dog receives a wide array of nutritional elements. Instead of chicken, try substituting turkey, duck, beef, bison, elk, or rabbit. You can also do a partial substitution: use 1 cup chicken and 1 cup of another meat. Use butternut squash, acorn squash, or spaghetti squash in place of the sweet potato. Substitute ¼ cup canned or cooked pumpkin in place of blueberries. Vary the fresh greens with romaine lettuce, grated zucchini, wheatgrass, collard greens, or other greens. If fresh greens aren't available, use canned green beans. Variations may impact the calorie count, so pay attention to your dog's weight.

bone appétit!

Beef, Bacon, and Sweet Potatoes

If your dog works hard, plays rough, or is training or competing in performance sports, he or she may need more calories than the average dog. This recipe supplies enough good nutrition for one day's worth of meals for a hard-charging 50-pound dog, and provides about 1,700 calories.

2 cups beef, muscle meat, not ground

1½ cups sweet potato, finely diced

½ cup green beans, fresh or canned

¼ cup bacon, cooked and crumbled

1 (3-oz.) can salmon in oil, undrained

1 egg, hardboiled and crumbled, with shell

1 cup plain yogurt

1. Cut beef into bite-sized pieces. Place in a large saucepan.

2. Add diced sweet potatoes and green beans. Add enough water to cover. Cook until meat is done and sweet potatoes are soft. Remove from heat.

3. Add bacon, salmon, and egg. Mix well.

4. Divide into meals and place in airtight containers. Store in the refrigerator. When serving, add a portion of yogurt.

Variations: Instead of beef, substitute bison or venison. Substitute ½ cup potato, ½ cup yams, and ½ cup sweet potato for 1½ cups sweet potato. Use peas instead of green beans. Use a 3-ounce can of tuna in oil instead of salmon. Increase eggs in the recipe, using two or three eggs. All of the variations may impact the calorie count; pay attention to your dog's weight.

bone appétit!

Slow-Cooker Beef, Bison, and Peas

This is an easy recipe to make and is eagerly eaten by all of the dogs who taste-tested it. This is another recipe for active or hard-working dogs. It supplies enough good nutrition for one day's meals for an active 50-pound dog, and provides about 1,500 calories.

> 3 cups beef, ground
>
> 1 cup bison, ground
>
> 1 cup green peas
>
> ¼ cup carrots, grated
>
> 2 eggs, hardboiled and crumbled, with shells

1. Brown beef and bison until cooked thoroughly.

2. Place cooked meat, green peas, carrots, and eggs in the slow cooker. Add enough water to cover.

3. Set the cooker on low. Simmer ingredients all day.

4. Divide into meals, keeping juices with meat, and place in airtight containers. Store in the refrigerator.

Variations: Use other vegetables in place of peas, including green beans, red kidney beans, grated squash, or pumpkin. These variations won't alter the calorie count significantly.

bone appétit!

Bison and Barley

Bison is available in most grocery stores. Although it's expensive, it can be a good choice for dogs who might be allergic to beef, as dogs with food allergies often need unique proteins and carbohydrates to avoid a reaction. This recipe supplies enough good nutrition for one day's meals for an active 50-pound dog, and provides about 1,300 calories.

1 cup barley

2 cups bison, ground or finely diced

1 egg, hardboiled and crumbled, with shell

1 TB. safflower oil

1. Cook barley according to the package directions until well done. Drain excess water and set aside.

2. Brown bison until well done.

3. Add bison, including meat juice, to barley. Add egg and safflower oil. Mix well.

4. Divide into meals and place in airtight containers. Store in the refrigerator.

Variations: Be careful when making variations to this recipe until you have identified the foods that trigger an allergic response in your dog. Work with your veterinarian as you try to identify the allergen.

bone appétit!

For Cats

A Finicky Feline's Favorite

Cats who have eaten dry kibble food all their lives may be reluctant to try new foods, but this recipe was accepted by several finicky felines. It supplies enough good nutrition for one day's meals for a 10-pound indoor cat, and provides about 300 calories. Kittens and outside cats will require more.

> ⅔ cups chicken, cooked and finely shredded
> 1 egg, hardboiled, shelled, and crumbled
> 1 TB. salmon, canned, in oil
> 2 TB. wheatgrass, finely diced
> 1 pinch cheddar cheese, grated

1. Mix chicken, egg, salmon, wheatgrass, and cheddar cheese.

2. Divide into three or four airtight containers (depending on your cat's feeding schedule) and store in the refrigerator.

3. Add a 100 mg taurine supplement to one meal before serving.

Variations: Instead of chicken, substitute cooked turkey, duck, or another meat. Use trout, herring, mackerel, tuna, or clams instead of salmon. Use mozzarella, Swiss, or goat cheese instead of cheddar cheese. Variations may impact the calorie count, so pay attention to your cat's weight.

meow, love, eat

Tuna Sashimi

This recipe is delightful—even the finickiest felines tend to devour it eagerly. It supplies enough good nutrition for one day's meals for a 10-pound indoor cat, and provides about 300 calories. Because the tuna is raw, mix it with the other ingredients just before serving. Do not store it once it's mixed.

½ cup tuna, raw
2 eggs, hardboiled, shelled, and crumbled
1 tsp. plain feta cheese
½ tsp. flaxseed meal

1. Slice tuna into very small, thin pieces (slightly larger than a piece of elbow macaroni).

2. Mix eggs, feta cheese, and flaxseed meal.

3. Immediately before serving, add tuna and a 100 mg taurine supplement. Mix well to prevent cat from picking out tuna and avoiding other ingredients. Do not store leftovers.

Variations: Substitute other freshwater or saltwater fish in place of tuna. Vary cheeses, including finely grated cheddar, Swiss, Monterey, mozzarella, or goat cheese. These variations won't change the calorie count significantly, but watch your cat's weight if you serve this recipe frequently because some cheeses have higher calorie counts than others.

Duck and Oatmeal

Contrary to popular belief, duck doesn't taste like chicken! This is a different, tasty, nutritious recipe for cats. It provides 325 calories, which is one day's nutrition for an average indoor 10- to 12-pound cat.

⅔ cup duck, raw, chopped into bite-sized pieces

1 duck egg, hardboiled, shelled, and crumbled

2 TB. oatmeal, cooked (leftover from breakfast is fine)

1 TB. cod liver oil (or other fish oil)

1. Sauté duck until well done and place in a small bowl.

2. Add egg, oatmeal, and cod liver oil, and mix well.

3. Store in the refrigerator. Before serving, add a 100 mg taurine supplement to one meal each day.

For Dogs and Cats

Raw Beef, Apples, and Greens

This recipe supplies enough good nutrition for one day's meals for a 50-pound dog of average activity, and provides about 1,300 calories. Adapt portions according to your dog's or cat's individual size and weight. Because this recipe contains raw meat, which may contain bacteria, and because apples oxidize quickly, make it immediately before serving. Do not store leftovers.

2 cups beef, ground

1 cup apple, finely chopped

½ cup applesauce, unsweetened

1 cup wheatgrass, fresh, finely chopped

½ cup goat cheese, crumbled

2 eggs, hardboiled, shelled, and crumbled

1 TB. flaxseed meal

1. Mix beef, apple, applesauce, wheatgrass, goat cheese, eggs, and flaxseed meal together.

2. Serve immediately.

3. For cats, add a 100 mg taurine supplement to one meal each day.

Variations: Instead of beef, use raw ground bison, elk, venison, rabbit, or other red meat. Instead of wheatgrass, use alfalfa, broccoli florets, collard greens, chard, or other fresh greens. These variations will not change the calorie count significantly.

bone appétit!

Leftovers in the Slow Cooker

This recipe uses the leftovers in your refrigerator or freezer, whether meat leftovers from last night's dinner or the remaining vegetables from a side dish. Avoid heavily spiced and greasy foods. The calorie count for this recipe depends on the ingredients used. For the ingredients included here, the recipe provides about 1,300 calories. Adapt the portions for your dog and cat according to his or her size and weight.

> 2 cups chicken, cooked and shredded
>
> 1 cup turkey, cooked and shredded
>
> 2 strips bacon, cooked and crumbled
>
> 1 cup green beans, canned or fresh
>
> ½ cup carrots, grated
>
> 1 egg, hardboiled, shelled, and crumbled
>
> 1 cup yams or sweet potato, diced
>
> 1 TB. flaxseed meal
>
> 1 cup goat cheese, crumbled

1. In the slow cooker, combine chicken, turkey, bacon, green beans, carrots, egg, yams, and flaxseed meal. Mix well.

2. Add enough water to cover. Cook on low heat until yams are soft (usually 4 to 5 hours, depending on the slow cooker).

3. Divide into appropriate-sized meals and store in airtight containers in the refrigerator. Do the same for crumbled goat cheese.

4. When serving, add some of goat cheese to the meal.

5. For cats, add a 100 mg taurine supplement to one meal each day.

Variations: Because this recipe is made from leftovers, each batch is different. Use other cooked meat, including beef, lamb, bison, venison, and rabbit. Avoid greasy and heavily spiced meat. Try using a variety of vegetables, including squash. Feel free to use more than one egg; two or three is fine. Substitute grated cheddar cheese for goat cheese. Variations will increase or decrease the calorie count, so pay attention to your pet's weight.

meow, love, eat

Chicken, Eggs, and Goat Cheese

Eggs are the perfect food; they contain amino acids in excellent proportions and are digested easily. This recipe provides about 1,200 calories. Adapt portions according to your dog's or cat's individual size and weight.

> 1 cup chicken, cooked and finely shredded
> 4 eggs, scrambled
> ½ cup zucchini, grated
> ½ cup potato, precooked (omit for cat recipe)
> 1 TB. safflower oil
> ¼ cup goat cheese, crumbled

1. Preheat oven to 350°F.

2. Place chicken in a bowl. Add eggs. Mix well.

3. Add zucchini, potato (if using), and safflower oil. Mix well.

4. Spread mixture in a baking pan. Sprinkle goat cheese on top of mixture.

5. Bake for 20 to 30 minutes, or until cheese is melted and begins to brown.

6. Divide into meals and place in airtight containers. Store in the refrigerator. For cats, add a 100 mg taurine supplement with one meal each day.

Variations: Use cooked turkey instead of chicken. Use cheddar cheese instead of goat cheese. Instead of safflower oil, use sesame seed oil or fish oil such as tuna or salmon. These variations won't alter the calorie count significantly.

bone appétit!

Index